The Sales Manager's
MENTOR

JEFF LEHMAN

MENTOR
PRESS LLC

Seattle, Washington

MENTOR
PRESS LLC

MENTOR PRESS LLC
An Imprint of Classic Day Publishing LLC
2100 Westlake Avenue North, Suite 106
Seattle, Washington 98109
800-328-4348
www.classicdaypublishing.com
Email: info@classicdaypublishing.com

The Sales Manager's
MENTOR

Foreword

Living in California, I'm no stranger to earthquakes. I'm familiar with them for another reason as well. An "earthquake"—at least in famous playwright Arthur Miller's vocabulary—is that moment when the customer stops "smiling back." It's the moment the sale, no matter how well sold or managed, screeches to a halt. It's the moment when a salesperson hears their least favorite word: "No."

We hate to admit it, but of course we've all been there. In my personal experience—from selling lemonade to software—I've encountered some of these so-called earthquakes. As someone who now runs a company in the sales automation marketplace, I hear often about how this misfortune strikes other businesses as well. Misfortune helps us appreciate the true value of a mentor because it causes us to seek ideas from others to help learn how to keep "No" from happening the next time.

While there are a myriad of reasons why certain deals are stymied, there's one fault line that's always easy to recognize. It happens when a company puts ultimate emphasis on the money coming in—while ignoring basic sales management principles of "how and why" it should happen. As Jeff comprehensively delineates in this book, a well managed sales organization is built upon a thorough knowledge of why it's in business, how its sales processes work, training and knowing its salespeople, and understanding the depth of its customers' experience. Creating a successful company begins with integrating and better managing the sales process throughout the entire organization. It ends in the creation of more profitable revenue.

What Jeff does here is share his mentoring tips on how sales managers can build a successful sales organization in the companies they work for. I have watched him accomplish this first hand as our mutual career paths have crisscrossed over the years. One of the methods he covers—and of course my favorite—is the use of customer relationship management (CRM) solutions. Working with sales managers on a regular basis in my own business, I hear first hand how their salespeople are constantly looking for ways to be better informed and share their information (good and bad) with C-level executives in order to gain better visibility. On the flip side, CEOs are also looking to gain their own improved visibility and accountability into the sales function.

An example of the utility of this book is that Jeff makes an important point when he suggests that solutions (like CRM) must be simple for sales managers to implement in order for salespeople to embrace them. In one of my favorite parts of this book he describes a situation where deploying a CRM solution was so difficult that the implementation manager went crazy—literally! Luckily we've come a long way from solutions dogged by exorbitant costs and impossible implementation.

Successful sales managers, as you well know, are action oriented. By incorporating hundreds of practical tips and real-life examples, this book guides sales managers and sales oriented CEOs on leading more effectively and selling more strategically. That's what makes this book unique and a worthwhile read. With Jeff's mentoring—drawn on 20 years of experience—companies can reduce the "earthquakes" and enjoy a more stable and profitable sales landscape.

Marc Benioff
Chairman & CEO
salesforce.com
San Francisco, California

From the Author

Who Needs a Mentor?

"Your manager is either your mentor or tormentor.
If they aren't working for you, they are working against you…
get out as soon as you can!"

Keith Grinstein
Vice Chairman, Nextel International, Inc.

Every sales manager needs a mentor from time to time during his or her career, but most don't have access to one. This book provides that mentoring and is based on 20+ years of observations and practicing what works and what doesn't in the real world of sales leadership.

Throughout the pages of this book I'm offering to be your mentor. I'm here whenever you need me, 24/7.

What makes me qualified to help you? Over my career I've helped:

- Many companies and investors obtain huge returns from their investments;

- Start-ups achieve a worth of billions of dollars;

- Companies make it through fast-growth periods or tough times;

- Formerly successful companies re-establish their paths to success;

- CEO's, peers, and fellow employees become very wealthy;

And I've helped:

- Make many people successful in their sales, sales management and leadership careers.

I've also made a number of mistakes along the way. I haven't gotten it right every time. Sometimes not even come close. But I have done a lot more things right than wrong. You can learn from my successes and mistakes here and I hope without having to make the same mistakes on your own, although sometimes that is part of the learning process.

The sad truth is that the world is littered with sales managers who have taken themselves a little too seriously and believed their own press releases. They have spent more time pumping up their egos than focusing on legitimately pumping up their company's revenue and true value. The latter two challenges constitute a full-time job, and a hard one at that. That's why you were hired.

Before deciding to write this book, I spent time at many of the major offline and online book retailers to see what books were available for mentoring sales managers. While there are over 100 books on the subject of personal selling (how to love and hug your customers, etc.) there aren't many on how to be an effective sales manager, much less a sales leader. Those books that do exist have been written more like textbooks than "I've been there and you can learn from my mistakes" advice. I've chosen to write from a practical point of view, to tell it just the way it happens every day. And I'm going to give it to you straight, just as you'd expect from any good mentor.

Writing about how to excel at being a sales manager and leader must be a pretty difficult thing to do, or else there would be more books on the subject. This book is my humble and unassuming attempt to try and unravel some of this mystery for you.

If you are new to sales management, a seasoned sales manager or a sales executive, there is something here for you. Even if it just confirms what you were already thinking, what you read here might help spark other ideas or solutions to problems that you might encounter, even if they haven't been covered in these pages. This book will certainly help you make more money than what you spent to buy it.

I'm thankful to all the sales professionals and superb managers, leaders, executives, and great presidents and CEOs whom I have watched lead and who have been my mentors. I have had the pleasure of learning from them personally and building great teams with them over the years. They taught me many things that I can only hope to effectively relate here.

The same goes for friends and family who have also been mentors to me in their own unique ways. On his 75th birthday, my father summed up good rules to live (and to manage others) by:

- Keep breathing,
- Be flexible,
- Roll with the punches, and
- Try to help other people.

I also want to thank all those people who lacked motivation in their jobs and whose bad attitudes showed me what not to do under any circumstances. Without "naming names," those lessons are here, too, and there are plenty of them.

And, finally, my thanks to Caffe Ladro in Seattle for being my second home and part-time office while writing this book.

Jeff Lehman
Seattle, Washington

Contents

Chapter Five

Chapter One

Making the Transition

Making the career transition from salesperson to sales manager, or from sales manager to sales executive, isn't as easy as it seems. The assumption is often made that whatever set of skills made someone successful at one type of job will work equally well when moving up the ladder. Unfortunately that couldn't be further from the truth: "salesperson" and "sales manager or sales executive" job descriptions aren't even close to being the same. The only point of commonality is that when you become a sales manager or sales executive you are still responsible for selling something—in addition to managing and leading a sales team.

No matter where you are in the sales management ranks, at the beginning of your climb or close to the top, there is always something new to learn. And seldom is there someone nearby to look to for helpful advice. It's rare that people at the same peer level with you, and those who are outside of the sales group will have any sales experience, much less the time to share it with you. Your sales management knowledge is cumulative. What you learn today may make a huge difference tomorrow, so absorb as much as you can now.

More than ever, companies need sales managers who can effectively manage *and* lead talented salespeople while taking more complete ownership of the revenue-creation process. Being this type of sales manager will take you a lot farther down your career path than you ever thought possible.

The heady days of great ideas that will ultimately … someday … hopefully … maybe make money are thankfully over. The emphasis now is on giving your customers what they need and knowing that you can make money from it. Return on investment, profitable sales revenue, lifetime value of a customer, and accountability are *again* all pieces of the sales success equation. Only with a competent sales organization, led by a true sales professional, can any of this occur.

There is plenty of room in every company for great sales management. It takes passion, motivation, leadership, and commitment to make revenue happen.

Chapter Two

The Revenue-Focused CEO

Picking the right CEO to work for can make all the difference in the world when it comes to your success in sales management. If you don't work with a "revenue-focused" CEO, your job will be that much more difficult! It can be done, but not easily. The "revenue focus" of successful companies comes from the top.

CEOs are often picked for their tactical leadership abilities. They can be brought in to: clean up a balance sheet, eliminate unethical behavior, keep a company profitable, make it profitable, rebuild a reputation, launch new products, increase revenues, turn a company around to sell it, maintain the status quo, take a company private, take it public, find additional investors, grow it from small to big, or downsize it. The list is endless.

Knowing why the CEO is there and how you can help them is a priority when looking at an employment opportunity. It has to be an honest discussion. The reason why a CEO is brought in to run a company may not put revenue creation as a priority. You should know that going in because this can immediately put a senior sales executive at odds with the company's goals. Make sure to set the expectations for your potential success accordingly.

There are generally three types of CEOs: the Revenue CEO, the Product CEO, and the Finance CEO.

- The *Revenue* CEO is focused on creating shareholder value and supporting profitable sales for the company. They are all about ROI (return on investment).

- The *Product* CEO is good at designing (or redesigning) a product and getting it out the door but not necessarily interested in how to make money from it.

- The *Finance* CEO is good at trimming costs, but not at building an environment that can generate long-term revenue or a sellable product.

In addition to providing strong and effective leadership, a successful CEO should incorporate qualities of at least two of the CEO-types above, as long as one of them is the Revenue CEO! Combining the characteristics of all three is ideal—and rare. To work for such a CEO is total nirvana. Additionally, a truly exceptional CEO hires smartly, lets their team execute, and makes changes quickly when there's a mistake.

How do you know you've found a revenue-focused CEO? He or she has many of the following traits (use this as a check list for picking your next CEO):

They:

☐ Have sold products in their career and understand what it's like to have to make a revenue number each month or quarter.

☐ Understand that the company is in business to make money.

- ☐ View "time as money" and don't procrastinate on creating revenue.

- ☐ Understand that successful selling is a function of having talented salespeople and sales managers, who have inventory (or services) to sell, and that the customers want these products.

- ☐ Drive their sales, product and marketing people to focus on creating profitable revenue.

- ☐ Respect the people who buy or use their products and balance that respect with the creation of revenue.

- ☐ Want to keep their customers, sales management and sales team happy.

- ☐ Listen to the sales executives they hire and the sales teams, who in turn, have been listening to the customers, in order to improve the quality of the product and the customer's experience.

- ☐ Make sales calls on customers, ask them for ideas, and implement those ideas if they make sense.

- ☐ Let salespeople and sales managers do their jobs without internal hurdles. Or, at least, work aggressively to minimize or eliminate those hurdles.

- ☐ Don't say *no* to profitable revenue opportunities, they ask *how* they or others in the company can help to make them happen.

- ☐ Hate bureaucracy or anything else that stands in the way of profitable revenue.

☐ Realize that it takes time to build momentum in creating a future sales pipeline.

☐ Understand that eliminating or changing successful products in the middle of a sales cycle can slow revenue momentum and destroy sales morale (and customer morale as well).

☐ Offer revenue-producing alternatives, or lower sales budgets accordingly, if they kill a product.

☐ Make hitting revenue numbers an overall company goal, not just a sales goal.

☐ Let people who control the revenue have "second to last" say in revenue-creating decisions.

☐ Partially compensate the entire company or at least the departments in the company that touch revenue directly (product marketing, product development, finance, etc.) for making overall revenue goals.

☐ Only support the creation of products/services that can be monetized in some direct way, unless that product is the rare (and mutually agreed to) "loss leader."

☐ Rarely take only the 40,000-foot view of how sales happen. Instead, they take a ground-level approach and strive to understand *why* sales goals aren't being met by digging deeper into all the surrounding issues.

☐ Don't view a sales organization as a "necessary evil" for their company's success.

☐ Have respect for the hardships of selling and being on the frontline when their company can't execute its product strategy properly.

☐ Ask how they can help when a sales team is struggling to build momentum. And then they listen.

Believe it or not, there are CEOs who claim to be revenue-focused but do very little of the above. The same goes for heads of marketing and product development groups. Investors, boards, and employees are all stakeholders in the success of their companies, and successful companies exist to make profitable revenue. There has never been any fault in *that* type of thinking. Without a top-down revenue focus, profits don't materialize, investors become disenchanted, and talented salespeople and sales managers leave to work for or start companies that *can* deliver.

It's one thing to say "make your budget or else" and quite another to be actively involved in the process of leading a coordinated effort to make it happen. Make sure that your CEO is, first and foremost, revenue-focused and you will have a much better chance at success.

How to Test a CEO for *Revenue* Focus:

There are a series of interview questions that you can ask to determine if the CEO you are or will be working for is revenue-focused. If the CEO isn't a "revenue hound" like you are, then your job will be more challenging. Not every sales management candidate will be able to interview the CEO. These questions can be adapted to the person you are potentially reporting to, or they can be asked during the hiring process.

Be observant throughout the interviews. It's more than just the answers to the questions that you have to think about. There are often less subtle forms of communication going on that communicate even more about the CEO you are interviewing.

When interviewing your next CEO, ask the following questions:

What is your goal for the company this coming year as CEO?

- Is he here to: clean up a balance sheet, eliminate unethical behavior, keep it profitable, make it profitable, rebuild a reputation, launch new products, increase revenues, turn it around to sell it, maintain the status quo, take it private, take it public, find additional investors, grow it from small to big, or downsize it?

- Listen to the order in which he responds. When someone responds off the 'top of their head' it is generally in the priority in which they are thinking about things.

- This has to be an honest conversation. If the CEO has a hidden agenda that can't be disclosed that's understandable. However, if you feel that the CEO isn't clear in his mission it will be more difficult to help him achieve his goals, and for you to achieve yours.

If you can't get into specifics, try this type of question:

Are you a revenue-, product- or finance- focused CEO?

- Which did he answer with first? That's often very telling. If he doesn't immediately say "revenue-focused" (or something close) as part or all of the answer, ask him to give you examples of how he is revenue focused.

- If he isn't revenue-focused, think long and hard about how successful you can be. A company's revenue focus has to come from the very top down.

If that question is too blunt, then use this next question:

What percentage of the company's overall focus is on creating profitable revenue, on product marketing, and on cost-cutting and finance issues?

- If the sales percentage isn't 50% or higher relative to the other two, it may be an uphill battle getting the company to be revenue-focused.

Here's another way to get at the answer:

What is the mission statement of the company?

- If *making money* isn't mentioned as part of the mission statement then you have just been given a large clue about the focus of the CEO and the company.

Has the CEO ever sold products directly before? What type of products? For how long?

- What did he sell? How successfully?

- This is very telling. If the CEO understands selling, you will start to know that here.

If the CEO hasn't sold directly:

When was the last time the CEO went out on a sales call? How often does the CEO go out on calls—every month or quarter? What happened on the last call?

- If the CEO doesn't make sales calls (too busy!?) you are starting to get the hint. If he or she does make sales calls, try to determine if the CEO listened to the customer and did anything with the information.

How involved is the CEO (personally) in the sales process?

A CEO can:

- Micromanage.

- Hire strong sales management and support the sales team 110% without micromanaging.

- Choose to be actively involved when asked.

- Be uninvolved.

- Be uninvolved and unsupportive.

How are employees of the company compensated for making overall revenue numbers?

—and/or follow up with—

What departments are compensated for the company's making the overall revenue numbers?

- If there is no overall plan for compensating the company for hitting the overall revenue numbers this is a red flag.

- It's even more obvious that there's a problem if the departments that touch revenue don't have an incentive to make revenue happen.

- The degree to which a company or department is compensated for helping to create revenue is also a strong indication of how seriously the company takes revenue and how motivated the team might be. Anything less than 5% of a total compensation package as a bonus for making revenue goals is a token amount that may not be enough to truly be motivational.

In general, is the exec level group in the company compensated directly for making the company numbers? How significant is the bonus? (Big money or token amount? What % of overall compensation?)

- This is more telling, because most smart CEOs will put their money, or the shareholders' money, where the revenue potential is. If product or marketing teams aren't compensated for hitting "the numbers," then chances are that revenue isn't the overall focus of the company.

Will the person who runs the sales organization in the company (potentially, you) have override/tie-breaker authority, below the CEO, in revenue-related decisions?

- If the CEO says that the head of sales doesn't have the override, be very careful. You will constantly have to fight over tiebreakers with your peers.

- If the head of sales does have override authority, then get it in writing.

- The CEO always has final say.

If the person who runs the sales organization doesn't have override authority, how will tough calls be made?

- If you get back some "group decision" mumbo-jumbo, then ask for more clarification. If it smells like a potential bureaucratic nightmare, it probably is.

How does the top sales job relate to the top product or marketing job?

- If you hear the phrase "You are partners in the decision-making processes," then put your antenna up. This generally can't be good news unless your partners are also a known "revenue hounds." Ask to interview your product and marketing peers before making a final decision on taking the job. You can ask the same questions of these peers that you've asked of the CEO. (A good CEO will include them in the interview process.) If you don't get the sense that your "partners" are truly revenue-focused, then you will most likely end up losing in a multi-way tiebreaking vote if the CEO is less than revenue-focused.

- Only a politically inclined marketing or product person will tell you what you want to hear. The genuine ones will be completely forthright and honest. If they do play politics, you will find out soon enough that they aren't there to help create revenue.

CASE STUDY: Observant Interviewing:

TRUE STORY: A Sales VP candidate was interviewing with the CEO for the first time. The candidate was trying to size up the CEO for the company's potential revenue focus. The CEO was verbalizing all the right things but something just didn't feel right to the VP candidate.

The CEO's mouth was making "pro-revenue" statements like: "We are partners in making the numbers and you will have my full support...," but the CEO's demeanor was saying something else. What was actually being communicated came across more like: "I hate salespeople, they are a necessary evil. Sales management is a low level job. I don't wish to dirty my hands touching anything sales related, but I have to fill this job." The CEO had a big smile while delivering a seemingly supportive message. He didn't say revenue negatives openly, but the VP candidate could just sense something wasn't right.

How did the VP candidate know? When asked about revenue focus, the CEO became more distant and vague. When asked product or finance questions, the CEO could give very specific answers. The CEO used generalizations instead of personally accountable or detailed examples regarding sales. The CEO did not know what was going on in the sales organization and it showed. The CEO also pushed back a bit from the table and crossed his arms and became ponderous when responding to revenue questions.

The VP candidate also asked about the job

description sent out in advance of the meeting. It made the job sound more like a lower level sales management job than a Sales VP job. The position had minimal authority to make things happen internally, but carried all the responsibility for hitting the revenue numbers. It wasn't considered "peer" level with engineering and product marketing. It was a "just go out and sell and let us figure out everything else"— type of sales job description. It was clear that the CEO didn't consider the sales job as important as other executive jobs. That was another subtle clue. It appeared to the VP candidate that what the company really needed was a high-level sales executive who would push hard for revenue creation inside the company as much as out in the field.

Then the VP candidate started looking around the CEO's office for more clues. (All good sales types do this.) On the conference table were piles of spreadsheets regarding finance and product analysis. No sales projections could be seen. There was not even a file folder with a sales heading on it. There were no white board notations about hitting numbers, goals, forecasts, etc. You can't always expect that these will be in plain view of outsiders but sometimes the absence of something is just as telling as something right there in front of you. If revenue is truly the focus of a CEO, then there is usually some reminder of it that is visible.

The VP candidate asked how the sales team was doing. The CEO said, "Great…our key metrics are up." (That was another vague answer.) "The sales team just needs to be managed better than they were," said the CEO. That was another warning sign. The buzz on this company in the industry was that they were falling apart. Most of it was self-inflicted—and mostly everyone in the industry knew it. It wasn't just about sales management. It was about company management.

The VP candidate asked the CEO who the last Sales VP was and what happened to them. The CEO couldn't remember that person's name (not a good sign). The CEO made a vague comment about the last Sales VP not fitting into the team—a "Chamber of Commerce" answer—meaning that it was appropriately spun to give no revealing or negative information.

As it turned out, the last Sales VP and the VP candidate had worked together previously. As soon as possible, the candidate called the former VP and asked what happened. It was true that the former VP didn't fit in. Why? The former VP wanted the company to be revenue-focused, and the CEO wanted the company to be more product-focused. Unfortunately for the CEO, the design of the company's products directly affected its ability to create revenue. The product marketing team wasn't revenue-focused either, so the former Sales VP kept running into a wall of resistance at every attempt to create profitable revenue. Products were being designed without any advance focus on revenue creation. Product marketing people were referring to revenue as that "ugly" revenue. Yes, that former Sales VP certainly didn't fit in—and for good reason! And now the candidate knew exactly why.

But wait, there's more!

Even more telling information came from staffers whom the CEO had the VP candidate interview. The Human Resources director was brutally honest about the fact that the company had no sales or revenue focus, and that it wasn't coming from the top, either. Even the lead engineer openly wanted the company to be revenue-focused as well, but noted the CEO wasn't supporting it. (Author's note: Have you spotted a trend here?) And guess who was running the product marketing group because the previous head of product marketing had been fired? The product-focused CEO of course!

You probably are wondering: Did the VP candidate get the job?

Yes. But before accepting the job, he demanded that the responsibility be much higher-level and the job description be more wide-reaching. That happened, at least on paper. The candidate took it as a challenge to try and turn around a good company with a solid product, in the midst of a management mess. All that was needed were basic blocking and tackling drills for the sales team. And most people in the company wanted to tackle the CEO, too, but not in a positive way!

The only way this company was going to succeed was with a top-down revenue focus. Did the VP candidate who was now the head of sales succeed? After a year or so, it was time to go. Frustrations had hit an all-time high. It was clear that the CEO wasn't going to come around despite the majority of the company (outside of product marketing) clamoring for changes. There was constant head-butting, but the Sales VP would not back down.

The CEO became less and less supportive of revenue creation and just did what he knew best: redesign the product just enough to get the company sold. That's not necessarily a bad strategy, but in this case it wasn't the most profitable. The company ended up being sold for less than it should have. Why? The key metric for measuring the value of this type of company was a multiple of sales. If the revenue had been higher the value of the company would have been higher—by a multiple. That seems like a simple math concept, right? With the focus more on redesigning the product and less on revenue creation, major opportunities were missed.

In the end all the warning signs were there from the beginning. The candidate knew that but took the job anyway. Why? It was the desire to make a difference and be part of a historic turnaround. The only problem is that it didn't happen. But it was a tremendous learning experience. Sometimes the way to get much better at what you do is to try something incredibly hard that has a high risk of failure. You can often learn more from failure than success.

LESSON LEARNED: If you get the sense that your CEO and peer-level management team aren't revenue-focused you are potentially starting in a bad place. The revenue-focused CEO is worth his or her weight in gold. No… make that platinum. It's not that you can't succeed in a product- or finance-focused company, but it will be that much harder to get what you need to win and make things happen quickly and smoothly.

Communicating *Revenue-Focus* from the Top Down:

Most companies are in business to make money. Sales drives the business. It's up to the CEO and the sales executives to act as great communicators and work to pull everyone together with a clear focus on creating profitable revenue. This focus has to come from the top down or the sales organization will not be successful. If other departments have an established culture that isn't pro revenue, it will be that much harder to be successful.

Great communication starts with a company-wide, revenue-focused mission statement. A mission statement is an internal "call to action" for everyone in the company. It isn't necessarily the same tagline that shows up in corporate ad campaigns. The mission statement should open all minds in the company to what the company does and why it exists.

Sometimes the exercise of building a mission statement is best done with guidance from facilitators. Some companies are so disconnected from their mission that they have departments operating in their own orbits where employees don't even know what it is or what the company's overall revenue-focus is. Some companies wisely put the mission statement up on the wall for all employees to see. Other companies hide it like it's a secret company formula. Don't keep it a secret: Get the word out to everyone in the company that you are in business to make money. No one should feel guilty about that, since money makes mortgage and car payments, makes charitable contributions, sends kids to college, pays taxes, pays for nice vacations, and allows ownership of second homes.

TRUE STORY: A sales manager is at her first day of work. She is part of the executive management team and asked to attend the annual company offsite meeting that charts the future course of the company.

During the meeting, the company mission statement is addressed. The company has lost some focus and hasn't been very successful financially. The previous management team preferred to be more "academic-" and "product-" focused than "revenue-" focused. The company has two sets of customers: the ones who use the product for free (the users), and the ones who provide marketing messages to those users for a fee (the customers). Both users and customers are important to the bottom line. There is a fine line between keeping both happy. Everyone in the room understands that balance is needed, but has different interpretations of what the actual balance should be (not the 50-50 balance that most people would immediately think of). There is no consensus.

As the discussion of the mission statement unfolds, it becomes clear to the sales manager that the company wants to make a product for users without much interest in how it can be monetized for customers. That's a revenue disaster waiting to happen. Since the mission statement will be rolled out to the entire company, it will be important to make sure that everyone is focused (at least internally) on the company's goal of making money. That would be a historic first for this particular company.

Multiple versions of the mission statement are put up on a white board. The team is getting closer to the final version. The mission statement is nearly perfect—except for one thing: Nowhere does it reinforce the idea that the company is in business to make money. Without that statement, years of non-revenue-focused company culture will continue to be perpetuated. The company will not be able to succeed.

The sales manager makes her case for using the mission statement to change the company culture to one with a revenue-focus. This is out of the CEO's comfort zone and expertise. It doesn't happen. For the next two quarters the CEO circulates the mission statement to the executive team for comments. Each time, the sales manager writes back: "Shouldn't we complete the mission statement by adding that we are doing what we do because we are a revenue-focused company and we are in business to make money and increase shareholder value?" The CEO continues to ignore that request. Two quarters after that, the company has to be sold. Go figure.

Chapter Three

———

*In*effective Sales Managers

It's the highly effective sales managers who always seem to get the job done—sometimes effortlessly. People want to be like them and like working for them. They do the right thing and through their decisions make sales happen. These are the true leaders.

Before you can determine what a good sales manager does well, you need to look at what ineffective ones are doing poorly. It seems a bit negative, but this section will sensitize you to what won't work and what not to personally duplicate. If you consider the opposite side of these traits, you will begin to see what makes for a basically good sales manager. But being a great sales manager and leader takes more than just turning these negatives into positives. Making a quantum leap will involve the tips that come in Chapter Four, starting on page 25.

How often have you seen these traits in *in*effective sales managers? Check all that apply.

They:

☐ Are conveniently in meetings, at lunch, or otherwise completely inaccessible when their input is needed.

☐ Constantly complain about being too "up to my eyeballs in alligators" to actually deliver anything they promise you.

☐ Immediately pass off a sales problem to someone else to solve and avoid getting their hands dirty.

☐ Are always at their desk and on non-work-related e-mail or instant messenger, when they should be out in the territory, listening to customers or listening to their salespeople.

☐ Come up with a set of sales numbers to present to upper management or to the board but they don't tell the sales team about it until after the presentation.

☐ Make important decisions without consulting their direct reports.

☐ Believe it's more important to their career growth to bond with their executive peers than take an active role in managing their sales team and selling the company's products.

☐ Think personal accountability for profitability is something related to their expense accounts.

☐ Will show up at a big deal signing so they have a "Yeah, I closed that deal" war story to tell at the next executive staff meeting.

☐ Show dismay, disdain and utter surprise when their direct reports tell them that they aren't going to make their monthly or quarterly numbers even after they've been given multiple early warnings and have been asked for help.

- ☐ Don't accept personal responsibility for anything.

- ☐ Undercut their own sales team on "sweetheart" deals so they can say "Look, I can sell this stuff, why can't you?"

- ☐ Reinforce their lack of interest in addressing sales objections by saying witty (and stupidity affirming) things like: "Just do what it takes to make the sale!"

- ☐ Will take days to get back to others—most likely by e-mail, asking for more clarification to effectively stall the process so they can vest more stock before someone figures out that they are actually doing nothing for a living.

- ☐ Spend time creating and watching a spreadsheet application that monitors how much stock they are vesting, calculated up to the second, of course!

- ☐ Make unreasonable, unilateral and arbitrary demands (like: sales must increase 15% or you are all gone!) without having a clue about market conditions or a plan to make it happen.

- ☐ Always insist on wanting to go on sales calls but never seem to be able to schedule them in.

- ☐ Play favorites with certain people on the sales team, or at least give that perception.

- ☐ Come up with cute ways of showing that they are actually doing something to motivate the sales team, like having a sales meeting where the team will walk on burning coals, do upside down tequila shots, or whack boards over their heads as a sign of team unity and commitment to being winners.

☐ Resign in the middle of a sales disaster (that they created) to take a better job elsewhere while claiming that they were the driving force behind the success of the sales organization!

☐ Thoroughly enjoy firing and ruining the careers of salespeople they personally dislike.

☐ Don't stand up to lack of support for profitable sales in the company, whether at peer level or in the executive ranks.

Does any of this sound familiar? It probably does. Have you seen this happen around you during your career? You probably have. These are all actual events that have occurred. The good news is that they did not happen all at once in one company!

Simply being able to see these as bad examples that you wouldn't want to replicate is a learning experience in itself, especially if you are doing some of them. If you have personally done or are doing any of the things above, and can admit to them and then just stop doing them (if possible), you will begin to make huge improvements as a sales manager and leader.

Truly great sales managers do none of the above. Instead, they work with their salespeople to help them sell, they spend time out in the territories listening to the customers, and they act as strong leaders.

Chapter Four

Over 300 practical career-advancing tips and real-life insights on sales leadership

Your job title may be Sales Manager,
but your real job is Sales Leader.

Let's assume that you are working for a revenue-focused company and learning to be a more effective sales manager or sales executive. Everything you learn along your journey will help you in some way. This learning will include both successes and failures. The following tips and real-life insights will help accelerate your successes and minimize those failures.

These tips have been learned over twenty years and have worked for countless salespeople, sales managers, and sales executives. Perhaps these will work for you and give you some new insight into how you might address situations that you encounter on a daily basis. Put them to work for you and make money with them!

These tips do not reference a particular company or a specific person. It's the lesson that matters most here.

The tips are divided over eighteen key sections. They are: Recruiting, Interviewing, Hiring, Human Resources, Sales Pitches, Sales Training, Sales Meetings, Sales Tools,

Motivation, Listening, Managing Salespeople, Quotas and Commission Plans, Managing Everyone, Managing Yourself, Career Management, Personal Selling, Personal Finance, and the Reality of Bad CEOs.

Some of the tips at the beginning of each section have been designated as MEGA TIPs and represent the most important tips in each section. Important tips throughout each section have been labeled as TOP TIPs. The remaining tips are considered standard tips and are not labeled.

1. RECRUITING

Recruiting never stops. There are many ways to recruit the best salespeople into your company. Here are some ideas on recruiting the right way:

MEGA TIP: Always Be Interviewing:

Even if you aren't hiring, interview anyway. You never know when you might meet a desirable candidate. No sales team is ever perfect, so keeping the team dynamic is paramount. The potential candidate might not be ready to make a move now, may not be needed, or may not be in your industry or a geographically desirable area, but later, who knows?

MEGA TIP: Know Exactly What You Need before You Recruit:

Not knowing exactly what you need before you turn to a recruiter or turn the HR department loose on finding candidates is a classic mistake.

EXAMPLE: Some people will just say to their recruiter: I need a West Coast VP of Sales to replace Bob. "They would be doing the same job that Bob used to do... can you find me another Bob?" "Oh, OK," your recruiter might say in return... and then, unfortunately, the process starts without a well-defined plan.

There is a better way: You write the job description. Often the hiring executive thinks it is the responsibility of HR to write a job description. It isn't, unless you don't care what you are going to get.

The first thing to do is pull out the job description that was used to hire Bob in the first place. There may not be one. It would make good sense to review what you have first.

- Did anything change while Bob worked for you?

- Look at what the job might have morphed into: Did you like everything that was going on under Bob? If not, now is your opportunity to change it.

- If Bob had been promoted or left on good terms, have him outline his successes and challenges and make recommendations on what should be done differently, if anything, with the new responsibilities.

When you write an internal job description, make it crystal clear what you are looking for:

- The responsibilities of the job,

- Whom the position reports to,

- The size of the territory,

- The number of direct reports,

- Percentage of travel,

- Level of previous experience required,

- Territory budget,

- Compensation range (base, commission, bonus, stock options), and

- Required industry experience and educational background.

You will save a lot of time and get closer to finding the person you are looking for by being as clear as possible in the job description. It's initial prep work that saves a lot of time in the actual hiring process.

Once you've created a clear description of the job, sit down with your recruiter or HR department and review it together. Edit it and come up with an ideal description and have the recruiters do the pre-screening. By closing the loop between the specifics of what you are looking for and matching that up with the available pool of candidates, you will cut hiring time dramatically.

Leverage the Salespeople in the Company:

The current sales staff will always have friends who are looking for jobs. Tap that resource. Most markets are very dynamic with good salespeople always on the move. They may dislike their current boss, want to move up the ladder, might be "underwater" on their stock options, disenchanted with the prospects of their current company, or it might just be time for them to make a change.

Leverage Your Current Customers:

Customers whom salespeople call on are also key sources for job candidate referrals. Other salespeople who have impressed a customer, worked with them for a long time, serviced them well, or simply have an effective style for the market they cover can be found just by asking the customers.

Customers will know who is a potentially great candidate and they will probably know who is looking. Reward them in some way if they help you find the ideal candidate.

TOP TIP: Find the Tough of the Toughest:

Hiring people out of other tougher selling environments is very effective in boosting the quality of the sales team. It can also motivate the existing sales team.

EXAMPLE: In the media sales business, selling radio time in a highly competitive market is considered a really tough job. Good radio salespeople have typically excelled in different media markets just by virtue of the competition and stress they have endured in the radio environment. It's often a good strategy to try to find such people and bridge them into sales jobs in other media categories.

This strategy can apply to hiring people from any tough industry and training them to work in your industry.

Another approach to finding tough salespeople might be to ask the purchasing people in the company who are the best salespeople who call on them. They might be ideal candidates for your next open sales position, or know other salespeople who are.

When You Need Executive Recruiters:

Hiring for most senior sales management jobs usually will require an executive recruiter, especially if the executive the position reports to is new to an industry.

There are a couple of strategic ways to use executive recruiters to hire the right people, and also to help you save money in the long run. It's best to use recruiters to hire the most senior level execs possible. Once that's done, those newly hired executives can open their databases to tap their network of contacts and fill the rest of the jobs that may be open or to upgrade the team. That's how you save money. For the 20-30% of the newly hired sales executive's base salary that it will cost you in professional recruiting fees, you will be able to make multiple additional hires, and no doubt find the "right" people that the new sales exec wants on their team. This represents an excellent return on investment for what was spent on initial recruiting fees.

How to Find an Executive Recruiter:

Most industries have a core group of high level recruiters who know the executives in their respective markets or industries and track them like hawks. These recruiters can be very aggressive and often deliver quickly.

Recruiting sources:

- If you are located in a major city that has no problem attracting employees, consider using national recruiters that track your industry.

- If you are in a smaller market that has a more difficult time attracting employees, consider using a more local recruiter who has access to many companies in your local geographical market.

- Another source of recruiters is industry trade publications and local business newspapers.

- Talk to the HR department and see whom they use.

- Network with peers in your industry and ask whom they have used.

- Do Web searches for national recruiting firms.

- Use online recruiters.

When you find a few recruiters you would consider, have the HR group screen them and ask questions like:

- How long have they personally been recruiting in the industry?

- Whom did they place most recently (or what level job was it)?

- What is their process for creating a candidate pool?

- What is their compensation structure?

- How quickly does their process move?

- If they have multiple executives in offices around the country, who will lead the search?

- What were the last three similar companies they worked with?

- What is their placement rate (compare completed searches to started searches)?

Create Common Motivations:

When you are using recruiters make sure that they are properly motivated and understand what you are trying to accomplish from day one. Be certain that they are clear on what you are seeking and can articulate it back to you. Also, that they know what you aren't looking for as well as what they should look out for when screening résumés. Keep everyone apprised of your thinking.

Your recruiters should be compensated and motivated appropriately to get you the best person. You want them to wake up every morning excited to fill your job openings before anyone else's.

360-Degree Networking:

Look to past and present contacts when you are recruiting. Finding good salespeople in any market is always challenging. Especially when you are competing with the potential riches that other companies might promise.

In tough markets the good people often stay put. In growing markets, competition for great people can be fierce. Go back through your database and see what people who have worked for you previously are now doing. Network with them. If you don't think they are right for you, ask them for contacts just as a recruiter would.

Recruiting friends of friends saves at least one step in the qualification process. They are somewhat pre-qualified—at least as far as character references are concerned. Buy your network friend a dinner or tickets to a play or sporting event if a friend they recommend comes to work for you.

TOP TIP: Make a New Contact Every Few Weeks:

Make it a goal to meet one new potential salesperson or manager every few weeks. Keep in touch with them. Discuss what they may or may not like about their current job. You will no doubt learn some valuable things along the way about what makes salespeople happy. This practice presents the opportunity to hone your interviewing skills. You should make it clear to the candidate that you are not looking to fill a position immediately.

TOP TIP: Develop a Farm League:

The worst thing that can happen to you is to have a salesperson quit with no back-up in sight. This strategy might sound a bit paranoid, but the departure of salespeople happens frequently for many reasons. The hiring process usually takes a few weeks from a cold start. Sometimes having that right person waiting in the wings when you sense that one of the salespeople who work for you is on the ropes can be the difference between making the company revenue number or missing it.

Making the Industry Event Connection:

Industry events are a prime source for making connections with some of the best salespeople outside your company. There are usually after-hours parties sponsored by industry associations or related companies. Go to them. Mingle. Get to know your competitor's salespeople. You may never know when they are thinking about making a change.

Salespeople love to tell war stories and talk about themselves at parties. Use that to your advantage the next time you go to an industry social event. Have a good story to start the process with. Once you've told your story, then be quiet and listen to others. See how they handle themselves, how others react to them, and if there is any chemistry for working with you.

Meet as many people as you can. Do mini "get to know you" interviews. Send them thank you notes or e-mails as follow-up. File their information away for future reference. Keep in touch with them.

Throw Your Own Recruiting Event:

Some of the best recruiting can be done in a casual party environment that you create on your own. Let's face it, good salespeople love to schmooze. Create an opportunity for that to happen in an environment that you control and you will have your hands full of potential candidates.

Throw an unofficial, pre-trade show, kick-off party or throw a survivor's party at the end (or attend similar events that others have planned). Also consider sponsoring a party at a local industry hang-out or a sports event. Have your existing salespeople each bring a few potential sales candidates to the event as the price of their admission. Keep it casual. You obviously wouldn't want to tell the potential candidates that it is a sales-recruiting event. Be low-key. That will create a more relaxed environment for subtle evaluation. Keep it easy-going and see how potential candidates react in a social setting. Make sure you collect business cards if the group is large. Always follow-up promptly with an e-mail and continue networking with the good prospects.

2. INTERVIEWING

Once you have a group of viable candidates, it will be time to start getting to know them. This can be a long or short process, depending on how well you and the HR team have prepared. Here are some ideas on how to conduct effective interviews.

MEGA TIP: Finding People Who Fit the Culture:

Ideally you want to find people that fit into the existing "DNA" structure of a company. If you've done a good job of hiring those around you, then they will have a good feeling about whether a potential candidate fits into your sales organization. Have at least 3-4 people interview a candidate in varying circumstances.

EXAMPLE: Interviewing over a cup of coffee at the local java joint might yield a totally different type of feeling about candidates than meeting them in a busy conference room at your company while people are constantly interrupting you or the sales team. Take the time to make a deep contact with the person you are interviewing. Get to really know this candidate in the time you have.

Relate to something that the candidate has done or is doing. Get him or her at ease as quickly as you can and you will find the "real" person all the faster. Make sure the candidates can interview in all sorts of environments (noisy office, quiet office, open cube environment, etc.). That will be an excellent indicator of how comfortable they are in less-than-perfect selling conditions. That will give you an indication of how well they can talk about your product or service in a similar environment. Have them come back for multiple interviews so you aren't making your decision solely on first-interview chemistry.

MEGA TIP: Avoid the *No-Fault* Candidate:

When you are trying to determine how a candidate fared at another company, listen carefully for the "It was always another person or the company's fault" answer. These are "No-Fault" candidates. They tend to be *prima donnas* who don't like to get their hands dirty, won't admit to their mistakes, and can't accept responsibility. Let your competitors hire them!

One of the more important things that you need to uncover about any candidate whom you interview is:

- Do they take responsibility for their actions?

- Are they contrite about mistakes they have made?

- What did they learn from their mistakes?

- Have the mistakes continued? (Is there a pattern you can detect?)

That's pretty heady stuff for an interview process but now is your chance to get these issues on the table. Try to listen for people who claim to have made no mistakes on their own and blame others for things going wrong. If you hear it in the interview, there is a good chance you will hear it when they aren't making their numbers or something goes wrong after you've hired them.

TOP TIP: **Don't Fall for Interview Hype:**

So many times it happens: A candidate has a great interview and then quickly fails in the job. The person comes across as impressive but then doesn't ultimately deliver. Don't let interview hype cause you to make a fast decision. In cases like these, the candidates have done a great job of selling themselves, but that's pretty much the only thing they are skilled at selling. They seem to have all the right answers. They've obviously been through this before. It takes more than just a good sell job by a candidate to be a great salesperson.

When you interview people who sound overly impressive, try to envision what they will be like six months into the job. What will you expect from them? Are you looking to them to deliver things that no other salesperson can? Are your expectations real?

Has anyone who you have ever hired worked out exactly as you expected from the interview? Probably not. Some do better, some do worse. It's the first impression that might get someone hired but it's how you train them, plus their day-to-day effectiveness, that helps them keep the job. Take everything in the interview process with a grain of salt, as they say.

One way to keep interview hype from creeping in is to keep all your questions as open-ended as possible.

Ask questions like:

- How do you manage your territory?

- How do you prospect for new accounts?

- How do you like to be managed?

- Who has been your worst manager and why?

- Who has been your best manager and why?

- How do you use technology to help you do your job more efficiently?

- What has made you successful in the past?

- How have you failed and what did you learn from it?

- Who has been most influential in your career and why?

This approach is better than your giving them a hypothetical situation to comment on that hints at what you think the right answer is. They will jump on that and tell you what you want to hear.

EXAMPLE: Instead of asking if they prefer close supervision or hands-off supervision, just ask how they like to be managed. This seems like a nuance, but the question, when posed in that way, can yield a more accurate and telling answer. Anything you do that gives them a hint as to what the "right" answer for you is will give them an opportunity to be a "yes person" in the interview process. You can always probe the answer more deeply in a follow-up question but start off vague and unstructured to see how they answer most questions.

Don't accept a fluffy answer. Always dig deeper. If they seek clarification of what you are asking, that is a good sign that they are listening and want to be as diligent as possible in answering.

As part of a deeper interview process ask these questions:

- What could you have done better in your last job?

- What was the biggest mistake that you might have made?

- Did you take responsibility for your actions?

Keep drilling on that answer until you feel that they have been appropriately revealing. Their answers will tell you quite a lot about how they think and operate.

TOP TIP: Résumé Inflation:

Sometimes people will just lie on their résumés. It's that plain and simple. This has happened at the highest levels, inside companies, sports, and politics and has become a huge topic in the press.

This means that you will need to review a candidate's résumé carefully, especially job titles and responsibilities. Pay close attention to figures (like: Increased sales 20%). Make sure that you check on their responsibilities with references or previous employers. Ask what the person's title was and what they did for the company. Leave the question open-ended to see if the job title matches what was on the résumé.

Here are some real examples of résumé inflation at work:

TRUE STORY ONE: A friend of a CEO called and asked her to look at a résumé of someone the friend's company was considering hiring. The CEO sent the résumé to her former Sales VP, since the candidate once worked for him, and asked for feedback.

The former Sales VP read the résumé and was astonished to find it belonged to a person he had fired for not smartly managing even a small sales territory. The résumé listed a very high level title with major responsibilities for company policy-making. It also said the person started the regional office where he once worked.

That seemed like such a huge stretch. Well, it actually seemed more like a huge lie, which it was. None of it was true. The former Sales VP set the record straight. The CEO's friend was very relieved. The candidate was immediately and unceremoniously nixed from consideration.

TRUE STORY TWO: A former executive was looking for work. A recruiter called a Sales VP from the former exec's previous company to confirm that the applicant had indeed been a vice president there.

That sounded odd to the Sales VP because the former executive had never been promoted to a position higher than a sales director. The Sales VP called the HR director and another company executive. Both confirmed that the person claiming to be a former VP was indeed only a sales director when he left the company. This particular person seeking the reference wasn't bad at his old job, and certainly didn't need to lie to get a new job. What compelled this person to lie is unclear. The executive ended up getting a job, but was offered a lower level title, and rightly so.

Lying about something as significant as a résumé is often a sign of deeper issues. Generally it's better to pass on people with falsified résumés unless you can get some clarification as to why it happened. If an honest mistake was made then second chances are merited. If you do hire people whose résumés you know were falsified but who are exceptional at what they do, then make sure they are clear that you will be keeping an eye on them.

In the Candidate's Own Words:

Using the candidate's own words to learn more about them can be a powerful tool. This is one of the more interesting interviewing tactics you can use. The idea came from a high level recruiter.

Here's the way it works:

As part of a screening interview, you or the recruiter ask the candidates what they think they could be doing better in their current job or what they would like to improve. Then you take this information and ask their references to comment on what you have "heard" about the candidate (not referencing that it came directly from the candidate).

EXAMPLE: The candidate might say: "I have a tendency to stick to my guns and see something through when I think it's right for the company."

The recruiter might spin this a bit to the negative side and say something to one of the references like: "We've heard that the candidate is hard headed. What do you think?"

This helps open the door for a more truthful and

accurate assessment from a reference. References don't want to say bad things about their friends but if something factual is already put on the table they are more apt to comment on it openly.

Ranking the Candidates:

Have your recruiter or HR person rank potential candidates on a rating system (A-B-C, 1-2-3, etc.). Review the résumés and decide whom you want to see. Quickly review the reject pile to see if anyone slipped through the cracks.

It's probably best to have the recruiter or the HR person do a brief phone pre-interview with the candidates before you speak to them. See how they measure up to the job description and see how their current compensation fits with what you can offer. The latter is very important. Many candidates are ushered through the interview process with no attention to compensation needs. It can be very disappointing for everyone involved if the candidate needs more money than the company can pay. It wastes everyone's time.

TOP TIP: Same Leopard, Same Spots:

Whatever your thoughts are on a candidate, don't overlook bad information about them in past jobs and assume that they have changed. Chances are they haven't changed much and that they will conveniently blame any faults on someone else.

TRUE STORY: A sales manager hired a candidate who possessed all the right stuff, as far as she could tell. Although there were some negatives, the candidate passed the reference checks, worked for another key company in the industry, and was highly recommended by the recruiter.

Once the salesperson started work everything started going wrong. He was constantly late to internal and external meetings, didn't have the contacts that he said he did, had no work ethic, wasn't interested in learning the product, and couldn't use a computer as he had claimed.

After doing some extensive "after hire" due diligence, the sales manager determined that the salesperson had the exact same patterns in numerous previous jobs which resulted in firings. None of the references or employers came clean about it. But of course the salesperson continued being in denial about his faults and constantly blamed others for his problems.

The final outcome should have been no surprise to anyone. The sales manager fired him.

The Good-Square-Peg, Good-Round-Hole Dilemma:

Take any answer you get from candidates during the interview process at face value and try not to bend the answer into being a plus for them because you like them personally or need to fill a position quickly.

Don't make a great candidate fit the job if there isn't one. A classic mistake is when someone who is a great marketer applies for a sales job. He gets the job and then fails because he ultimately can't close a sales deal. Why? Because the person filling the job didn't take him for who he was (a marketer) and what he was good at (marketing). The sales manager made a stretch to fill the job. The moral of the story is that if something doesn't feel right about the candidate's fit for the job then tell the candidate so. Have him or her respond to it, but don't let them sell you on why they can do it. It's your job to make that call.

How Would the Candidate Handle a Problem?:

Give job candidates a "situation" and ask how they would handle it. The process they choose to solve the problem will give you an insight into how well they might succeed at the company.

Here are some ideas on where to come up with potential problem questions:

- A hypothetical situation with multiple issues,

- A real-life situation that you recently encountered (this will show if they think like you, or are smarter, etc.), or

- A situation that they might face in the first few weeks on the job.

If you end up hiring a candidate, see how the responses given to you in the interview relate to the problem solving skills exhibited in the first few weeks on the job. This will tell you if you have a straight-shooter on your hands.

TOP TIP: Advance Knowledge Is Power:

It pays to have inside information on candidates (good and/or bad) before they come in and meet you. You can ask a question that you know the answer to (like the circumstances under which they left their last company, etc.) to see what kind of spin they put on it.

How to get the scoop on candidates in advance:

- Preview their résumé to see where they have been and what they have accomplished. If your marketplace is a small community, chances are that people will know people and they will know how your candidate faired in previous jobs, if they learned from their mistakes, and if they have shown progress. Find out. This will help you determine how truthful someone is being in the process.

- Type your candidate's name into one of the popular search engines and see what comes up. That may give you some valuable information. Good recruiters use this trick frequently. Just make sure that you have the right person for names with common spellings!

Strategic Misrepresentation:

Some people are masters at stretching the truth in the interview process. They take just a little too much credit for work that others have done. How do you know when this is happening? Chances are you don't, so you have to be a little preemptive. If the answer you get to a question doesn't sound right, dig deeper.

If candidates tell you that they worked in a group "with a $2 million sales budget" ask what specific responsibility they had for that budget. Have them confirm they were personally responsible for that revenue. If you are still unsure of their involvement, then address that in reference checks.

Selling Tests:

To test natural sales ability, consider asking a sales candidate to sell you something on the spur of the moment—a napkin, a cup, their car keys, anything on your desk, etc., (let them choose it). This exercise can be very revealing. You may find a natural salesperson in the rough. You may find that a seasoned salesperson isn't all that good "on their feet." This will also tell you if a candidate can go with the flow and adapt to changing conditions.

As you move sales candidates farther along in the hiring process have them sell you something in a more formal way. Your product would be a good choice. Give them a few days to find out more about your product and come back in and present to you. Don't give them any hints, unless they ask first.

The presentation itself won't matter as much as:

- How resourceful they are in learning about your product and your competitors,

- Preparation of the presentation,

- Structure of the presentation,

- If they sell in a positive way,

- If they have command of whatever presentation method they choose, and

- If they ask for the order.

Preparation is a large percentage of the success of any presentation. Here's what to look for:

- Did they research your website or get any product literature?

- Did they talk to your customers?

- Did they talk to other salespeople?

- Did they try to buy the product themselves, etc.?

This exercise is one of the most revealing tests of how resourceful a candidate could be in selling for you. It's the process they go through that's more important than how polished their initial sales pitch is.

3. HIRING

If you find candidates whom you like, get them hired as soon as possible. Here are some ideas on what to look for and how to negotiate with them when it's time:

MEGA TIP: **All Candidates Being Equal: Seek Out the Technology-Literate:**

Technology is ubiquitous. Not only do people need to be great salespeople, they also need to be technology-literate—in that order.

Policies will vary on how much technology can be used within a company. Laptops and cell phones (and possibly two-way pagers) are a must for a sales organization. Knowledge of presentation software, search engines, a word processor, spreadsheet, and a web browser are "must haves." Knowing how to use most of their features is equally important.

Make sure that you understand how technologically savvy a candidates are before you hire them. Make technology-literacy part of the screening process. It will save you weeks in getting a new salesperson or manager acclimated.

Questions to ask:

- Does the candidate you are considering know how to use technology?

- Which operating systems are they familiar with?

- How do they deal with things when they break or crash?

- How much downtime did they have because of their computers in their previous job? What did they do during the downtime?

- What software programs are they familiar with? Have they had formal software training? On which programs?

- What types of e-mail programs do they know? Have them describe some rules of e-mail etiquette they use.

- Ask them for a tip or two on some of your favorite software programs to see if they really do understand them well.

- Have they used an LCD projector and do they know how to hook up their computer to it?

MEGA TIP: Creative Reference-Checking:

Most people aren't going to give you references that are potentially damaging to their job prospects.

But chances are that you will have to check referen.... as part of hiring them, so make this process work to your advantage.

There are two ways to use references:

The first way to check references is to find other people who may know the person through the reference that the candidate gives you. In most industries the "six degrees of separation" rule applies (i.e., someone will always know someone who knows who you are talking to). Ask the reference what other peers your candidate worked with and what they thought of this person and how they ranked compared with other peers. Ask if you can get their contact info (if they don't work there any longer) and contact them to see what they think. Ask those secondary references for similar input.

The second way to use references is to assume that they will give you a good recommendation and tell them that, "should the candidate be selected," would they give you inputs on the following:

- How can you best manage this particular person?

- What do they like or dislike about selling and managing?

- What should you look out for?

- What are their hot buttons, landmines, and opportunities for growth?

- How did the person giving the reference manage or work with the candidate?

- In what kind of environments does the candidate excel or become frustrated?

- Would they hire the candidate again, *and in what capacity?*

Answers to these questions will give you a strong insight and a better base to start with when it comes to managing this person.

TOP TIP: Leaving Room for Cream:

When you are negotiating a compensation package with a potential candidate, don't start with your best offer. Leave a little room for negotiation. If you sense that you are dealing with a savvy salesperson who likes to negotiate, then start at about 85-90% of what you can offer on all fronts (salary, commission, bonus, stock options, etc.). Be prepared to go up in key areas, or offer other perks. Have your limits. If there is some give-and-take, then everyone will win and feel as is they got what they wanted. That's a better way to bring a new hire into the company. And when it's time for annual reviews you will know what you are going to face.

TOP TIP: *Quid Pro Quo* Salary Negotiating:

When a reasonable compensation package has been offered and a negotiation process is underway an interesting approach is to follow the *"quid pro quo"* rule. If a candidate asks for more of anything (salary, commission, bonus or stock options), you ask for something more in return to balance it out. This presumes that your initial package offer was a fair market rate or maybe even slightly more than generous.

EXAMPLE: A new sales candidate wants $20K more in their annual commission plan... ask if she is willing to take that increase in the form of an increased budget or a "kicker bonus" for being over the annual budget so that the bonus is paid on the back-end. Or simply ask what more she would be willing to do to get the additional compensation. (Be careful of communicating any sexual innuendo here!)

If you both make compromises during a negotiation and feel as if you both have a good conclusion, then you have created an environment of mutual respect that will carry forward into the job from day one.

REMEMBER: Never *give* something without *asking* for something in return.

TOP TIP: Hire Experience:

Hire the best, most experienced salespeople with the best business networks possible. "Most experienced" doesn't necessarily mean the oldest. Experience is relative. You may be pioneering a new market and the only salespeople who are available have minimal experience.

The competition is often the best place in which to look for experienced salespeople. Experienced salespeople are worth their weight in gold when they deliver sales. And remember that when you hire them, you also hire their network.

Generally, the experienced salespeople will cost you more in terms of base salary. In the end, when you add up training, and ramp time costs of the less experienced salesperson, the cost is generally lower.

The Experience Hurdle:

The downside of hiring experienced salespeople is that it makes it difficult for younger and possibly more talented salespeople to get the experience they need to become sales rock stars. There is no great wisdom on getting around this problem. There is nothing wrong with hiring younger salespeople but it's better to focus on making strategic hires of experienced people first and then fill in around them with exuberant and somewhat less experienced but still potentially talented salespeople. That is a stronger strategy.

Here are a few ideas:

SALES SUPPORT: If the sales organization is highly structured, put younger talent in the role of sales support first. Keep them moving through a series of tasks and programs to build on their experience. Make the experiences somewhat redundant. They will learn more. Doing basic sales tasks right the first time (and only once) is often beginner's luck. New trainees should master the sales support experience, not just quickly experience the experience. That usually means at least six months in a beginner salesperson function. This also helps weed out those who can't get their arms around repetitive tasks (also referred to as "work").

WING PERSON: Another approach might be to put a sales trainee under the wing of a top salesperson. A top salesperson could probably use additional support on more complicated accounts. This will allow a very talented trainee to get firsthand experience but not stray too far from thoughtful mentoring. It is also an excellent reward to a salesperson producing at the highest levels in the company.

SMALL ACCOUNT MANAGER: A final idea is to set up an inside sales team that handles smaller accounts. Most likely it would be centralized, mentored by a leading, inside sales manager, and have a formal and structured training program to bring in new sales talent and groom future, outside salespeople. Interestingly, it's some of the smaller accounts that require a higher level of personal attention. Anyone new to sales would find this an invaluable experience.

The Marketing Edge:

Consider hiring a salesperson with previous marketing experience. Some of the best salespeople have marketed products first in their selling careers, and some of the best marketers have sold products previously.

Creating a Hierarchy and Careers:

If the sales team is set up in a tiered way with a senior salesperson teamed with a junior salesperson, consider a hierarchical hiring-and-training program that grooms the junior salesperson to take on the role of the senior person in the future.

If the sales team is set up in a triple tiered way (Sales Assistant + Junior Salesperson + Senior Salesperson), consider a similar program that trains each of the lower two people to do the next-level job.

Hire with upward mobility in mind and work to create a career path for the sales team.

Hiring Bonuses:

If you use the existing sales team to provide people you hire, then reward them for it. This assumes that you are relatively happy with your existing team and trust their judgment.

Set up a referral program with the blessing of your HR team. Maybe it's a $500-$1500 bonus for referring each new hire who successfully completes 90-120 days of employment. The specifics of the program should be entirely reflective of your company's culture and compensation models.

Be careful that you don't turn the sales team into recruiters who can make more money through recruiting instead of selling your product or services. Consider a limit on the number of people they can refer directly per quarter or year. If they are really smart, they will get around this by referring to other friends in the company and negotiating a split-fee deal on the bonus. If they are that resourceful, then you have to give them some credit!

Welcoming a New Salesperson:

Once a new salesperson is hired make sure to welcome him or her properly on the first day. Check in with the new hire at the beginning of the day, maybe take them to lunch, and then check in with them before he or she leaves. Remember back to your first day at any new school and you'll see why this is helpful.

Use your time together to set expectations. Personally introduce the new salesperson to other people on the staff, walk him or her through the offices and show where everything is, and who the "go to" people are for various needs, etc.

Prepare a kit that might include hats, t-shirts, manuals, HR materials, etc. The idea is to make the newcomer immediately feel appreciated and welcomed as a team member. You might also include the newcomer in some of your regularly scheduled meetings (where appropriate) while he or she is getting acclimated.

4. HUMAN RESOURCES

Human resource issues keep every sales manager busy. Here are some ideas on annual reviews, and dealing with problem personnel and terminations, as well as harassment issues:

MEGA TIP: Do Annual Employee Reviews:

Salespeople love feedback, so do reviews religiously. Make it a point to give constructive feedback and tell them how to get to the next level in the company. Help them chart their own course. Giving them focus will make all the difference in the world to employee morale.

Annual reviews are usually the *last* thing anyone in sales management wants to deal with. If you deal with them quickly and completely, they can make your life a lot easier. If you do take an interest in doing the reviews, you will quickly separate yourself from most other managers in your company and your employees will appreciate your interest in them.

Have the salespeople do a self-review of their previous year. Next, they should lay out 3-5 areas where they feel they need improvement, and set 3-5 goals that they will work hard to accomplish over the next year. Review all of this with them to make sure it maps to goals that you would like them to accomplish. Agree to the goals mutually.

MEGA TIP: Do Upward Reviews:

You ask your direct reports, and possibly even their direct reports, to tell you anonymously what they think of you and your sales management style. At first blush it appears that this might be the dumbest idea in the world. Is this insane? But how can you get better at what you do if this doesn't happen? These reviews are more valuable than the ones that come from just about any boss you will ever have.

TRUE STORY: When the sales manager asked if the sales team could do an annual review on him, the HR Director thought it was a wacky request. The sales manager wanted it done anonymously to get completely honest feedback, to do a better job for the sales team.

The HR Director and sales manager created a review form that touched on all aspects that they felt were important. HR had the final say on the questionnaire. It was sent out and the response rate was excellent. So was the feedback. The sales manager listened and made very visible improvements where the team felt they were needed.

In a staff meeting later in the year, the sales manager thanked the sales team for the anonymous ideas. This showed them that he was listening to them and respected their thoughts. Those are two key ingredients to the two-way communications necessary in a sales organization.

As extreme as some of the points of view may be from a sales team they are your peers and you need to listen to them fully. There is more truth to be found in this type of review than any other. When you hear the same themes over and over again, then you need to take them seriously. Don't put yourself in denial mode, or the entire exercise will be useless. Take the information for what it's worth and make the necessary changes. The way that you respond will speak volumes about how you feel about your team.

TOP TIP: **Take the Review Process Seriously:**

Much to the dismay of many of your managerial peers, you should strive to get your annual review forms and ratings done before anyone else does. Make it a personal goal. The sooner you do it (and do it well) the less you will have to worry about it. This will show the employees that you care and the HR department will love you. It's similar to doing your taxes early and getting the refund faster. It feels good and you can go on and do other things. Waiting until the last minute (like the night before—and you know who you are!) is human nature. It also lowers the quality of your reviews and that does a disservice to the salespeople.

TRUE STORY: At one company, the employees were able to rate the heads of departments they worked in for overall satisfaction and satisfaction with how they were being managed. One sales manager's department scored in the top three of twenty-five departments for employee satisfaction. That department was one of the newest at the company. There was a direct correlation between how much the sales manager visibly cared about the sales team and how satisfied the team was with its job experience and the sales manager's leadership.

Employee Assessment Check List:

Here are key points that should be considered when doing annual reviews:

- Performance against Sales Budget
- Close Ratio
- Work Quality
- Communication Skills
- Interpersonal Skills
- Reliability
- Product Knowledge
- Resourcefulness
- Team Work
- Problem Solving
- Leadership

Consider using a numerical scale to rate each point. Make sure that you define what the numbers mean. You can rank on a scale from 1-5 or 1-10 (decide which end of the scale is "high/important") or use short essay questions. The essay questions might be more telling depending on how many salespeople are doing reviews.

You can also use a letter-based ranking system, like: Outstanding (O), Exceeds Expectations (EE), Meets Expectations (ME), Below Expectations (BE), etc.

How often these are done may be decided by company policy. If there isn't a company policy for this, make a departmental policy. Doing reviews annually for salary changes is reasonable.

TOP TIP: The Employee Self-Review:

Salespeople should write their own version of the annual assessment so that their sales manager can understand how employees view their job and contributions to the company. The sales manager should write a parallel review to see how close the two are.

Here are ideas on what to include in a review:

- Describe job responsibilities.

- Describe major strengths in their current job.

- Describe major contributions to the company.

- Areas where they need to improve.

- What help is needed to get their job done.

- Last year's 3-5 goals/objectives and how they did against them.

- Next year's 3-5 goals/objectives that they want to accomplish in "X" time frame (usually in the next six months if there is a mid-year check-in).

Reviews like these can be handled in one of two ways:

- The sales manager and the salesperson can write the reviews simultaneously, or

- The sales manager can comment on the salesperson's review once it is written.

Keep in mind that waiting for the salesperson to finish the review before the sales manager makes comments will lengthen the process.

HINT: Set an earlier deadline for your employees.

It's better to do the reviews in parallel so that the sales manager can add more original thoughts before seeing what the salesperson is thinking.

TOP TIP: **Do a Six-Month Check-In:**

One way to keep the salespeople and sales managers focused on meeting their goals and improving on their performance after their annual review is to do a six-month check-in. Let them know a month in advance that the review is coming so they (and you) can plan for it.

If possible, mid-year reviews should be tied to additional stock option or bonus awards. Annual reviews are usually where salary increases take place. Some companies require six-month reviews, some don't. Even if it isn't company policy, it's a good idea to do them anyway.

In the six-month review cover the same points that were made on the annual review but on a more casual basis. The "check in" can be done in as little as 15 minutes and often over the phone (but *never* on e-mail unless absolutely necessary).

Ask how the salesperson or sales manager feels about their progress. Make more suggestions on how they can improve. Get agreement that the improvements make sense and will be worked on. Make a revised action plan. In that plan, it's not a good idea to lower a budget number unless there is a major company-wide sales issue.

You'll be surprised how much additional progress can be made with a six-month review. Make sure that the salesperson or sales manager understands that mid-year reviews aren't necessarily for increasing compensation or stock options (unless that's how your company does it). It's mostly to check on their personal performance.

TRUE STORY: A CEO wasn't sure that a salesperson was going to make his goals and keep his job. The salesperson was approaching his first six months with the company and wasn't even close to hitting the pre-agreed to (and greatly lowered) sales expectations. Panic was setting in.

It was time for the sales manager to have "the talk" and put the salesperson on warning. The sales manager made corrective suggestions and gave a heartfelt pep talk. She told the salesperson she was behind them 110%. The salesperson had no idea that the sales manager cared. Over the next few weeks there were constant check-ins and guidance, and improvement was made. It was enough to save this salesperson—but only because the salesperson took it upon himself to make the necessary changes after being given the appropriate guidance.

Re-Calibrating Great Expectations:

Some salespeople and/or sales managers think they are farther along the "getting promoted" curve than they really are. In fact, they are doing a fine job, but are being pushed by their egos, spouses, families, or significant others to ask for more responsibility than they may be ready to take on.

Re-calibrating their thinking can be complicated. It's best to tell them the truth about their skill sets and work with them on a plan to get them closer to what they need and what you need them to do.

Give them shorter-time-frame tasks or smaller tasks to accomplish as a way of giving them faster feedback. When the task is complete, provide a fair critique of what they did or didn't do on these small projects to move the ball farther ahead. Be constructive. If they aren't ready to get to the next level after the project is completed, tell them so. Tell them exactly what they will need to accomplish and how long you think it will take them to get to the next level, based on what you know about their skill set. Let them see that there is an end in sight. Be patient with them and let them find their own way under your watchful eye. Be prepared to "hold them back a grade" and extend their re-calibration time in order to get to the next level—or accelerate them if they are overachieving. If you make a promise then deliver on it, so long as they have delivered. If you can't deliver, then tell them why.

Confidential "one-on-one" conversations are important here. Tell them what experiences you personally had that might help them to understand that what they are experiencing is truly normal. Over time they will be more at ease with themselves and more productive, as well as loyal.

TOP TIP: Rid Yourself of the Bottom Feeders:

Sales teams are an ever-evolving group, a revolving door for some sales managers. The top performers perform admirably and make your day while the bottom feeders suck resources out of the system and make your life miserable. The great middle can go either way. Your challenge is to move the lower range of salespeople up the ladder toward "top performer" status.

It's wise to make the bottom-end-of-performance spectrum for the sales team a clearly marked one-way ticket out the door. Do this as fast as is reasonable and legally possible. The question is: Where will the "cut line" be? You must be sure that you have done everything possible to save those on the bottom tier from their demise. It's never a good idea to fire people who are victims of poor planning and bad execution on the part of sales management.

In the end, sales numbers generally tell most of the story. They don't lie. Have a full grasp of the picture that the numbers are painting. Try to make sure that everything is proportional across all territories so that the performance numbers can be a fair judge of success. That will eliminate a lot of finger-pointing and lengthy termination processes. Also, try to supply all the support possible to help people be successful. Ask them what tools they need. This is important. If they tell you the tools they need and you deliver but they don't, well...case closed!

It's all about how salespeople choose to do their job. Only fire them if you have done everything you can to help them and yet they still fail, and they know it. Here are some of the reasons they may fail:

- Maybe they just aren't great salespeople after all.

- They weren't a good fit with the product or customers.

- They had too many distractions in their private lives to be focused on selling.

At some point these issues can no longer be your problem. If salespeople keep the company from making its numbers, they are a liability that you can't afford to have. You will still need to ask important questions like:

- Did you give them enough training?

- Did you give them enough time to ramp up?

- Did you give them enough tools to do the job?

Make sure you do your homework before you summarily cut the bottom percentile of the sales organization. Cutting the bottom 5-10% usually feels about right, but see how many people are just over the edge before you pull any triggers. Don't forget that you have to replace them with new salespeople who will need training on your products and sales process. All that time spent making changes will cost sales.

TOP TIPS: The Reality of Bad Hires:

Bad hires are often made along the path of a stellar sales management career. Once you figure out that you've made a bad hire, it makes no sense to keep the person in suspense or make either of your lives miserable for any longer than necessary. For all the recruiting that you may do, you may also have to do some un-recruiting from time to time.

Always take the high road when you are letting someone go. The short version of this is that you will need to document all the problems and honestly (graciously) tell them why they didn't meet expectations, and that while they aren't bad people, they should probably move on to a better-fitting job. It's nothing more than complete honesty without being demeaning. A bad hire was probably a great salesperson before working for you, and will no doubt continue on and be a great salesperson afterwards. That's the best assumption to make. Sometimes there just isn't a fit or the chemistry just isn't right. Acknowledge it in a professional way and move on.

When it's time to ask someone to move on it's best to document the performance issues thoroughly. As soon as you sense a problem, contact HR to make them aware. Also, make your boss aware that you are "on the case." Start taking notes regarding performance issues (anything from being late to meetings, to not getting call reports in on time, to missing sales quotas—whatever your measurements are).

Have a very specific conversation about why the salesperson is being terminated. Be kind because you don't want to scar a failed salesperson or sales manager for life. It's not always 100% the employees fault. Even in that rare circumstance where it is, it still pays to be professional. The person you fire today may become a customer tomorrow, or may go on to do great things in another profession, or be *your* boss one day.

If you have built up a lot of anger and resentment regarding how bad this salesperson or sales manager is and you'd just as soon yell at them and fire them on the spot, then you've probably waited too long to address the problem. Move quickly to keep everyone's sanity and remain professional.

TOP TIP: Fire Them Yesterday:

There's an old adage in sailing that says: If it's getting windy and you think it's time to put up smaller sails, then you probably should have already done it. The same goes for people on the sales team who must be fired. Once you've done everything you can to save an employee and you find that it's not working, don't wait a second longer to fire him. Keeping someone around who doesn't meet your needs or can't do the job isn't good for either of you.

The process of firing a salesperson will be different in each company. One thing that is universal is that the longer you wait, the more it will cost the company in lost sales. As soon as people become a liability, you need to manage them like any other liability. Yes, it sounds cold and callous, but this is business, and you have to do what's best for it. If salespeople aren't helping the sales team achieve the company goals, then they are hurting you. Many salespeople have said after being terminated that leaving a company was the best thing that could have happened to them. Many have gone on to excel in other sales organizations.

TOP TIP: Termination Day:

When you bring a salesperson in for "the termination meeting" start by asking how he or she feels about the job they have been doing.

The conversation can go one of two ways:

1. The salesperson can be in total denial and feel that he (or she) is doing a great job, although their numbers probably won't show it. He will have plenty of excuses. That is the appropriate time to raise the issue of a "disconnect" between what the company requires and what the salesperson is delivering. If you are a performance-based selling organization, the numbers usually say it all, unless something has changed dramatically with the product. There may also be some extenuating circumstances that are causing the problem, but chances are, you wouldn't be having the termination meeting if that were the only thing. Lay out your documentation about the salesperson's activities. You can start asking questions like:

- How do you feel about being so far behind on your numbers? Why do you think it's happening?

- How comfortable do you feel about selling the value that the products provide to the buyer?

It usually doesn't take too many questions to start uncovering (and getting the point across) that the salesperson is failing and not fitting in. Try to avoid telling salespeople that they are getting fired without first letting them get their head wrapped around why it isn't working. They will figure that out soon enough. You may get some push-back and excuses. That's to be expected. In the end you need to be clear and firm that there isn't a mutual fit and that they are being terminated. Then lay out whatever their severance plan might be.

2. The other way it can go is that the salesperson tells you he doesn't feel that he is doing the best that he can. The more astute salespeople will take this approach mostly in anticipation of what they think is about to happen to them. This is a less likely scenario but it does happen. It's best to try and determine why they think they aren't doing their best.

If they haven't been well trained or had enough time allocated to them, then take that as important feedback. Assuming that you truly believe it, not everyone can be simply taught to do everything without thinking on their own. They have to apply themselves. If you think they can be saved, then take some monitoring steps to see if that's true. Make it a very short leash, though. Do a two-week performance evaluation. Check-in every other day. Review goals and what's happened. Be up front every step of the way and be honest with salespeople about their chances of success.

Once the microscope is on the failing salesperson

or sales manager, they may more fully understand that they aren't cut out for this type of sales work. But if you think they are worth saving after some form of attitude adjustment, then go for it. In the end it's the company revenue numbers that they are helping you deliver (or not), so you will need to make the call about how well they are contributing.

Dealing with RIFs:

Dealing with a reduction in force (RIF) can be painful. It requires tremendous focus as the team will have to get smaller and handle more responsibilities. This is often much more complicated than firing a single salesperson. Firing an individual salesperson is usually done for performance issues (i.e., they didn't make their numbers or they did something else wrong). Doing a RIF usually means that a lot of hard-working, good-minded people will need to be let go to keep a company or a division afloat. Keeping the proper perspective when doing a RIF is important.

Here are some ideas on preparing yourself to do a RIF:

- If you sense the company will be doing multiple RIFs, use the first one to get rid of "dead wood" and underperformers. This will also ease the pain of having to fire these people individually.

- Realize that the company or division must do this to survive. Don't take it personally. In many cases, a company may get ahead of itself or do projects that are "out there" so the process of reeling in a bit is sometimes very healthy.

- Make sure that everyone who has to leave understands that this is a company decision, not just yours (although you must pick the underperformers or those whose talents won't be suitable to the new group). Try to smooth the pain for those who must leave. Offer to be a reference if that is appropriate.

- Those who are staying behind will have to be treated differently as well. They may feel guilty that they still have their jobs when the person in the cube next to them doesn't. Reassure them that they were handpicked to help the team move forward. Get the business "back to normal" as soon as possible.

TOP TIP: Knowing When a Salesperson Might be Leaving:

Sometimes the departure of a salesperson can take you completely by surprise. This can create a HR nightmare if you don't see it coming. Here are some early warning signs:

They:

- Are out of contact with you for periods of time and basically hiding out.

- Begin doing a minimal amount of work, just whatever it takes to get by.

- Do not negotiate with you on next quarter's budget numbers.

- Stop asking you for assistance in getting difficult deals pushed through.

- Send messages through the "grapevine" that they might be leaving, but deny it if confronted.

- Have their résumé on the street. (That's a big hint.)

- Were once very verbal about company issues or politics, but they stop giving you new ideas or fighting for what they think is right. (Essentially, they have given up.)

- Start to display a sense of entitlement about what they should earn or how their variable compensation (commission) plan should work.

- Start asking for higher compensation for the same amount of (or less) effort.

- Don't take on new challenges that create a promotion path for them.

- Tell you what you want to hear and then don't deliver on it.

- Start taking a lot of time off (especially sick-days).

- Have a diminishing sales pipeline.

- Aren't excited about taking new products to existing customers.

- Start asking you questions about the future of the company.

- Issue ultimatums, hoping that you will fire them.

- Become obstinate and argumentative.

- Cease being a team player.

- Bad-mouth you or their managers to their peers.

- Ask when they can next exercise stock options.

- Call HR (or have their significant other do it) to get information on extended healthcare benefits.

Keeping the Keepers:

There will be times when some of your star performers want to move on. The reasons can be varied but boil down to: the need to make more money, feeling slighted about not being promoted, not being included in the latest projects, and feeling stagnant in a job they have been doing (well) for a while.

Without them, your team will be of less value. What do you do to keep these keepers? Many times, all it takes is some personal attention from the top. That may include you and executives above you. The key is having a heartfelt (*honestly* heartfelt) conversation about how they fit into the company and what they are looking for. In some cases it might just be a little more money, more responsibility, more "love" from you or the company. Weigh the advantages of giving them what they need compared with the cost of losing them. Don't let emotions rule the day. It's still a business decision after all and you can't throw a sales organization out of whack just because of one person. That's not to say you can't skew things just a little in your favor when necessary.

But They're *Your* Idiots!:

There will be days when you feel that you have nothing but idiots working for you or around you. Just remember, if they work for you, and whether you hired them or not, they are your idiots. So are they really idiots, then? Probably not. It just feels that way.

Resist all temptation to judge or classify anyone, especially the salespeople, as idiots, morons, dolts, etc. Try to understand why they might be acting the way they are. If they are doing something seemingly stupid because they are enforcing a company policy then do what you can to change the policy. If something is happening that fosters stupid behavior, then get to the root cause and fix it.

If the "idiots" work in another department and you think they truly are idiots, don't forget that the same company that hired you hired them. That makes you a potential idiot in their eyes as well. Is everyone an idiot? Doubtful! Everyone needs each other to be successful in a company and that couldn't be truer for the sales organization. So resist the temptation to call people idiots. It will never help you accomplish anything.

As a leader and a manager it's up to you to figure out why good people could be doing idiotic things and help keep it from happening again and again.

TOP TIP: Sexual Harassment:

Some sales managers and salespeople do not take the concept of sexual harassment seriously. Don't be one of them. Here is a simple rule: Don't tolerate harassment on any level. It can go unnoticed because it takes on many forms that aren't within the norm. The classic version of sexual harassment is a manager expressing interest in an employee who doesn't share the same interest. If a manager's advances make another employee uncomfortable, the potential is there for a lot of trouble. A *lot* of trouble.

Harassment is not always just between two employees. It is possible for an employee who isn't being harassed to feel uncomfortable because another employee is.

EXAMPLE: A sales manager is sleeping with Salesperson A (who happens to work for them) and Salesperson B feels that A is getting an unfair advantage when it comes to perks and account assignments. That discomfort is real in the mind of Salesperson B and should be avoided at all costs.

Denial and rationalization are powerful sentiments in these situations. They can blind someone from making realistic decisions. Sexual harassment doesn't necessarily follow gender lines the way that you think it would. A male salesperson can feel harassed if a female counterpart is sleeping with her boss (male or female). See how complicated this can get? It's better just to play it clean and avoid the opportunity for a problem.

There isn't any form of sexual harassment that doesn't hurt someone in one way or another. The most important advice that can be offered here is to stay away from it at all costs, unless you have to deal with it, and act professionally.

TRUE STORIES: Here are some of the more stupid moves that sales managers have made in the area of sexual harassment.

There are sales managers who have:

- Thought the annual sexual harassment seminar is the appropriate place at which to tell dirty jokes.

- Kept a computer database on the sexual skills of staffers they have slept with.

- Thought they were e-mailing a humorous response to a few friends about a new staffer "wanting" them, only to find that they sent the message to their entire division.

- Thought it would be hysterically funny to videotape a female salesperson's chest while she was practicing her sales pitch in training classes.

- Thought no one was paying attention at a drunken sales meeting/dinner while proceeding to "get involved" with another staffer in the restroom.

- "Hit on" staffers and vice versa.

- Slept with their assistants (You can repeat this one about 5 times).

There have also been:

- Staffers who claim harassment because of jealousy or to ruin someone's career; and

- Sales assistants who had their desk in the middle of a big office area (with no cubicle or partitions) and felt compelled to share, in vivid detail, their weekend sexual conquest stories with friends over the phone.

How do you effectively deal with these issues as a sales manager? The first rule is to not be involved in these situations yourself (that seems awfully obvious, doesn't it?). The second is to not turn a deaf ear, when it is happening around you.

Here are some guidelines:

- Investigate all sexual harassment claims discreetly through the human resources department as soon as possible.

- Make sure that the harassed party knows that you are on the case, looking to resolve it as effectively as possible, and that it will be dealt with confidentially.

- Keep *your* love life and sexual needs out of the office.

- Keep all issues confidential between the employee, human resources, and you. Do not discuss any details at any management meetings. Word will travel fast and both parties may be irreparably damaged.

- If you see something developing that doesn't look good to you pull the offending party aside and express concern as a friend and boss about the perception others are having. That may shock the offender into stopping or seeking help. Try to nip it in the bud. Don't accuse, just inform and make suggestions. Make sure that HR is aware of how you are approaching the problem.

- Don't drink excessively (preferably not at all) at company events.

- Don't make liquor the only theme of any company event, even after hours.

- Realize that harassment isn't just between two employees. It involves *every* employee who witnesses or simply hears about it, directly or indirectly.

- Sexual harassment can also extend to customers.

- Have a written "zero tolerance" policy on sexual harassment. Fire people when you have to.

- Help members of your staff get counseling when necessary. Encourage them to get help and make it easy and confidential for them to do so.

- Realize and acknowledge that in high-stress environments employees will be drawn to each other. As a rule, these situations shouldn't be tolerated, but people are human, and real relationships in the workplace are sometimes possible. It's just potentially a lot messier when people meet inside the company.

- If relationships have to happen (sometimes people do fall in love!) encourage discretion and professionalism. In most cases, "hooking up" inside the company rarely has a happy ending (although one can always hope for the best) and if it is going to occur at all, it should be out of public view.

Alcohol and Other Substances:

Harassment isn't always sexual in nature. Employees who don't wish to drink alcohol or do drugs can be forced to at social events in order to be considered part of the "in group." That obviously creates huge issues. Avoid that behavior at all cost, too.

Company-sanctioned parties that orbit exclusively around a drinking (or drug) theme aren't really suitable for a business environment. This isn't a prudish point of view, it's realistic. Calling a company party "The Friday

Afternoon Beer Bust" is no longer appropriate. Calling it the "Friday Afternoon Attitude Adjustment Hour" or "TGIF Party" or "Staff Mixer" doesn't draw attention to a drinking theme and is more appropriate.

Many people who have drinking and drug problems can't admit it, and events that are solely alcohol related give them an excuse to overindulge. Such events may also put recovering substance abusers in an awkward situation. Both scenarios can cause personal humiliation and cost job productivity. You don't need to run the sales organization like a nunnery (unless it is) but realize the impact that some very simple choices can have on your image, the employees, and the company.

5. SALES PITCHES

Why have a sales pitch? They give a sales team something to focus on and rally around.

Building a sales pitch should be a team exercise. It is very much like a mission statement in that it's hard to get everyone to agree to just one version. Get your smartest people together and start tossing ideas around. Reserve the right to take all the input and create the final version on your own. This is an iterative process but there is only one quarterback who can get this done—you or someone smart who works for you.

Some salespeople will use a pitch as a direct sales tool while others will use it as a reference point for building their own presentations. Whatever works for the salesperson and brings in the sales is the right way to go.

Role-play any custom presentations that your sales-people create so that you are sure a consistent message is being delivered. The goal of having a usable sales pitch is so every salesperson will be on the same page. That is the hard part. It does require some monitoring to keep sales-people from overstating or being inaccurate with their presentations. Keep tabs on all versions of the pitch. You may learn some very valuable info from your team and be able to incorporate it into future versions of the sales presentation. Always keep an open mind in doing this as it helps create ownership of the presentation by the entire team.

Here are ideas on the process of creating sales presentations:

MEGA TIP: Nail Down the Key Selling Proposition First:

Of all the points that you can have in the pitch there will be a single most important one. It's the one that will set the company apart from its competitors and something that the sales team must know by heart. You may have an idea of what you want it to be but you need the entire team to buy into it. Without that sense of ownership of the key selling point, the sales effort will be less successful.

Start the process of determining the key selling point with a high-level team session. Determine in advance what you think the key selling point might be, or at least an overall theme or the direction it might take, *before* you start discussing it with the sales team. That level of lead-ership is required to move this process along and to a high-impact conclusion. Then keep an open mind to hear more ideas, once the discussion starts. The ideas could be new products, new competitive features, and new ways to position or present the product, etc. The key selling point could be something that's already in the sales presentation but needs further emphasis, or refinement, or has been misunderstood and needs correction. Ultimately it's your call since you're the sales boss!

Have everyone with a vested interest get into one meeting room to do this exercise. This could include product and marketing people but it's primarily a sales exercise. Initially, this is a silent, individual exercise. No group-thinking yet. Have team members write answers on slips of paper. This will make sure that you get everyone's point of view.

Then have them write down answers to these questions:

1) What is most unique about what the sales team sells?

2) What are the benefits to the customer of what you are selling?

Then put all the answers on two separate white boards. (Put all the answers to one question on one board.)

Next, debate the merits of the items on each list. Rank them in order of importance. Put the best responses to 1) and 2) into a brief sentence. It should look like this: Company X's product (name) is unique because it: 1) _____. The benefits to you (the customer) are that: 2) _____.

EXAMPLE:

Our widget is unique because it: lowers the time to do X.

The benefits to you are that: it will
costs by XX% and lower your headcount

You are beginning to unearth the best k
point. Next, read it out loud to see if it makes s⟨   ⟩u
may want to tweak it many times. Set some sort of
framework on how much time will be spent on this exercise. Try to leave at least one-third more time than you
originally scheduled for the meeting to get this right. It
always will take longer than you think and you want to
give ample time for people to sort it all out and share
their opinions.

If the group isn't naturally gravitating towards the key
selling point you think is the most important you will
want to understand why. It may be time to assert some
leadership and start debating the merits of what you consider important to the sales team and the customers. Use
logic to make your case, but don't bully people into
accepting your vision of the world. They may have the
right answer, not you. It has to be a shared view. Get
agreement from the group that everyone is heading
down the right path. It may turn out that what your team
thinks is a better solution than what you came up with,
to wit, the old adage "two heads are better than one"

EXAMPLE: At one company, the sales team created an extensive list of what was unique about the
company's products and what the benefits were to
their customers. Many of those "unique things" had an
impact on every customer, while a few were important to only some customers.

After a rigorous debate, the key selling point was

established. This particular company was in the business of acquiring and marketing a large volume of low-cost Internet advertising banners from thousands of high quality small to medium web sites across a wide spectrum of content (sports, games, finance, etc.). The sites were all "clean," so there was no possibility of ads showing up on adult content sites.

The company also had the ability to optimize the placement of those banner ads on participating websites where they would get the most response. That would mean better quality "clicks" on the ads or sales or leads or whatever metric was important to the advertiser.

Through optimization, the customer would get a more efficient ad spend and at a significantly lower cost. The company also had multiple ad products to help an advertiser meet its goals. There was a lot more to it, but you get the idea.

The final version of this company's key selling point went something like this:

> "The company has created a unique way to aggregate high-quality ad banner inventory from many small-to- medium-sized websites and to optimize the placement of interactive ad campaigns over those sites so that you the customer will get a significantly higher ROI (Return On Investment) from your online ad spending.

It seems simple enough but it took hours of input and debate to get there. Once everyone was behind the key selling point, it became a huge success.

MEGA TIP: The Structure of a Sales Pitch:

Creating a sales presentation doesn't have to be rocket science, unless you *are* selling rocket engines. Planning it out does make all the difference, though. It's hard to build anything without a plan, even a rough one.

Here is a basic, six-point sales pitch plan:

- Timely, Topical, Unique Opening

- Market Info/Competitive Conditions

- How the company can help the customer create more customers

- Executive Summary

- Proposal

- Close

TOP TIP: Laying Out the Key Selling Datapoints:

You start building a pitch by establishing the key selling datapoints that will resonate with your customers. Then have the sales team rank them in order of importance. Some ideas may hit the cutting room floor as you strive for just giving customers what they need to know to buy from you.

The key selling datapoints could include:

- Current market conditions affecting the need to have the product.

- What people who currently buy the products think of them.

- Case studies on how the product is used.

- Anything that's new and exciting about the products.

- What the customer's competitors are doing in the marketplace.

- Latest market research information that makes a case for the product.

- Insight and analysis on the latest news stories in your category.

Have a free-form discussion about all the key selling datapoints. Write everything down on large sheets of paper and put them around the room so everyone can see them. Get everything on paper—no matter how insignificant it might seem. Once you start piecing everything together, the presentation will take shape.

TOP TIP: Powerful Proof Statements:

To add another dimension to the sales pitch, have the sales team write down "proof that it works" points that back up the key selling proposition. It's best to do this individually on a sheet of paper. The "proofs" are small anecdotal success stories, or if your product isn't well established, they might be analyst statements supporting how good the product potentially is.

EXAMPLE:

- XYZ Company increased sales 10X by using our product/service!

- ABC Analysts say that this product represents the next wave of "innovation" in this marketplace.

You get the idea…

Next, get all the "proof that it works" statements on a white board. Have the sales team pick the most powerful ones. There could be three, five, ten, or twenty. This is how you involve the general sales team in the process and get their buy-in. They must believe and know that what they are saying is true.

TOP TIP: Creating a Unique Opener for Your Pitch:

Don't bother with writing a formal opening as part of a core sales presentation. It will sound too "canned," unless you find something that works well, that you can easily recycle, and that all the salespeople can deliver well.

Openings are great places to raise comments on current events and engage your customer so that you are creating a two way conversation, not a monologue.

The opening can be one of the most creative parts of the pitch because it captures attention and sets the tone of the presentation. If you lose someone at the beginning of a presentation, it's difficult to get them back.

Things to do in an opening:

- Use a "current events" opener from the daily newspaper or industry trade publication.

- Frame what you are about to discuss and give a quick outline.

- Set up key points that you will want to address at the closing.

Minor Points:

- Check on how much time you have to cover the presentation (this shows respect).

- Tell the customer to ask you questions at any time (if you have time to field them).

- Address any issues from previous meetings (if appropriate).

Here is one example of a unique opening:

TRUE STORY: A company had just done a major product redesign and was showing it confidentially to its top customers. The product had a new logo, but the sales team was prohibited from having new business cards because the new logo wasn't yet released. So, the sales team turned that seeming lack of coordination from the marketing department into an advantage.

The sales team made sure that they passed out their current business cards first (with the old logos on them). Then they flipped open the first page of the new sales presentation and there it was: the new logo. They started the presentation with: "As you can tell from the logo on our business cards and the logo on the presentation, something new is happening at the company and you are one of the first customers to see it!"

That little nuance with the business cards made the customers feel special and casually opened up an entire discussion of the new product. It could only be used for a few weeks but it flowed well into the presentation, which is exactly what the sales team was trying to accomplish. The first time someone tried this on the sales team it was completely ad libbed. The sales team could have never scripted this. It worked so well that numerous salespeople in the company started using it during the product redesign launch.

TOP TIP: Piecing It All Together:

Build a rough outline of the presentation by using the six point format from earlier in this chapter:

1. Timely, Topical, Unique Opening;

2. Market Info/Competitive Conditions;

3. What the company can do to help the customer create more customers;

4. Executive Summary;

5. Proposal; and

6. Close.

Start filling in these key sections with the information you have gathered. This is always a work-in-process. Go for the main points you want to get across first and make sure to summarize them. Then flesh out the details to the degree to which customers need to know them. This will form the basis for your presentation.

TOP TIP: Getting All the Information Organized:

Getting everything in one place to build a pitch is a big challenge. The use of presentation software is good for overall organizing. Use the outlining feature to get all your points into the pitch structure. Don't worry about how pretty it looks or how much information is on each page. You can change all that later. Right now it's the message that matters most. There are plenty of style guides and tips available to help make it look good. That's really the role of your marketing department.

Once you have everything in an outline format, begin reviewing it to see how it flows. Are there any snags? Does it make sense? Have salespeople who haven't seen it determine if they can follow the logic.

TOP TIP: Creating Presentation *Flow:*

After you've ranked and prioritized all your presentation information, develop a good flow for the presentation. Once you do this, you are a third of the way there.

Flow is always subjective. It's usually the simple, logical, straightforward approach that works. You are trying to craft a presentation that makes an undeniable case for why your products are important to your customer. It requires that the presentation be pieced together to enable the buyer of your products to walk down a path of inevitability.

Like any good comedian, you'll want to keep it light and airy, to the point, and memorable. Towards the end of the presentation you'll want to loop back to key information that you set up in your opener or in the informational part of your pitch. That puts it all together and sets up for the close. Have you noticed how good comedians set up a punch line early in their monologues and then go back to it for the big laugh at the end of the joke? The same concept applies here.

Get agreement from your immediate team that you have the right flow and that all paths lead to a strong close and opportunity for the customer. Assuming that the flow works for everyone, you can start building a formidable presentation.

TOP TIP: Setting Up the Proposal:

The next step is to build a quick summary of the points that you are going to cover just prior to the proposal. This should be considered the "executive" summary. Pulling this together will really test how well your flow works. Try saying it out loud so that you can hear how it actually sounds. There has to be logic and flow that you feel comfortable with.

Next, create a reasonable proposal to your customer with supporting reasons for why this proposal one would make the most sense. The focus should be on what's good for them, not you.

TOP TIP: Writing a Narrative Road Map:

Once you build a pitch that everyone is happy with, write a narrative to go with it. It's best to make it a separate document. There are a few reasons for this. Some salespeople might forward the sales presentation to customers. If your narrative is part of the overall presentation, there may be points you'd rather have just the sales team see. Mistakes like this have occurred!

On the narrative, make key points slide by slide so that your salespeople know where to emphasize a point. Keep it brief. Give tips on where objections might occur, and any details on any statistics that you reference.

Presentation Reminder Tricks:

One small method you can use to help salespeople move confidently through a sales presentation is to put small colored dots into the corners of select pages of the presentation to act as cues. The cues would remind the salesperson to do or say certain things in the pitch on that particular page. These cues would be also referenced on the narrative pages, but on the presentation they would appear as inconspicuous dots. A small red dot (an alert color) might be a signal to ask the customer if everything you have presented until then is making sense—just a simple check-in point. A small green dot (the color of money) might be a signal to do a trial close, to see if the customer is interested.

TIMED SALES PITCHES:

One-, five-, and twenty-minute pitches represent an appropriate range of presentations that all salespeople can use depending on the complexity of the product you are selling, the sophistication of the customer base, and how much time is available to present.

One-Minute Pitches:

By creating the key selling point or points, you have set the groundwork for a series of sales pitches of varying lengths. The first in the series is the one-minute pitch.

One minute is actually a long time, when no one is talking. Look at the face of your watch for one minute (do it right now) and see if it doesn't take a long time to tick off sixty seconds. Don't count them out loud or to yourself. Just watch the seconds go by. Sixty seconds is a long quiet period of time…isn't it? But as soon as you start having a conversation, sixty seconds will fly by. So, keeping brief and to the point are key.

Typically a one-minute version is called the "elevator" or "cocktail party" pitch. It should be effective enough to get the customer's attention and, you hope, get a longer meeting at a later time. Those are generally the only goals you can seek to accomplish in sixty seconds or less.

Practical Application of the One-Minute Pitch:

Start practicing the pitch with a basic run-through. Have each salesperson give his or her best minute on what the company does, why the products are important to the customer, and why they would want a longer meeting sometime in the future.

Pick one salesperson to start (the one who you think will do the best job). Time the pitch and critique it. Keep things moving quickly. Keep the selection of the next person random. Have the one who just pitched pick the next person until you've covered everyone on your sales team. Have them practice saying the pitch in different ways that work for them personally.

All you are really doing here is practicing the key selling point over and over until it becomes second nature to the sales team. Be mindful that you really don't want the pitch to become a boring, canned monologue!

Hint for making one-minute pitches work best: Leave room in this one-minute version for some interaction with the customer. That makes the minute go by fast and the interaction is incredibly valuable.

You might want to have a few of your stars practice it for the entire room and then have a break-out session where people practice the pitch. You could have them draw "industries" out of a hat and tailor the pitch to that industry. The proof points they pick will depend entirely on what they think will work best to get the customer's interest and open the door for the salesperson to request a meeting.

EXAMPLE:

SALESPERSON: Hi, I'm with 123 Company. Nice to meet you...

FUTURE CUSTOMER: Nice to meet you, too. What does your company do? I've never heard of them!

SALESPERSON: (GIVE KEY SELLING POINT)

If they don't ask what your company does you can always say:

Are you familiar with what we do?

(FROM THE EXAMPLE GIVEN PREVIOUSLY)

We've created a unique way to aggregate high quality ad banner inventory from small- to medium-sized web sites and optimize the placement of your banner ad campaigns over those sites so that you will get a significantly higher ROI from your online ad spending.

Then ask: *Does that make sense?*

FUTURE CUSTOMER: Uh, I'm not sure I get it...

SALESPERSON: Basically we help our customers create more of their customers more effectively by optimizing their ad campaigns and helping them spend their marketing budgets more efficiently.

(PROOF POINT) And it has been working well because our top ten advertisers have all increased spending with us over the last six months. Maybe we can talk more about this in a day or two?

FUTURE CUSTOMER: Sure, that sounds interesting.

SALESPERSON: Great, let's exchange cards and talk soon, maybe aim for a brief meeting next Tuesday?

...Now, can I buy you a drink?

COACHING TIPS: Constant practice will further fine-tune the one-minute pitch. It will seem different on paper than when it comes out of a salesperson's mouth for the first few times. Be prepared for most salespeople to attempt their own take on the "company's" version. Assure everyone that they will stumble initially—it's all very normal. This will calm most people down.

There will be a strong desire on the part of the sales team to start filling out this pitch—and make it longer during the one-minute version. It's a normal reaction, but don't let it happen. That comes next with the five-minute version. For now, you just want to get down the basics.

Training in front of peers is always tougher on a sales team than being in front of an actual customer. This is why it's so important. The one-minute pitch needs to roll off their tongues naturally and with confidence. With a lot of practice, it will.

Five-Minute Pitches:

These are a bit more elaborate, but you can't start the five-minute version until you have mastered the one-minute version.

Five minutes is actually a really long time, too. A lot can go right or wrong in five minutes. It feels *at least* five times longer than the one minute of silence you might have practiced earlier. But once a salesperson gets rolling, the time will go by fast.

Try to say nothing for five minutes. Look at your watch *(again)*. It might well drive you crazy. For a salesperson (or anyone) to stop talking for five minutes is painful. Excruciating! Think of it as an exercise in listening. A salesperson talking non-stop for five minutes could be equally painful, to your customer. A balanced presentation and mutual exchange of words is the most even-handed approach. How do you execute on that?

When building a five-minute presentation you naturally start with the one-minute version, the DNA for all your pitches. The five-minute version is a logical extension. Once the potential customer expresses interest in learning more, you can respond with probing questions so that you know how to fill out the pitch to a five-minute version to benefit their needs the most. Maybe they desire more proof. Or more clarification of exactly how you do what your company does. They may want to know more about the benefits they get from working with your company. If they buy your product on behalf of one of their customers they may need more background on the market you serve and the competitive climate.

Five-minute pitches are designed to cover virtually all the essential information that a customer needs to know to buy your product. Or at least steer them directly down that road. If you don't make key points early on in the presentation, you will lose the customer's attention. It's best to not belabor points. After all, your customer has a lot of selling information coming in every day. Brevity will actually stand out, in a positive way.

Five-minute pitches are used when a potential customer wants to hear more on the spot. They can also be used in a more formal presentation setting. Let's say that a customer wants you to come in and do a 30-minute meeting. That might be the best place to use your 5-minute version of the sales pitch. Why? Chances are that it will take time to settle the room down. People will, of course, be late, you'll need to make the introductions and get the group focused, and you might get a number of objections and questions along the way. If you can get your point across in five densely packed minutes (elapsed time), during a thirty-minute meeting, it may border on a miracle. If the room comes to order quickly and you get through the presentation quickly and without objections you might want to use the time to ask more questions to strengthen the key points of why you should do business. *Just don't forget to ask for their business before you leave!*

Once you've made the five-minute pitch, probe the customer for what was the most interesting point they heard. Then you might want to give a more elaborate anecdote about how another customer has used the product in a similar way. The sales pitch is the salesperson's to weave in the best way possible to get closer to the sale.

Here are other ways to build a five minute pitch (tailor as necessary to address specific customer needs):

- Go deeper into key selling point(s).

- Expand on customer benefits.

- Supply more proof that the product works.

- Add an anecdotal customer story.

- Give a little of the company history, if appropriate.

- Share the vision of the company.

- Have more interaction with the customer.

- Give more background on the market you serve (for third-party buyers).

- Present the appropriate proposal.

- And *most importantly:* Always ask for their business!

While you want to encourage the creativity of your salespeople in the five-minute presentation, it's still not a lot of time to stay on point. Make sure that the key points you have agreed to with the sales team are front and center in your presentation. From then on the, presentation will most likely be customized for each particular customer.

Twenty-Minute Pitches:

Who would want to sit through a twenty minute one way conversation that some would call a sales pitch? Not many! People squirm and cringe when the laptop is flicked on and the title page of the presentation pops up. They have been psychologically damaged by years of presentations that drone on and on and are only being given because presenters liked hearing themselves speak! One way to avert this is by giving a quick overview of what will be covered, how long it will take, and then asking the customer if that sounds good to them. Once expectations are set, it's up to you to deliver. When you take this approach, the customers smile and are grateful.

The real goal of a twenty-minute presentation is to have an exchange with your customers and to delve more deeply into issues that concern them. The actual twenty-minute sales pitch is more like the ten-minute version of the five-minute pitch (got that math?) with responses to more specific issues the customer might have attached to it. Make sure that you know what the issues are before you start. Get on the phone or e-mail and ask the customers *in advance*. Make sure they know that you aren't going to be there to waste their time. Planning ahead usually goes over extremely well with customers.

Typically, when you are making a longer presentation you will have more people in the room listening to you. Many will be decision-makers. Some may just be there to try to figure out how to say "No." Make sure you know who will be there and what their interests are in what you are selling. Preparation is at least fifty-one percent of the work here.

When you make a longer presentation you have the opportunity not only to ask for the order (multiple times), you can also lay out a plan for doing business and tell how you plan on delivering on your promises.

COACHING TIPS: Practice this type of presentation over and over. Have the salespeople work on their "opener" and on transitions from point to point or page to page of the presentation so that it flows smoothly. In some cases it's as much about style as it is content. Keep the core pitch to ten minutes. Work with the salespeople to anticipate what questions the audience might ask (more on this later). Rehearse the responses over and over. Throw more objections at them. Keep asking "why" and "what if." They have to know and understand the material, cold.

MEETING TIPS: Why is it important to keep your twenty-minute presentation to ten minutes? It's mostly for practical reasons. As in any group presentation it takes quite a bit of time to get multiple people into a meeting room. It's the same set of issues as the five-minute presentation. The more people who need to be at the meeting, the more the task of assembling them is similar to herding kittens. The last one to arrive usually defines the starting time of the meeting. Most people are happy to show up late but reluctant to stay past the agreed-to ending time. It's human nature, if you know that you can adjust to it.

Once the meeting starts, someone (maybe you) will

inevitably want to go around the room and make introductions. It's a nice idea, but this is usually a brutal waste of time. So don't fight human nature, just plan for it! Use this as an opportunity to collect/exchange business cards or get everyone's name and e-mail address on a note-pad that is passed around.

Someone will always ask a lot of questions. This may happen during presentations you are in. Some questions may be important to answer then and there, especially if this person is an opinion leader. Otherwise try to defer the question to an offline discussion after your presentation. (Politely!)

6. SALES TRAINING

Once you've hired a great team you have to train them so they can start producing revenue for the company. The real question is how you do it efficiently and effectively.

For years, many sales managers taught the selling concept of ABC. ABC = Always Be Closing. Here's an updated version of this thinking:

- Always Be Listening (more on this in Section 10, starting on page 160.)

- Sell the customer what they need.

- Close when appropriate.

Great salespeople don't always come "pre-wired" from the factory" ready to sell the way that you want them to. There should be constant training, regardless of the quality of the product or how good the salespeople are at selling it.

Sales training is one of the most important things a sales manager can do. Why? Marketplaces change rapidly and you simply can't go out and sell every deal on your own. A well-trained sales team is much more effective in the field than one exceptional sales manager.

Here are ideas on training and keeping the sales team sharp:

MEGA TIP: **Make Sales Training Happen Regularly:**

For sales training to be successful, it has to happen regularly. How often will depend on how seasoned the sales team is and how often the company's product line changes.

The sales team will never learn a consistent message if you don't train them on it regularly. Few people can get away with running the Boston Marathon without serious training for it. Many sales teams don't fully appreciate the value of intensive sales training until they get back out into the field. What might seem like a waste of two or three days is quickly forgotten once something a salesperson has learned gets put into practice and helps handle a customer problem or close a sale.

TRUE STORY: A sales team was doing quite poorly. They hadn't been together or trained in nearly two years. No wonder! Their new sales manager did an intensive two-day training session filled with pitch training and marketing presentations. It was grueling, intense and a lot of work. In the end, the sales team was thrilled and their spirits were renewed, and sales productivity began increasing.

MEGA TIP: Teach the Sales Team Everything You Know:

Teach the salespeople all you know. Don't hold back. Many sales managers worry that there won't be much left for them to do if they teach the salespeople all their tips and tricks. This is a myth. To dispel it really just remember that all knowledge is cumulative so you can never teach them everything you know. You are always learning, and as you teach them you also learn more from them. Everyone gets better at what they do when giving their all to the process.

Each salesperson will use your information in different ways. Don't expect retention of more than 10%-20% of what is taught at any given time.

When you are training/teaching them, make a point of being clear about what you want the sales team to remember and use out in the field.

TRUE STORY: A sailing instructor always used to stomp his foot when reviewing a key question that was going to be on the final written exam. Usually the foot stomping started after a few points prior to one final point. It was an interesting way to emphasis a point—certainly memorable. Everyone who was taught by this instructor passed the test and became more knowledgeable sailors.

Throughout the course of sales training, you will be sharing minor and major points with the sales team. Make sure that you label them clearly. Prioritize for them. It will add clarity to review the major points at the end of the day.

It also is beneficial to summarize for the sales team more completely, at the end of the training sessions. Give them, on paper, the main points they learned. Encourage them to tack the information up in their office, their cubicle, on their computer screen, or carry it in their brief bag. Constantly drill them on the points and refer back to them. Repetition helps learning.

TOP TIP: Create a "Best Practices" Manual

One of the more effective ways to train a sales organization, especially one that is growing or churning salespeople, is to have a reference manual full of "best practices" that everyone should follow. The trick with these manuals is making sure that people actually use them and that they are updated regularly.

Assign the responsibility of maintaining the manual to one person only. When a set of best practice manuals is made up, it's best to have a fair number of extras for new hires and replacements.

What goes into a "best practices" manual? Here are some ideas:

- Company-wide phone contact lists.

- "Who to call for what" lists.

- Departmental organization charts.

- Company order forms.

- Outlines of the process for placing orders, making changes, cancellations, etc.

- Site map for the company website.

- Guidelines on using the company intranet or requesting information inside the company.

- Code of Ethics for dealing with customers.

When possible, all these items should be available online so that updating can be done centrally.

TOP TIP: **Be a Constant Sales Coach:**

Most sales managers can't be on the playing field and coaching at the same time. There aren't enough hours in the day to do both jobs. The sales team is out making most of the plays, not you. Go out on sales calls with them but resist the temptation to do the call for them. The only exception is if your meeting has been pre-arranged for the specific purpose of having you present. In those cases, teaching by example is a good form of coaching.

If salespeople get in trouble on a call, you can always bail them out and call it a learning experience. But you are the sales manager and, in the end, teaching them to sell better through their own efforts is better than doing their job for them. They will become over-reliant on you and so will the customers.

Sales training is team coaching, and if done in a real-world environment, can help salespeople handle most of the customer objections they will face before going out in the field. Your job is to give them the tools to do the job when you aren't there.

TOP TIP: Make Training Useful:

When you take aggressive salespeople out of the market for a few days, you must provide an excellent program for them to learn from. Sales meetings have to be packed with tons of value or people will feel that their time was wasted.

Solicit input from the sales team (especially sales managers) in advance on what topics they would like to cover. This helps to understand what is on their minds. Try to address all the issues while taking into consideration overall goals for the sales meeting.

Leave plenty of time for:

- Presentation practice.

- Feedback from the group.

- Introduction of new initiatives.

- Team-building.

- Mixing and mingling.

TOP TIP: Sales Meetings and Cell Phones Don't Mix:

There is a very simple rule for sales meetings and sales calls: Salespeople should turn off cell phones and pagers except during break time or when they aren't in front of the customer. Why? It's pretty self-important to think you need to keep your phone on for that "I'm a big shot so everything has to stop" call when you've got a room full of people who are there to learn something. It's also just plain rude. The customer does not want to listen to the salesperson's phone ring, especially if the phone rings a favorite adventure movie theme song, again and again.

Another option is to allow salespeople to set their phones to silent mode. But if they do get a call, don't let them run out of the room to return it—that's what breaks are for. Not only is it disruptive, they will almost always miss some opportunity to learn something new.

If a salesperson has communicated to important customers who might be calling that they are in a sales or other customer meeting, the customer will certainly understand if the call is returned within two hours instead of two minutes. This is just a simple form of good manners and managing customer expectations. Encourage changing voice-mail messages to say that the salesperson is attending off-site meetings or in sales calls for the day.

For those salespeople who continue to forget to turn their phones off in sales meetings, establish a "ring tax" of $10-$20 each time their phone rings. Donate the money to charity or throw a sales manager's party after the meeting.

TOP TIP: **Go with the Best First:**

On sales training presentation day, it's a good idea to have the best presenter go first. This will raise the bar for less experienced salespeople, and everyone will pay much closer attention in the early going. Presentations will usually get better over the course of the day as people scramble to include great new ideas into their versions.

If you manage a large group and aren't quite sure who

the best presenters are yet, ask the regional sales managers. Or you might consider having members of the sales management team pitch. You might want to do the pitch yourself. You are never too high up the pecking order to pitch the company's products and teach others how.

TOP TIP: Stand and Deliver:

"Stand and Deliver" sales meeting presentations are often best done as full-blown, twenty-minute pitches with all the bells and whistles. In these scenarios you ask non-presenting salespeople in the room to take on specific rating assignments regarding critiquing of the pitch. Try rotating assignments with each new presenter. Have the salespeople doing the critique take notes on a rating sheet. They will make comments after each pitch is completed.

Here's how the rating assignments might look:

- Ability to get across key selling points.

- Ability to stay within pitch structure.

- Objection-handling skills.

- Factual accuracy.

- Avoiding "self-serving" comments like "I think" or wasted words such as: like, um, uh, etc.

- Using sales tools effectively.

- How poised and comfortable the salesperson was with themselves and the material.

- Asking for the customer's business.

Prior to presenting, have the salesperson review the goals of the pitch. After the pitch has been made, cover the key feedback points above and open up the comments to everyone else in the room, if there is time. Personally take the "last word" to summarize key successes and recommendations regarding the pitch. Follow up with the salesperson the next time you are in their territory or at some set time (maybe 15-30 days) after the sales training.

Keep to a strict time schedule for these presentations. The initial presentations typically go more slowly because more comments will be made. By the end of the presentations, you will be able to streamline the critique process.

Consider saving some time the next day for a few additional re-pitches that show improvements from the previous day.

TOP TIP: Training with Sales Tools

Sales tools cost a lot of money to make and require constant attention to update. If salespeople are trained to use sales tools as a part of sales training, they will be that much more likely to use them out in the field. The use of sales tools in a sales training setting is important because it creates a habit of use.

Sales tools are as useful for the salesperson as they are for the customer. But that is often forgotten because the salesperson knows the content inside and out, and the collateral pieces backwards and forwards, yet doesn't have them top-of-mind. These marketing pieces are eye candy to a prospective customer however, and should be used to add "color" to a sales presentation whenever possible.

NOTE: Sales Tools are covered in Section 8, starting on page 133.

TOP TIP: Avoiding the "I" Word:

If salespeople use the word "I" in selling, and especially in sales presentation training, (i.e., I think you should do this because...) then the salesperson will come across to the customer as being self-serving. This is not good. The customer will see this as a proposal that lines only the salesperson's pockets.

Train salespeople to present a proposal with reasons why it's in the customer's best interest to adopt it. Putting the customer first should always be paramount.

It's very natural to just say "I" all the time, so always have salespeople monitor themselves. It is especially important to draw attention to such mistakes in sales training sessions and correct them in a positive way.

TOP TIP: Eliminating Wasted Words:

Giving any sales pitch is just as much about delivery as it is about content. Coach the salespeople on eliminating "well", "you know", "um," "like," "uh," and other "mind farts" out of their presentations. These wasted words use up valuable selling time and make a salesperson look less than professional. Count the number of times they say these time wasting-words. For the severe offenders, have them guess how many times they've said them. Then tell them what the actual count was. They will be amazed. Hearing as many as 70 "ums" in a five-minute presentation is not out of the question. That probably isn't even close to the world record.

Most salespeople don't even realize that they are

doing it. That's often because they are more nervous than relaxed and not fully connected to the material they are covering or the product they are selling. Once they know the product well, and understand it, they will have a more convincing delivery. Time and experience matter immensely here. The good news is that with some focus this transformation from an "ah-um-er" to an eloquent presenter can happen quickly.

TRUE STORY: Wasted words aren't just limited to "ah," "um," and other nonsense words. They can also be something more important—like the customer's name. A long departed salesperson left behind a file copy of a follow-up letter sent to a customer. In nearly every other sentence the salesperson had used the customer's first name. By the end of a three-paragraph letter the customer's name had been used at least two dozen times. It was a pathetic display of over-personalization. It is flattering, and often effective, to use a customer's name in a presentation or follow-up letter, *but two dozen times?*

The best way to keep this from happening to the salespeople you manage is to make them extremely self-conscious in a positive way. Videotape these sales presentations and play them back so salespeople can hear the mistakes. Once they see them, chances are they will work harder to stop using wasted words.

Pair up salespeople who physically work near each other and have them repeat the wasted words to each other when they hear them (but not in front of a customer). Over time, the offending salespeople will cure themselves.

TOP TIP: **Presentation Software Skills:**

Not everyone is extremely proficient with presentation software, and that becomes painfully obvious around the time people start thinking about an upcoming sales meeting. Giving the sales team a pre-packaged presentation is a start, but most will want to customize it to their needs.

It might be a good idea to have a trainer come in once a year and do a few hours of presentation software training with the sales team. Use the current sales presentation as the basis for the training. Have the trainer teach tips on how to best navigate the presentation, make quick changes and updates, etc.

Things to consider when salespeople use presentation software:

- Don't overcrowd information, like charts and graphs, onto a slide.

- Using the customer's logo adds a custom touch.

- Background colors and fonts aren't as important as the content of the message.

- Sometimes a simple white background with minimal graphics is best.

- Keep the number of words on a slide to a minimum.

- Animations, fades, and wipes can be helpful in the "opener" slide of a presentation but when used on every page, or worse, for every sentence, they can be distracting.

- Integrating brief video clips can add "punch" to a

presentation so long as the topic is action-oriented and interesting, and launching the clip is easy.

Giving people more comfort regarding the use of technology will yield a more proficient selling organization.

TOP TIP: AV (Audio-Visual) Projector Skills:

One of the more annoying things when salespeople are making a presentation happens when they approach the podium and try to connect their laptop to an LCD projector.

As obvious as it seems, salespeople should practice connecting up their computers as part of sales training. Knowing which key to hit to move the image onto the "big screen" is important. There is also often a sequence for connecting a LCD projector and turning it on. Most of this process is standardized these days.

TRUE STORY: A salesperson approaches the podium to make a presentation, connects the LCD projector, and then can't get the image up on the wall. The presenter starts mumbling, "Well, I've done this before. It worked last time. I've never used a projector like this before. Ummmmm, is there anyone here from the AV department?"

Situations like this are completely embarrassing and start the presentation off on the wrong foot.

Consider this approach when training salespeople:

- Practice hooking up the PC to the projector in advance.

- Put the sequence on a 3x5 card if they are unsure of the process.

- Tell them to skip the commentary if something isn't working. They shouldn't say things like: "It was working when we practiced this." Or "I'm not very good at this." Being quiet while setting up makes the process go faster and creates anticipation in the audience.

- Once they've hooked up successfully, have them take a deep breath, look at the audience, and get started.

- If something does go wrong during the presentation they shouldn't begin apologizing. Just have them quietly fix the problem and keep going.

TOP TIP: **Getting Agreement:**

In sales pitches of any duration, make sure that the salespeople take time to get ongoing agreement from the customer. Not getting agreement along the way and getting complete disagreement at the end of the presentation is worse than dealing with small differences that can be handled along the way. This will ensure you that the customer understands the concepts you are trying to get across.

Asking for agreement is similar to a trial close. It's a way of checking in to make sure everyone is on the same page.

In a longer presentation, salespeople can ask for agreement multiple times. Asking for agreement shouldn't create an awkward moment. The biggest mistake made is sounding condescending and saying something like: "Does this make *any* sense to you?" That's probably not the best approach because who will say "No" to that question? It's better to just mention it as a casual transition point in your presentation. Something like: "That was a lot to cover. Do you have any questions or thoughts on what you've seen so far? Do you agree with what you've heard? Are we on the same page?"

Getting agreement gives you a sense that the person you are presenting to is walking down the same path with you. Once you get agreement on your key points, you are that much closer to a strong close when you make your proposal.

To Close or Not to Close:

The close isn't a "thank you" to the customer for listening to the proposal and an obligatory "we'll follow-up with you" comment, or worse, dead air and a hopeful smile. It's an opportunity to ask what the customer thinks of the proposal, ask for the business and offer some mutual next steps. It's also a huge opportunity for you to say that you are open for business and ready to help them. Encourage the salespeople to tell the customers they want their business!

TOP TIP: Training on Asking for the Order:

Salespeople should never forget to ask for the order. Unbelievably, most don't, so it's important to get constant sales training on the subject.

TRUE STORY: At a sales-training session, a sales manager awarded points for multiple aspects of making a sales presentation. There was a twist: If salespeople didn't "ask for the order" as part of the presentation they wouldn't be in the running for an award, no matter how many points they earned.

Before asking for an order, salespeople should make sure that the customer is ready to do business with the company or they'll end up looking like a dolt. If the meeting momentum is going in the wrong direction and enough of the customer's questions haven't been successfully answered enough to sell them, then the salesperson should hold off.

If the customer is nowhere near ready to buy, asking for the order would make the salesperson seem to be operating only out of blind ambition. That would look extremely stupid. If the salesperson only gets halfway down the sales path, then he or she should take the opportunity to immediately reschedule another meeting. A proposal can still be made to the customer but characterized as a "straw man" proposal for them to review. The salesperson should reassure the customer that it is not yet *the* proposal (although it might ultimately be) but just something for the customer to see and get an opportunity to get a feel for what is in their best interest.

Once the Customer Says YES, Then Shut Up!:

One of the classic rules of selling is to shut up once the sale has been made. Chatty salespeople can fill the customer's mind with all sorts of useless blather after the decision has been made. Salespeople who are overly talkative often give the impression that they don't deserve the sale so they are covering for their insecurity with extra words.

The only exception to the "too much information" rule is when customers need a ton of information to back up a purchase decision. Often, this isn't their fault, they are just messengers for the company and, no doubt, some internal company policy (or a level of paranoia) requires extensive back-up information. It's usually better to start with the "need to know" approach, see where it takes the sale, and then provide as much additional information as is required and as quickly as possible.

Part of regular sales training should include practicing when to shut up. When salespeople are making their pitches in sales training, consider randomly stopping the pitch three-quarters of the way through to tell them that you agree with them and that you are completely sold. Then see what happens. They may want to keep pitching you until they are finished with "their" presentation. If that happens, use it as a good example of when to shut up. Once you have said you are sold, an aware salesperson will go right to the proposal level and have the "customer" sign right on the spot.

Understanding All the Objections:

One thing that catches salespeople off guard and can kill a sale is not having an answer when the customer throws out an objection.

An objection is nothing more than a misunderstanding about the value of a product or service.

Objections can be legitimate or placed in the minds of customers by competitors. As part of the sales training process, spend time going around the room and collecting all the objections the sales team faces every day. Do this with silent input first (have them write the objections they get on paper and hand them in). That way, all objections will get listed.

Put all the objections up on a white board and have

sales team rank them in order of frequency with which they are heard and their likeliness to kill a deal.

Go around the room and have everyone work on the answers to the objections. Take one at a time. Work the objections to death. Make sure someone is writing all the responses down. Send out a summary as soon as possible after the sales meeting.

Make objection-handling training an ongoing process. Create an objection handling-booklet for all the salespeople. It's best to have it as an online file that can be constantly updated. Keep an open-door policy on handling objections. Make sure that you hear them all the time. Create an e-mail group to present the new ones and get feedback.

TOP TIP: **The Objection-Handling Process:**

When salespeople handle an objection, make certain that they repeat that objection back to the person who just said it before they respond. This is extremely important. Practice this religiously in sales training. Be sure that what the salesperson heard was what the customer actually said or meant. Often, that action alone will eliminate or change the objection.

Over time, the ears of salespeople will become attuned to the key words of an objection and they may complete the objection in their mind and begin spooling up the answer before the other person is finished stating it. Unfortunately, they may not respond to what the objection actually was because they were too busy thinking up their answer and not listening to the customer. This is a common problem. So, repeating the objection *after listening to it* is a "must do." Once the person objecting hears the objection again he or she may decide that wasn't what was meant or take back the objection altogether. That's the best scenario. At a minimum, a salesperson gets additional clarity on the objection and can address it more effectively.

ROLE PLAYING: When an objection is made, here's how a salesperson should be trained to respond:

Customer says: We've been reviewing all the products that you sell and while we like you as a salesperson your company's products are just too expensive.

Salesperson responds: Let me make sure I completely understand what you are saying: Our products are simply too expensive? Or do you feel that the value you would be getting once you buy these products isn't worth the price? Or is it that the list price is too high or the discount structure isn't deep enough?

Wait patiently for their answer.

Customer says: The retail price of the product seems OK, it's the discounted price that isn't good enough.

Salesperson responds: OK, I understand, the discounted price isn't good enough. If you would be willing to buy a slightly higher level of volume I can go back to our pricing team and see if we can extend a much deeper discount. Does that work for you?

Customer says: Well, OK, that's a start!

Try having competitions (for cash prizes) at sales meetings for who is the best objection handler. Just make sure the objection is repeated before a response is made!

TOP TIP: Create Core Concept Reminder Cards:

The sales organization should have a set of core selling concepts that everyone helps create, fully understands backwards and forwards, and which can be explained with consistency across the team. These concepts need to be used as part of their sales training.

These reminders are nothing more than 3x5 cards, each with a different point, that can include: key selling points, company mission statement, top goals for the sales team, and rules for treating the customer well. They should be simple, straightforward, and not capable of misinterpretation.

Some salespeople may choose to put these core concepts on small laminated cards and carry them in their wallet or put them in their offices or cubicles—whatever works to serve as a constant reminder of what the sales team stands for.

The goal here is not just to display these reminder cards for everyone else to see, but to live by them and make a conscious effort to make them happen on a frequent basis.

Trash Talking:

When making sales presentations (or sales calls), encourage salespeople to avoid bringing up the competition. The only exception is if a customer asks you, but even then the salesperson should be weary about taking that bait. Be aware that the customer may be fishing for information on behalf of your competition.

The rule here is: Every minute a salesperson spends

discussing the competition is one less minute that they get to talk about your product.

In sales training or in the field, if a salesperson immediately starts slamming the competitors, try to steer them off that subject as soon as possible. Have a one-to-one talk about it afterwards.

Some customers (and competitors) love to do nothing more than gossip about the industry at great length. That may be how the customers spend their time, but it's not the best use of salespeople's time. Encourage salespeople to stay focused and "on topic" when confronting these situations.

Fight Politely:

When it comes to placing doubt about the competition in the thoughts of your customer, three words come to mind: Fear, Uncertainty, and Doubt.

When used quickly and effectively, these words can save a potentially lost sale or increase an existing one. It's one step short of trash talking, so be careful here. It's probably best to practice a series of vague one-liners that salespeople can use to deflect a competitive conversation back to their interests. This is somewhat of an art.

To use Fear, Uncertainty, and Doubt effectively, a salesperson needs to first be on top of market knowledge, and not trying to manipulate information. If salespeople are trained to say to a customer who mentions a mega-conglomerate competitor, "Are they still in business?" they will look foolish, or worse—like smartasses. This sometimes works when said tongue-in-cheek, because humor can be a great deflector.

TOP TIP: Role-Playing:

Encourage live role-playing in sales training meetings. Sometimes it's a good idea to let the sales teams decide just how they want to do this. This way they can be more creative and gain better ownership of the concepts they are practicing.

TRUE STORY: One sales team took the cocktail party (one-minute) pitch theme seriously and during a sales meeting, created a mock cocktail lounge in the meeting room. They dimmed the lights, set up a "bar" and had some background music playing from a boom box (Hint: the clock radio from your hotel room makes a nice substitute, just be sure to give it back!).

Once the mood was set, they did a stellar job of presenting their one-minute pitches. Each salesperson took a turn at talking to a "customer" about what their company did and closed their pitch by offering to have a more complete follow-up meeting. The salespeople established a goal of creating interest in the company with their one-minute pitch and securing a future meeting. It worked brilliantly.

Presentation Downshifting:

Be prepared to adjust the time salespeople have available for a pitch in a sales-training environment. This happens all the time in the real world, so why not in sales training? You might have the sales team prepare for a twenty minute pitch but then only be able to give them 10 minutes. See how they handle the "on-the-fly" changes.

"In the Field" Presentation Triage:

If you are out in the field and a sales presentation is running long, make sure your salespeople know what parts of the presentation you are comfortable having them skip, so they can get right to the point.

Much as you would prioritize key selling points you want to get across to the customer, you'll want salespeople to prioritize what parts of the presentation are "must keeps," if time is running short. This kind of triage can save a sale. If the salespeople have brought leave-behinds (which they should always have) they can always refer the customers to the minor points there. What stays and what goes in an abbreviated presentation will be a function of how well the salesperson knows the pitch and the customer's needs, and what ground has been previously covered.

Practice what stays and what goes as part of sales training.

One-On-One Sales Training:

After a major sales meeting, consider doing intensive one-on-one, out in the field, follow-up training sessions for two hours, once per month. This will provide 100% attention to salespeople who may be underperforming or who had trouble grasping concepts during the more formal sales training.

Avoid *Stepford* Salespeople:

Some sales executives and CEOs think that the best way to develop a sales team is to have everyone memorize the sales pitch and deliver it in a highly structured and unilateral way. Everyone brings a particular skill set and life experience into their selling and sales management careers so let them be themselves. Salespeople will have tactics and strategies that work for them that just wouldn't work for others. Training them to be identical isn't making the best use of their individual talents.

When you think of your sales team as a family (yes, even including that crazy uncle) you can begin to realize that all kinds of personalities can combine to make a sales family successful. Some salespeople are wildly successful despite having quirks that drive you personally crazy. That's OK. *Viva la différence!* Put it to good use for you.

Everyone in a sales family should have a style that works best for him or her. Knowing your own personal style and those of your sales team and developing them to maximize sales should be a priority. Keeping them from expressing a personal style may only hold people back.

It never hurts to expose salespeople to unique ways in which others have sold. Smart salespeople will see a new way of doing business for what its true value is and decide if it can work for them. But if they aren't exposed to how others sell successfully, they can't learn from them. Try setting up roundtable meetings, either in person or with conference calls so people can exchange ideas on how they sell and service their customers.

Bringing in a successful salesperson from outside the sales organization can often shed new light and give a different perspective.

7. SALES MEETINGS

Sales meetings are an all-important part of any sales culture. They can be a huge waste of time or very memorable and invaluable to the sales team. They don't happen automatically and their success is often predicated on their being well prepared and topical.

Sales meetings have different purposes and can last from a few minutes to a few days. This section isn't necessarily about how to run a sales meeting, although some tips will be offered. The ideas here are more about the various types of sales meetings you can have and what they can accomplish:

MEGA TIP: Use Sales Meetings for Quality Bonding Time:

Try to do at least one motivational, offsite, bonding event each quarter. This is best done during sales training or at some point when the sales team is together and people have time to get to know each other. It doesn't have to be a budget buster. It could be karaoke or bowling. In fact, it's the kitschy stuff that becomes the most memorable to people. Make sure that you have a few disposable cameras to record any silliness. The pictures will come in handy at the next sales awards dinner.

Bonding events shouldn't be offensive to anyone. Sometimes you can tack them onto the end of a grueling trade show or company-sanctioned customer event as a ward. They can be for the sales team only or include the spouses, significant others, or families (depending on company policy). The culture you want for the sales team will dictate the right approach.

The underlying reason to do these events is to reward your sales team, foster cooperation, and help everyone to know each other better.

MEGA TIP: The Annual Sales Meeting:

One major piece of advice comes to mind when planning the annual sales meeting: If the meeting is big enough, get a meeting planner or designate someone to own it from start-to-finish.

Have your sales managers (or salespeople) share ideas on how to structure the meeting, the location, the topics covered, training, time allocated to each topic, guests to be invited, evening events, and other entertainment. This will help the sales team take ownership and give them a stake in its success.

At the end of the day you will have final say over the agenda and the budget. Getting input from various groups will help ensure that there are no unpleasant surprises along the way.

TOP TIP: Pounding Sand—the Sales Reward Trip:

A great strategy for building team camaraderie is to create a sales reward trip for teams that make their annual sales goals. Consider making the trip extra special if all salespeople or divisions make their company goals. The overall goals should be "stretch" goals that are achievable, but only with everyone pulling together.

TRUE STORY: It was time to decide where the team was going to go as a reward for making the company sales goal. One creative sales manager divided the room into two to determine the location of the trip. One side of the room was labeled HOT and the other was COLD. Members of the sales teams were asked to pick if they wanted to have their reward meeting in a HOT or COLD climate. Once the salespeople in the room had voted on climate, they voted on destination. HOT won and the destination was sunny Mexico. The amount of lobbying that went on between sales team members was a team-building exercise in itself.

Once the decision had been made, there were constant themed reminders sent out by the sales manager and the marketing team regarding how close to goal (and the trip) the team was getting. As the deadline approached, the volume of the motivation was pumped up even more. Salespeople were helping others close sales right until the last minute. They made their goal and they all made the reward trip.

TOP TIP: **Just Desserts—the Annual Sales Awards Dinner:**

One of the most successful team-building and motivational events is the Annual Sales Awards Dinner. Typically they are done at the end of an offsite sales meeting or locally at the end of the sales year. Salespeople love to have their tab picked up every once in a while!

Some award ideas:

- Give out awards that are serious (top salesperson of the year) and fun (biggest budget sand-bagger of the year).

- Additional award ideas: Most Improved Player, Rookie of the Year, Single Biggest Sale, Biggest Up-Sell of an Existing Customer, Best Customer Service, Most Creative Sale, etc.

- Establish a series of local awards and let the sales managers give them out in their own territories.

- Make it an evening of fun and humor. Hire a comedian or magician.

- Include spouses and significant others if possible (but be aware that they may not get all the inside jokes unless you explain them).

- Not everyone has to win a serious award. Even the people who aren't the top salespeople overall or in their regions are part of the team and are fair game for poking honest fun at with silly awards.

- Depending on the size of the team, make sure that you acknowledge as many people as possible or at least the people whom you'd like everyone on the sales team to emulate.

TRUE STORY: A company established a top salesperson club to reward the stars. At a gala event, salespeople were acknowledged as the "Best of the Best" across the entire company. Unfortunately the morale at the company was not in good shape. These awards were a ticket right out of the company door for the top salespeople, and directly to the competition with better pay. Uh-oh.

TOP TIP: The Revenue Meeting Hot Seat:

The threat of monthly humiliation in front of a group of sales peers is an unfortunate but *great* motivator for salespeople and sales managers with numbers on their heads. Fear is not a good motivator. In fact, you should never make a fear-based threat to anyone on your sales team. But there is an effective way to use the concept of *fear avoidance* as a motivator. Fear of humiliation among your peers is a huge motivator for sales managers.

Here's how it can work for you:

Have monthly, sales-team revenue meetings where regional sales managers meet and spend a half-day going over sales results and plans for the month. Each sales manager should be asked to stand up and talk about their budget numbers, where they are against their goals and what their future sales "pipeline" looks like. Just the fact that they have to stand in front of their peers and discuss why they might possibly be sucking wind in their territory is a huge motivator that can cause them to always be working harder to make their numbers. In other words: They are putting the pressure on themselves to get the job done.

This strategy has helped turn around some great salespeople and sales managers.

TRUE STORY: Every month one poor senior salesperson had to get up and try to explain to the rest of his peers why he was only at 30% of goal. He had great credentials and talent but was miserable at the prospect of failing (as most of us would be).

The sales manager was close to exhausting every excuse in the book for not hitting their numbers. He was running out of time (especially with his boss). In the end his motivation came from within. The ego drive had kicked in. He got mad for letting down not only himself but his peers as well.

The sales manager *never* wanted to be at the bottom of the territory rankings again. He was kick-started with the help of the very team he was feeling humiliation in front of. He began quietly asking other sales managers how they filled their pipelines and managed their accounts. The peers gave help. Within a year he was one of the top sales managers in the country.

Mini-Regional Meetings:

On an alternating basis use half- or full-day mini-regional sales meetings to introduce new members of the sales team or other dignitaries in the company, new products, present sales pitches, and to promote new ways of doing business. These can be very helpful when the sales team is large or budgets are tight. You also want to be sensitive to salespeople's selling time.

When there are a number of people who are new to the company, go around the room and have everyone introduce each other. Get new team members acclimated as soon as possible.

Regional Dinners:

Take regional teams to dinner when you are in their territory. This can be a great team-building experience. Use the casual dining experience as an opportunity to listen to what salespeople are thinking about. Keep it light but purposeful. Ask a lot of questions. Get to know the salespeople. If you sense problems within the staff, use another time and place to dig deeper.

Make sure that you schedule these dinners in advance and be sensitive to people with families or other after-hours schedules. Try not to occupy an entire evening if possible. Don't let sales dinners get out of hand. Most people take a dim view of drunkfests and loose behavior. Such behavior can ruin more than one sales career. Even if an out-of-hand situation doesn't involve you personally, you could ultimately be legally responsible. It does tarnish your image if it happens under your watch.

Some of the information that you pick up during regional dinners and sales meetings will come in handy for that occasional humorous reference that can be made to keep the atmosphere light. Use the info carefully. Don't humiliate people. Humor, when done with a spirit of camaraderie, will draw the team more closely together.

Teamwork Off-Sites:

If a sales team is experiencing difficulties with personality conflicts, or in communicating and working together and can't work it out on a day-to-day basis in the office environment, try taking them out for some fresh air. Some *really* fresh air.

There are numerous team-building schools that use the outdoors as a change of pace and environment to get people working together and/or to pull as a team in order to survive. These can be life-changing and include courses out in the desert and woods or on ocean-going sailing yachts.

Running a Sales Meeting:

Running a sales meeting is a bit like being an emcee of a TV show. You are just the ring master. If you plan on taking an active role in the meeting, consider designating someone to do the emcee job for you (it could be the company's marketing director).

Regardless of who emcees the single biggest contribution you can make to a sales meeting is keeping it on schedule. There are numerous reasons for doing this. The primary one is respect for the time of those attending. Other reasons include getting through all of the agenda and ending the meeting at the agreed time. An overscheduled, rushed meeting sends a message about the managerial skills of the people who planned the meeting.

Meeting Icebreakers:

The mood in a room can make or break a sales meeting. Warm up a sales meeting quickly. When salespeople are taken out of their element and put in a room with other people, it can be disorienting. Icebreakers help people know more about each other in a casual way.

Here are some ideas for ice-breakers:

- Have people draw the names of other salespeople out of a basket and uncover some "fun" facts people don't know about them and report back to the group.

- Take a few minutes at the beginning of the meeting to have salespeople do mini-interviews of the person on their right or left. Then have them introduce the people on their right or left.

- Consider having people go around the room and introduce the salespeople to their left or right, but with a unique twist. They introduce these people without knowing anything about them, so they will have to make up some outrageous "facts" about them. This can be very humorous. Just make sure that it doesn't get out of hand. After this exercise, have each person go back around and introduce themselves to the group for real.

- Give all the people in the room a few questions that they must answer when they introduce themselves:

  - What city were you born in?

  - What was the last movie you saw?

  - What was the last book you read?

Modulating Meeting Intensity:

Sometimes meetings can be so intense that they start to drag a team down a slippery slope. Sales numbers can be off, morale can be down, products can be delayed, and internal systems might be working right. One way to keep things light during these tense meetings is to use the concept of "humor-iliation," with emphasis on the *humor*.

Keep the meeting light. Pick on members of the team who *are* hitting their numbers. Kid them about how they made their numbers. (Accusing them of sleeping with their customers is definitely not a good idea.) Keep it good natured and others will see that it's much more fun to be part of the "fun" team than to be in the "dumpster" with bad numbers.

Consider making casual "fun" bets on the outcome of revenue at the end of a quarter.

EXAMPLE: Make this casual group bet: The sales manager that is the farthest off budget for a territory will, at the next company off-site meeting, be the "drink-buying gopher" for the person who is the closest to their territory budget number. Someone will certainly want to take that bet!

TOP TIP: Sales Meeting Feedback:

Sales meetings are designed for salespeople to learn something. They can also help you learn. Feedback from sales meetings is important and there are a few different ways to get it:

THE FINAL SESSION: Save the last session of the sales meeting to go around the room and get feedback on any topic that the salespeople want to discuss. This can be open-ended and not necessarily cover the content presented in the sales meeting. Allow for plenty of time.

FOLLOW-UP SURVEY: If you want feedback on the content, duration, quality, entertainment, or accommodations of the sales meeting, you can cover that as part of the final session or create surveys that are handed out at the end of the event. Include a blank envelope that the survey can be placed in.

Getting 100% feedback can be a problem with follow-up surveys. A few ways to ensure that feedback happens are:

- Don't approve individual employee expenses until the feedback questionnaire is returned. Ask that they be returned with the expense reports and put a deadline on when the expenses are due. If they have been placed in a blank envelope, they can be separated from the expense report and placed in a folder. This maintains their anonymity.

- Don't approve the group's sales meeting expenses until all survey forms have been returned. Have an assistant call and follow-up on all the surveys until they are in.

- Create a reward for every salesperson who turns in a survey.

8. SALES TOOLS

Sales tools are an important part of any sales arsenal. There are many to choose from and they can shorten the distance to a big sale. Basic sales tools that companies create to help sell products are just part of the equation. Just because tools are created is no guarantee that they will be used.

Sales tools also come in the form of electronic devices and can either add to or complicate your life. Customer

Relationship Management (CRM) tools can also be valuable for companies that use them.

Here are some ideas on the value and use of sales tools:

MEGA TIP: Salespeople Should Always Carry Sales Tools:

Salespeople should always have appropriate sales tools with them at all times, no excuses. The desire to travel light and leave them back at the office is very tempting, but the idea of slowing down a sale because of inability to illustrate a point or offer an appropriate "leave behind" piece is unconscionable.

Salespeople who use sales tools out in the marketplace should be acknowledged for integrating sales and marketing. A great salesperson will use whatever pieces of the sales presentation are needed to make the sale. And although they may not use every marketing material available to them to move a sale along, they still need access to them.

MEGA TIP: Create a Sales Toolbox:

Every salesperson should have a binder with copies of the following items:

- Sales team contact numbers including: e-mail address, cell phone, fax and office numbers, etc.,

- Sales order forms and price sheets,

- Pitches,

- Pitch narratives,

- Research,

- Marketing brochures,

- Product spec sheets,

- FAQ (frequently asked questions) about the company,

- Print-outs of the company website,

- Press releases,

- Annual reports, and

- Any public financial documents.

These items should be kept current by a designated person on the staff. It's preferable to have the sales tool books numbered and "assigned" to each salesperson. They remain property of the company if they leave.

Ideally all this information would be kept online with protected access for the salespeople. The information can be easily updated in a central location without having to send updated copies throughout an entire sales organization.

TOP TIP: **Home-Made Sales Tools:**

Many marketing departments have been driven crazy by salespeople creating their own sell sheets, presentations, and leave behinds. This is usually done to fill a void. Fortunately for the salespeople, some customers like them and they do help make sales. "Necessity is the mother of invention," as the saying goes. Allowing numerous home-made sales tools out in the field is not always the best way to run a sales organization, but if the marketing team is ineffective the sales effort shouldn't suffer from it.

If a sales team is creating its own sales tools and they are working, give them to the marketing department so that the entire sales organization can take advantage of these resourceful tools.

TOP TIP: **Filling the Sales Toolbox:**

Selling something, like building a bird house, can be fairly simple—if you have the right tools in the toolbox. Knowing what tools to have is often the hard part. The marketer who listens carefully and fills the tool box with the right stuff is very important to the sales team.

The best marketers are those who have had the opportunity to sit in front of a customer and actually try to sell something first-hand. You should demand, or at least suggest, that your marketing people spend time out of their offices and out in salesland. Sales tools would be much more to the point if more marketers were closer to being salespeople. Sometimes you don't need a lot of tools to make sales happen or to fix a sales problem.

Here are some general tips on effective sales tools:

- Keep them brief and to the point.

- Use the "single subject only" theory when creating them: One major topic per marketing piece.

- Keep them on the front side of one page only.

- Be consistent in graphics, no matter what the sales tool is (business card, stationery, screen presentation, proposal, or leave-behind). This conveys an overall picture of professionalism.

- They shouldn't be created in a way that makes them un-faxable. This is a minor point that is often missed in the creative development process.

(Examples: putting black type on a red background, or making the type too small or fancy.)

- Create blank logo sheets with consistent graphics that can be run through a laser printer when you need to put a sales kit together. This also allows sales tools to be updated more frequently with minimal waste.

- Make sure that all sales tools are available as a plain Word file, a Word file with company graphics inserted, and a .pdf (Adobe Acrobat) file for e-mailing to customers.

- Do not overwhelm a sell sheet with too many words, graphics, typefaces, or charts.

- Salespeople should highlight what customers need to know with a highlighter marker.

- Salespeople should take the time to create generic custom pages or presentation slides for customers. They will be amazed at how often the customers will use them in *their* presentations.

- Offer to create or modify presentations for the customers if it will help sell the company's products and services.

Getting Organized

There is no shortage of tools available to salespeople for getting organized and communicating. Picking the combination that works best is a personal choice. Tool options include: cell phones, PDAs (Personal Digital Assistants), handheld PCs, laptops, phone/PDA combos, phones with cameras, wi-fi connections, etc.

Weigh the value of each tool and look at how you plan to use it before you buy. New technology is fun but putting your sales team on the line as a guinea pig isn't fun, especially when something goes wrong—company-wide. Additionally, the nuances of determining whether one piece of technology works with another are often overwhelming. Sometimes you don't know until you've hooked one device to another that they aren't compatible.

TOP TIP: Using Customer Relationship Management (CRM) Tools:

Customer Relationship Management (CRM) tools are often software or web-based solutions that are designed to integrate sales processes so they run more smoothly throughout a company. They are especially helpful if the company is revenue-focused.

CRM tools can be as simple as a customer database stored in a Palm Pilot or as complex as a company-wide, web- or network-based solution. CRM is about keeping closer tabs on the relationship between company executives, sales managers, salespeople, and customers.

CRM allows:

- Sharing of historical information.

- Upper management a higher-level view of what's going on in sales.

- Sales managers to have more accountability.

- Salespeople to do less paperwork and more selling.

- Everyone who touches sales to be on the same page and do the best job for the customer and the shareholders.

Currently this is a market in it's infancy with huge potential upside for the companies that adopt CRM solutions.

The major components of an integrated CRM solution will include:

- Sales Force Automation (SFA),

- Customer service and support,

- Marketing automation,

- Document management,

- Contract management, and

- Ongoing analytics.

The key components which are reviewed when evaluating a CRM solution are:

- Product usability for end-users,

- System administration,

- Overall product features,

- Product quality,

- System response time,

- CRM supplier's help desk,

- CRM supplier's sales staff,

- Fair price for the value received, and

- Overall experience with the vendor.

As you can see, there are many moving parts to CRM. What should matter most for sales managers is usability for end-users, specifically salespeople. If the salespeople don't enter information into the CRM database and then put it to good use, it won't work for the entire company.

The age-old problem with adopting any new technology lies in getting salespeople (or anyone else for that matter) to use it and weighing the value of that use against the time and resources needed for implementation.

Basic thoughts on CRM:

1. CRM should solve problems in an elegantly simple way:

TRUE STORY: Before CRM existed the way it does today, a resourceful company created a very simple revenue-reporting system that was linked to its order/delivery database. It would tell executives, up to the minute, what sales were by product line, just by going online to a single Web page. It was basic, timely, top-line information that was all that upper management wanted to see.

At the sales management level, there was another set of tools that gave the sales managers more detail on territory and salesperson performance against budget.

At the sales-process level, a set of tools was created for sales coordinators to provide more uniform quality of service across the customer base.

BOTTOM LINE: If a CRM implementation can't be done simply and with minimal disruption, it can do more harm than good to a company's sales structure.

2. People actually using CRM have to see its value:

It's not that the available CRM solutions aren't potentially great. They are often brilliant, which is why it has become an important industry. The challenge is getting salespeople and sales managers to change their well established habits and biases and see the true value of using CRM.

Most salespeople base their value to the company in relationships that they have with their customers. And most of that is tucked away nicely in their heads or in their own personal databases. The thought of transferring this knowledge to a database for all to see creates a feeling of expendability and accountability that salespeople aren't accustomed to and often can't handle.

TRY THIS: Put yourself in the shoes of a salesperson and imagine having placed all your personal trade secrets about a customer in a database that your manager can now view. Then imagine blowing a sale and not being able to spin it the way that makes you look good as a salesperson.

Now imagine being constantly micro-managed on every account that you have and every sale that you make. This is what salespeople are often thinking when they see CRM coming down the road. They start to wonder: "What do they need me for if this is going to be automated?" It's not what they should be thinking, but it is human nature. This is what causes salespeople to passively smile and agree with the concept of a CRM solution when the dog-and-pony show presentations are made to them—but it's also what causes them to not spend a lot of time entering information into the database that could help them do their jobs a whole lot better.

In the mind of a salesperson CRM is a trade-off. Salespeople think: "Do you want me filling in a database or do you want me making sales calls and closing business?" The answer, from the sales manager's perspective is, "Both, of course!" But with the salespeople it's: "Pick one or the other!" Salespeople are generally creatures of habit and if they are used to making money in a certain way, using a certain process, they are likely to keep on doing it that way.

All good salespeople have a little bit of insecurity running through the bloodstream. This makes them perform and show their bosses, and the world, how good they are. Sales managers love this. But it also gives salespeople a feeling that if they have to expose all their knowledge about their territories, that will make them an interchangeable cog in the wheel part or a commodity. That alone will keep them from fully embracing a move to CRM.

BOTTOM LINE: For anyone, particularly salespeople, to be enthusiastic about change, they have to recognize a tremendous amount of value for them personally.

3. Test your CRM options:

What *sounds* great might not always *work* great. Most companies that consider integrating multiple internal systems into a single CRM solution will test them first.

One of the best ways to contribute to testing is to ask some of the sharpest sales support staff, salespeople and sales managers in the company to act as part of an evaluation team. Since they will be the primary users of the solution, their input is invaluable when it comes to streamlining processes or improving on existing ways of doing things. Because they know how the systems work, they can troubleshoot for the CRM vendor and provide insight into the company.

BOTTOM LINE: CRM vendors should be prepared to provide short-term test programs for companies considering an implementation. Companies should also be prepared to spend some money to do these tests depending on the complexity of the solution they are considering. This is one process that shouldn't have to be repeated over-and-over.

4. CRM implementation has to be easy:

TRUE STORY: At one company, the implementation team that installed the CRM solution had no idea of what business the company was in or how the sales organization was set up. Each time the company's staff taught the CRM implementation team their business, the project seemed to get a new implementation manager (turnover was clearly an issue for this company). This ultimately became very frustrating, but not just to the company. The last implementation manager who handled the account literally went insane and had to be committed (!).

BOTTOM LINE: When exchanging old thinking for new, there has to be a quantum leap in terms of what is gained. Part of what makes change more acceptable is the ease with which it happens. Never underestimate the value of orchestrating a simple implementation and minimizing downtime for a new solution.

TOP TIP: **Selling CRM to the Sales Team:**

Internal pioneers of new technology score points with their managers. Their peers will likely embrace the changes more readily if these pioneers like the solution. Nothing could be truer when it comes to the implementation of a CRM solution.

The one point to stress with salespeople is, the closer you get to implementing a CRM solution the more they will need to be portable into new roles—if they ultimately want to get better sales territories or climb the management ladder.

Portability and transferability of sales territories make salespeople all the more promotable.

If salespeople can package their territory so that it's easily transferable to their peers, they are much easier to promote. This is actually true even if there isn't a CRM implementation happening. Though they should always think this way, very few salespeople understand this concept. It's all about creating an easily accessible territory that can be passed on quickly if a promotion opportunity exists.

9. MOTIVATION

Creating an environment where motivated people can give their absolute best work and motivate others around them should be a top priority. Encouraging and rewarding the personal motivation of top performers will carry over to the rest of the team and generate better overall performance.

Here are some ideas on motivation and how it can work within a sales organization:

MEGA TIP: **Show Appreciation for Great Work:**

Thank salespeople when they go out of their way to do their job. Acknowledge them. Give them a genuine thank you. It makes a *huge* difference in the way people respond. If a company is well run and streamlined, then there is no job that isn't important. Make sure salespeople truly understand that the job they do is important, no matter what it is. Practice random acts of "thank you-ness" to people, with little or no warning. Be spontaneous. The alternative is that you could be doing the job yourself, which might not be the best use of your time.

Showing appreciation goes outside of your department. Extend it to the departments that you work with most closely. Make key people of other departments "honorary" members of your team—for doing a great job or for putting up with your team's foibles.

MEGA TIP: **Create a Sense of Urgency:**

Never put off until tomorrow what you can accomplish with a little extra effort today. Meeting sales goals quickly starts by creating a sense of urgency at the top of any sales organization. Creating this urgency means taking personal responsibility for doing everything as fast, and mistake free, as humanly possible.

Creating the proper environment in which to make things happen quickly is your responsibility. Here are some ideas on how:

- Be your own role-model by beating deadlines that you set for yourself.

- Set deadlines for salespeople on jobs to be done.

- Pitch in to help salespeople beat their deadlines.

- With minimal micro-managing make sure that the salespeople are held to their deadlines. Check in on agreed-to timeframes.

- Reward those who beat their deadlines with verbal and (if possible) financial rewards.

- Tactical ways to create urgency:

    - At the end of each day, create a list of tasks to be accomplished tomorrow.

    - Spend a few minutes prioritizing the list.

    - Before going home, spend 25 minutes blasting through as many tasks on the list as possible.

    - Reprioritize the list and leave it for the first thing the following day.

    - Teach your salespeople this method.

TOP TIP: Infectious Motivation:

If you are visibly psyched about your company's opportunities for success your team will be too. But it has to be genuine. It's up to you and your team to translate the value and excitement of your product or service to your customers. How do you do that?

- Talk to your current customers. Find out why they are excited about your product. See what unique things they are doing with the product. Enlist your marketing team to turn customer enthusiasm into testimonials.

- Shop your competitors. Look at all the things their sales team does better than yours, and look at what yours does better.

- Find out how your best salespeople are selling the product and have them tell the team how they do it.

- Look for every product review or news story on your products. Showcase them for everyone to see.

- Bring your best customers in for lunch at sales meetings so the sales team can ask questions. If the company's product has end-user consumers, then get feedback from those customers so that the salespeople will hear first-hand how the product is used. This can be done as a series of anonymous focus groups that can be packaged to show to the sales team.

- Hold a competition among your customers for the most unique use of the products.

In the end, if you aren't personally excited about the product, it will be that much harder to succeed. If it's a product or service that you can personally use, then do it with gusto. Tell the sales team about your personal experiences in using it (depending on the product, of course!)

TOP TIP: Fun and Cool:

Make day-to-day life enjoyable for the sales team. Help the members get in touch with their fun side. It makes hard work a lot easier to do. Encourage a fun social environment.

TRUE STORY: A "fun and cool" committee was established by some key employees to help create a positive and vibrant culture for the company. This company was going full-bore and everyone who needed to (which was mostly everyone) was spending long hours at the office. The company was becoming a first home to many people. More "fun" was injected into the environment and the company became known for its culture. Once the word got out, people wanted to work there.

The company did some of these things for fun:

- Served bagels on Fridays with all the trimmings.

- Papered a graffiti wall and supplied big markers for writing comments.

- Created special nicknames for conference rooms.

- Had employees create their own cubicle name plaques.

- Put a "nerf" basketball hoop on the wall.

- Installed foosball and pool tables.

- Provided latte and vending machines.

- Had cubicle or office-decorating parties for birthdays.

- Held "theme" dinners during late-night work sessions.

- Held monthly company meetings at an off-site venue followed by a social get-together.

- Held on-site company meetings in the main atrium, when needed.

- Had a company holiday party in a unique and memorable venue.

TOP TIP: **The Culture Club:**

Creating team culture is a team effort. Establish ground rules for the appropriate culture for the environment in which the sales team is working. Then have the sales team build and reinforce it. Putting your foot down and trying to single-handedly create a culture won't work. No one will buy it. It will be perceived as your culture, not theirs. The sales team needs to own part of the process, with your guidance. They are the ones doing the work, after all. It's up to you to make sure that the culture doesn't put the sales team at odds with other departments in the company or even with your customer base.

Building a culture and keeping it going in an up economy is a lot easier than in a down economy. As markets head temporarily downwards, marketing budgets can be cut to conserve cash. The company culture can take a hit because there is less funding to do fun things. Down times are not best for cutting morale-building motivational programs, especially when the sales team needs to be rallied to make their numbers. Think of alternative low-cost ways to keep the culture intact. The core of a company's culture is its state of mind. There doesn't have to be a lot of money associated with culture maintenance. Just make sure that you allocate for it, keep it in the forefront, and continue to reinforce it.

TOP TIP: **Remember the Spouses:**

There are usually members of a sales team who are great motivators but often forgotten in the day-to-day process of selling. They are the spouses and significant others who give up their mates to the job. You may spend more time with members of the sales team than their spouses do! Don't forget these "silent motivators" when it comes to acknowledging the success of the sales team. This will add to the overall morale of the company and draw attention to a widely unknown fact: that spouses and significant others are also integral to the success of a company's sales effort and the motivation of salespeople.

There are many ways to reward spouses and significant others. Depending on your budget or company policy, you can:

- Invite them to the annual "fun" sales meeting or allow spouses to join in at the end of a sales meeting held at an exotic location and remain for the weekend.

- Give them small gifts at the end of the year that are appropriate to the role they have played.

- Invite them to the annual sales meeting award dinner.

- Include them in a fun night out.

- Verbally acknowledge their contributions in front of a group of people, and thank them.

- Make them an unofficial part of the "extended" sales team and award them with a plaque, trophy or gift certificate.

Do this as frequently as possible, while keeping it special.

TOP TIP: Restarting an Existing Sales Team:

When your car battery dies you get out the booster cable. If the battery isn't 100% dead the cables usually work. You can give the sales team a "boost" by hiring people whom you want the rest of the team to emulate. This will raise the bar for the existing sales team. It's one of those not-so-subtle motivators. The lower performers on the sales team will get the hint quickly that you are upgrading the quality of the group and that they need to keep up.

If you hire new stars in an organization, let them know that they are part of the restart plan. They are kingpins of the new sales organization. Quickly point out the successes of these new team members to the rest of the sales staff. Have them stand up at sales meetings and tell people how they sell, what worked for them, and how they did it. Give them the floor and let them talk about it. Let them motivate others.

Picking an Enemy:

Every competitive sales team needs an enemy to beat as a motivational tool. Make sure, however, that they aren't slamming the enemy in sales calls. That wastes selling time and is unprofessional. What you are ultimately trying to accomplish by picking an enemy is getting the sales team appropriately focused on prevailing over a competitor by selling more of your products and services. It's not so much that they hurt a competitor as it is that they advance the successes of the company they work for.

If you are using market share as a success metric, then you will need to have readily available and timely information to know what progress is being made. If you aren't playing the market share game, having an enemy can still play a motivational role.

Pick the list of competitors carefully. Pick the comparison metrics even more carefully. Motivate the salespeople to focus on these metrics though an incentive program. The incentive you pick will be a function of how the marketplace rewards your type of business successes. If you are in an established market where the metrics for competitive companies are obtainable, then start there. But it pays to be even more focused. Tie market share rewards specifically to large, top target accounts in each territory in addition to rewarding attainment of overall market share. Or, you can set rewards for selling a certain mix of product or hitting certain price levels. As you knock off each one of those top customers, give appropriate financial rewards and public accolades to the deserving members of the sales team.

When the Enemy Hasn't Shown Up Yet:

If you are in an emerging market where new competitors pop up or go away every day, it may be very hard to pick an enemy to focus on. Where the playing field is wide open, competitors sometimes aren't even there yet. Significant percentage increases in sales each quarter would be your typical goal here. The market share game is yours to lose, and not moving fast can be fatal. Trying to find published sales numbers and competitors to compare market share against won't be available, or if they are, they probably won't be accurate or timely.

Having an "enemy" to focus on without visible competitors or historical information might not be possible. This type of environment requires some fast thinking when it comes to building the right motivational/compensation models. The best approach may well be to reward the number of new accounts brought in over a period of time (month, quarter), the amount of upgrade sales for those accounts over the next few quarters, and publicly showcasing (in sales meetings) the innovative thinking of salespeople that went into finding, creating and closing those accounts.

Free Motivation:

CFOs and CEOs often cringe when motivational programs are created because it is often assumed that these programs will be added on to existing commission plans. They don't have to be. As part of the quarterly commission planning process, build sales contests and other motivational programs into the existing budget before the quarter starts.

Salespeople shouldn't be paid more to do the job they are already supposed to do. Create levels of additional motivation within an existing compensation plan that give the appearance of additional bonuses. One rule of thumb might be to hold back 20% of the quarterly commission (based on hitting a budget number) and allocating it to a special bonus program. That way, the sales team will still be paid the same commission at 100% of budget but there's an added opportunity to create more motivation to get there.

Friendly Competition:

Competition usually comes from outside the company, but can also come from within. Either way it can be highly motivating.

Always know the competitors. This will sound odd but considering sending cards or small gifts to them during the holidays. This will surely drive them crazy (or at least make them nervous) and maybe even endear you to them.

TRUE STORY: One holiday season a company's sales executive sent a fleece blanket to all the high level sales executives at competing companies. It was a class move that set him and his company apart. It also created some long-term relationships and let competitors know that the company was professional in the way it competed.

It doesn't hurt to be in communication with your competitors from time to time either, if only on an infrequent and casual basis. Competitive communication should, however, never be used as an opportunity to collude.

TRUE STORY: A competitor's salesperson had created a very negative (and inaccurate) presentation to go after a company's successes. One of the more enterprising salespeople at the company intercepted it in the marketplace and gave it to her manager.

Rather than confront the competitor's salesperson or have the sales team out in the field showing the competitor's handiwork to everyone, the company's sales manager e-mailed the CEO of the competitor to let him know that his salesperson was hurting their reputation. The CEO thanked the sales manager and took care of it immediately. The offending piece was never seen or heard of again. And neither was the competitor's salesperson!

Viva La Différence!:

Sometimes bending the rules and being more accepting of other people's quirks is a good strategy in the workplace. Some people like to bring their pets to work. (This would be subject to company policy.) Some salespeople like to go work out and then come back in their work-out clothes to finish up. This is do-able in some situations and company environments but not all.

TRUE STORY: A salesperson who was into exercising insisted on rollerblading during the summer months, then coming back into the office, after hours, to finish up. She put her rollerblades back on while she was working on proposals. This helped to get a little bit more of a work-out and get back and forth to the printer and the copier faster.

The salesperson's manager thought it was amusing

watching her glide back and forth in front of his office without moving her feet. In this case, the sales manager let company policy slide so the salesperson could glide. And the proposals were done faster.

Comrades in Arms:

Events like incentive sales dinners and sales reward trips can build a team if done properly. These are usually tied to annual sales goals, and sometimes the success of new product launches. They can be as simple as a gift certificate for a night on the town, or a three-day weekend to some exciting location for the salesperson and a significant other. Being acknowledged as a great salesperson is often all that it takes to get someone excited about doing his or her job, while others are motivated by an exciting destination (and talk about it to everyone, once they return!).

As mentioned earlier, various rewards should fit financially into an existing incentive program whenever possible. When well implemented, they create camaraderie, which promotes retention. These events can also subtly motivate underachievers to do better. It raises the bar for everyone. The idea here is to move the average success rate of the entire sales team to an even higher level—and then to acknowledge and reward stellar successes and grow even greater overall group success.

Naming Your Team:

Creating a team name opens the door for all types of team building. It gives the sales team something to rally around.

Some sales managers prefer creating one team nickname across all divisions and territories and then focusing their energy outward of the company and on the competition. (The competition can have nicknames, too, like, the weasels, rats, etc.)

Other sales managers prefer to have nicknames for individual internal teams (one for the west coast team, east coast team, different product launch teams—you get the idea) and then have them compete against each other in a good-spirited way.

Always put the nickname to a vote. Make sure everyone has a vote and buys in. Don't pick names that might be offensive to any group (except the competition!).

TRUE STORY: One company used fish-related nicknames for just about everything. Conference rooms were named after fish, nameplates for doors were designed to look like fish, dinners were held at restaurants with fish names, team award trips were tied to a fish theme. Logo hats, towels, squish toys, etc. were all designed to promote the fish theme. It worked!

Talented marketing people can take a very simple theme and turn it into an amazing rallying point for an organization. Trust the marketing pros in your company with this kind of work.

Sporting Events:

Company-sponsored sporting events are more than just a customer entertainment expense. Use sporting events for departmental rewards and interdepartmental mingling. Usually company employees get invited to these events when all the customer invitations have been exhausted. It may do more good to reward those departments around you than the customers.

Invite people from different groups inside the company so that everyone gets to know each other. Be aware of the political impact and any hurt feelings when you put together your guest list. Sometimes it matters symbolically whom you invite first even though you know they can't make it. That will extend the usefulness of the tickets you have available. This builds trust and helps break down the internal "us vs. them" departmental attitudes that can destroy the effectiveness of an organization.

The Clique-Free Zone:

There is nothing more offensive than a clique of sales managers or salespeople who laugh and talk behind everyone else's back. This is a negative clique because it's only part of the group. An entire sales team that hangs out together is not considered a clique. Cliques are generally demoralizing and de-motivating to just about everyone outside that group. Don't succumb to them by letting them exist or have any clout, and don't tolerate them no matter how good these salespeople may be.

Once the rest of the team identifies that a clique exists, they will either try to join it or do anything possible to give the clique members grief behind their backs (call it the anti-clique!). You will then have a full-scale political war of egos on your hands. There are better things to do with your time. You can't dictate who can be friends with whom. But you can take every opportunity to surgically break up cliques throughout the course of a sales meeting. It's best to do this only if the clique is creating a problem for you or challenging your authority.

If you see a clique forming do whatever you can to bust it up. When you do sales training or sales dinners, split the cliques up.

There is nothing wrong with salespeople forming informal friendships. Sometimes these groups can accomplish a lot and help each other. This just shouldn't be done to the exclusion of peers at the same level or as a "put-down" to others.

TOP TIP: **Bring in Fresh Ideas:**

No matter what you are selling, energy-efficient windows or car insurance or real estate, it's always motivational to expose the sales teams to innovative ways that salespeople from other walks of life use to sell their products. New selling ideas can come from people who buy the product telling you how they would like to be sold, or they can come from salespeople in other industries who are particularly good at what they do. It pays to know sales executives from other industries. Trade notes, exchange ideas, and apply what might work to your particular industry. Have them come in for lunch and tell your sales organization how they help their customers.

Stock Options and/or Bonuses:

The debate about how a company should account for stock options is always changing, but suffice it to say that salespeople should share greatly in the upside they are helping create for you and the company. That's motivational, isn't it? If options are available, then give them. Many companies are looking at cash compensation as an alternative to the accountability of stock options. Whatever the right answer is to that question make sure the sales team gets its fair share. Every department is valuable to a company, but salespeople are on the front line. They bear the brunt when things don't work or aren't delivered on time. They constantly hear the word "No" and that's not always just from the external customers. Having the resilience to take that kind of abuse makes them fairly unique. Get them what they deserve.

Salespeople are motivated by winning. When they win, money follows. Give them additional rewards for doing a stellar job each year. It's usually best to time these six months after salary increases.

10. LISTENING

The ability to listen is underrated and is a talent every sales manager should have. Most sales managers know they should do a better job at it and want to, but don't know where to start. Here are some ideas on how to listen better:

MEGA TIP: Have Kind Ears:

TRUE STORY: A salesperson told her sales manager he had "kind ears." The manager wasn't sure just what that meant.

The salesperson told the sales manager that he:

- Listened without judging,

- Asked clarifying questions to help the salesperson think more about the issues she was facing,

- Asked how she felt about whatever situation they were in,

- Asked how she thought problems should be solved, and

- Gave her ideas on how she could lay out all the facts and draw a conclusion in an unbiased way.

That's what "kind ears" were.

Having "kind ears" is a way of guiding the thinking of salespeople without telling them exactly how to solve their problems. It lets them figure it out on their own.

As a sales manager, being able to give personal anecdotal examples (good and bad) to help salespeople think through issues even more deeply is also helpful.

In the end, listening is one of the most important management skills that you can develop. That means listening until the other person is finished talking—not merely until you hear a few key words that begin to trigger your response before the other person is finished speaking so that you miss what is really being said.

Consider using this well-worn rule of thumb:

You have two ears and one mouth and they should be used in that proportion. (This is also true when making sales calls.)

MEGA TIP: Always Ask the Sales Team What *They* Think:

If the sales team isn't happy, it won't be effective. Ask team members frequently for their opinion. Create an environment where they can actually give opinions easily, and without recourse. That could be through a suggestion box, an anonymous e-mail address, or feedback to their bosses and then to you.

Once you get the information, acknowledge it and thank people (as a group) for speaking up. Also, take time in sales meetings or weekly updates to review the information that you've been given and what you are going to do about it. Let the sales team know what you can or cannot do. Make their suggestions happen whenever possible and they will know that you are on their side and are a "can do" kind of manager.

TOP TIP: Help Create, and Further, Careers:

Always help great salespeople get to the next level of their career by asking what motivates them and what their plan is. Then listen to what they have to say. Try to help them meet their goals. If you know what they want to accomplish and they have the drive and talent to do so, that will help you as you build the sales organization.

Keep moving proven performers up whenever possible. If they aren't ready to move up, tell them why. They will cherish their contact with you, and your honesty. They will become your strongest supporters, and they will be more valuable team members. They will also be good early warning systems if things are going wrong in the sales organization.

As you move from one job to the next, keep in touch with your best salespeople. When they are looking for work in the future you'll want to be the first person they call. Most people like to be challenged and well led. When you create that environment you will help others as you move up the ladder.

TOP TIP: **Practice Genuine Empathy:**

Salespeople have a hard job. Remember when you were one? Don't forget that you will always be one! They can't always win every deal. They can't always get the highest price for the company's product or service. They, and you, won't always be happy with their personal performance. They have the constant pressure of numbers on their heads. They will get frustrated and ticked off at bureaucracy from time to time (OK, maybe all the time!). You need to understand that all of this is going on in their heads. Once you get to an elevated management position, you can't forget what happens every day. You are now the person who can (you hope) start making smart changes.

It's important to practice real empathy with salespeople when things don't go as planned. Not phony empathy. That's easily seen through.

FOR EXAMPLE: Isn't it annoying on a personal level when people make fake and chatty conversation just to try be endearing to you and gloss over a problem? It's a waste of everyone's time. It's just as obvious to others if you do it to them. Salespeople can pick up on it in a New York nanosecond. So don't even think about doing it. When appropriate, let them know that you honestly feel their pain.

TOP TIP: Random People Checks:

Every once in a while pick a few salespeople and do a random "How are you doing?" call. It's not part of the official review process—it's just showing the salespeople that someone cares about how they feel about their jobs, their lives, etc. It can also help you uncover issues that may be brewing and affecting attitude and performance.

Ask if they need anything from you. If they do, help them get it. Go out of your way to help. Don't ever be hesitant to ask what they might need from you to do their job better. Don't assume that they will figure it out on their own. It never hurts to ask them a few leading questions to help them figure it out on their own. Ask questions like "If we had a one-sheet brochure that fully lays out our product offerings, would this *really* help you make clearer presentations to your customers?"

Use any downtime that you have in your day to accomplish your check-ins. They don't need to take long. You'll learn a lot and create a tremendous amount of goodwill with the sales team. Make sure that you rotate around to as many salespeople as possible in order to get a balanced assessment where no one feels overburdened or slighted.

TOP TIP: Turning Whining into a Positive:

Always listen to complaints that people have. But do so with one simple caveat: *If people are going to complain about something they must be prepared to offer a solution to that problem.* This takes a lot more thinking than just complaining. It requires people to dig down deep and think about what is causing the problem and whether it can be fixed. If it can be fixed, then what effort would it take to do so?

By having the "tell me how you'd fix it" *caveat* you are turning people's negative energy into a positive and doing some potential good for solving problems.

Get Healthy Feedback:

At the end of any meeting, try to have plenty of time for people to discuss whatever issues they want. It can be about some policy decision that was made, something going on in the company, complaints about other departments, etc. Anything and everything is fair game. This shows the sales team that you are listening.

When salespeople raise issues, make sure they are written down and responded to in a reasonable time-frame (within 24-48 hours). Listening to them is one thing, responding is another. Always close the session by recapping your expected follow-up.

Looking for the Real Inside Buzz:

Ask salespeople directly what they think the "buzz" is inside the company. You are trying to capture an overall feeling within the company, not just hone in on specific issues. Ask if things are going well or poorly. What are people thinking? See if it matches what is being heard higher up in the company. Try to do this without being a gossip monger. Just listen without expressing an opinion. Ask probing questions as necessary.

If people aren't opening up and you sense that there are truly problems, you can raise a widespread issue that you know exists and ask for feedback. This way people will know you are willing to hear what they say and this will get them talking.

This can also be done in one-on-ones or by telling people to e-mail with an anonymous alias (usually set up by your HR department). Talk to the sales managers before doing any group meetings with the sales team. The sales managers can often speak on the team's behalf. Or, you can simply ask the sales team what they've heard from around the company, instead of asking for direct feedback.

Mi Problema, Su Problema:

When the customer problem is a mutual one (i.e., both sides have helped create the problem) a little different approach is required. It involves listening.

Mutual problems require mutual problem-solving. It often doesn't hurt to take slightly more than your share of the responsibility to resolve the problem. The customer is always right—right? Well, not always, but that's the rule. If you can't mutually solve the problem, then ask for a fair compromise. Try to mediate the problem equitably.

If it is a severe problem where both parties goofed then make it clear that the problem can only be solved if both parties make some changes on a go forward basis. You each have to come part way.

If the problem has gone "nuclear," then it doesn't hurt

to take some time to let emotions cool down. Cooler heads always prevail. And some things that could be said in the heat of a discussion might permanently damage the relationship.

Dismissive Disorder:

Don't be immediately dismissive of suggestions for changes that come from the sales team. This is especially true in front of a group of sales managers. Acknowledge the idea, ask for feedback from the group, and if you can accept the idea on the spot, do so immediately. If you'd like to think about it (and you have every right to) then say so, but follow up as soon as possible after the suggestion has been made.

Sometimes the ideas are great, sometimes there is a lot of parochial thinking or a hidden agenda. Take down all suggestions. Sometimes partial ideas can be more fully formed into really big ideas. You can determine later if they are valid for the sales team. Listen for now, without making any judgments as to what could work.

Let everyone involved know if they were or weren't able to be accommodated. Sometimes a simple and logical explanation is all salespeople are looking for.

Know Thy Team:

Salespeople are humans too, and not emotionless robots that respond to your every whim. The better you understand them, the better you understand how to motivate them, monetarily and psychologically. You don't have to invite them over to your home for dinner or know their deepest darkest secrets, but getting to know them outside of the work environment is what will often set you apart from other sales managers. It may also help you understand what's best for them as they move forward in their careers.

Some ideas on getting to know your team members:

- Take them out for coffee or to lunch individually to find out what they are about.

- Ask them what they like and don't like about their job.

- Learn about their hobbies, their families.

- Try to get as much emotional intelligence as you can so that you understand where they are coming from and why they respond to things the way they do.

- Don't use this info against them. Show them how what you know about them will help them in a positive way.

Getting Feedback, Using Feedback:

Getting constant feedback on the sales management team is important and sometimes has to be done confidentially. If you hear grumbling in the ranks, it might be a good time to solicit some feedback. It could be about anything—from how salespeople are managed, to what they are selling, or how they are being asked to sell it, or how they are being paid. If you can talk to the salespeople directly, then do so. Sometimes sales team members will feel that they can't raise an issue directly for fear of political retaliation and would prefer to do so through other feedback channels. If you feel them holding back, you may want to have the HR team poll the salespeople through an anonymous questionnaire for more direct and realistic responses.

Give your HR people insight into what you are hearing from the sales team and what more you'd like to know. Let HR write the questionnaire in a non-biased way that delivers accurate and actionable feedback. Make certain that the salespeople understand the survey is truly anonymous and confidential so that comments will not be attributed to any individuals directly.

HR should aggregate all the information into summary form so that it can't be tracked back to any employee. This might include editing some language patterns or misspellings so they aren't traceable.

After your HR people have done the feedback research give it a thorough, non-defensive read. It might be painful, but illuminating. Read it without rationalizing responses or trying to explain away the problems. The problems are real if others think they are real. The question is: "To what degree are they real?" No amount of rationalization will make them go away.

Share all the results with your sales managers. Create a mutual action plan to solve any problems. Review it with the salespeople and let them know that you, and the rest of the sales management team, are working to solve these issues.

Try to read the results as though you are a dispassionate third-party observer who is going to use the information to make consulting recommendations. Then implement them.

If you see that your staff has negative opinions of you or your sales managers, confront these issues head-on or nothing will improve. Do it quickly, before something else creates a distraction and takes precedence.

Managing Nervous Nellies:

Sometimes there is that one employee who feels the need to share with you everything that could potentially be going wrong with the company. It's like Chicken Little saying the sky is going to fall! Generally, while these people seem like "nervous Nellies" and may annoy you with their paranoia, they can be a tremendous "early warning" system for you if trouble is brewing in the ranks.

There is usually something to their concerns. Maybe it's just not as big of a problem as they see it. Listen to what they say. Try to benchmark what they are telling you against something going on in the company that you know well. See if they are "off the charts" in their assessments or if they are providing you a true window to an impending problem. Be open-minded. Once you are calibrated to their sensitivities, you will know the value of their information. Don't dismiss them immediately, since they can possibly help you in the long run, but don't fall victim to them, either. If what they are saying makes sense, check out their story and use the information to your advantage.

Feedback and Behavior Modification:

If you sense that the productivity, camaraderie, and

attitude of the sales team are starting to diminish, you should ask *them* why. Start with your direct reports. Acknowledge that you sense motivation is suffering. Ask what they think is going on. If everything seems peachy, but you still think there is a problem, then ask the salespeople below them. Try to figure out where the disconnect might be. Allow the salespeople to respond anonymously. Whatever you learn, get it out on the table. Don't point fingers, just look for how to improve the problem and move on.

It might also be time to have Human Resources help you uncover the problem. If you are doing annual reviews fairly soon, insert specific questions into the review process to test your suspicions about why things aren't going the way you would like. The response rate to the questionnaire alone may tell a revealing story. If it's unreasonably low, you might find that there is a morale problem. Do everything you can to get the maximum number of responses: It will create a fairer picture of what's going on. Typically, the people who are more dissatisfied are more verbal about it and can greatly skew results toward the negative.

Listening to Issues:

The downside of group camaraderie is that it often allows negative attitudes to be shared across a sales group more readily. If that has to happen at all, it is at least out in the open and not part of the undercurrent. This is where being a true sales manager comes in. If you are close with the sales team, you will get to hear most of their issues. The trick is to not join in creating the issues yourself; just listen and see what you can do to help.

Use feedback to help solve internal conflicts but don't engage in upper-management bashing. Doing so would put you clearly in the "monkey in the middle" position in the company. You can't win there. (Do you remember that game from grade school where two people would throw the ball over the head of another? The monkey was on neither team, and played only to get out of the middle.) You are a member of a team—the sales management team, so you can't be perceived as being in the middle.

11. MANAGING SALESPEOPLE

The ability to lead others is what separates great sales managers from great salespeople. Managing others well is a huge test of personal ability. Sure, salespeople "manage" others to help them make their individual goals, but sales managers have direct reports and are no longer solo performers. They are now leaders. That's a big difference. The good news is that if you manage others correctly you write your own ticket for a long time to come. If you do poorly there is still good news, you can always go back to being a stellar performer on your own. Here are some ideas on effectively managing others:

MEGA TIP: Focus on Leading, Not Just Managing:

Occupying a management position doesn't automatically make you a leader. Focus less on the pure act of management and more on leading the team forward. Most people prefer to be led, not managed, anyway. Although throughout this book, it's assumed that good management is the same as leadership, the truth is that you won't get anywhere as a manager unless you do a fantastic job of leading people.

REMEMBER: Salespeople *have* to work for a sales manager, but they *want* to work for a sales leader.

MEGA TIP: Give 'Til You Get:

Be generous, within reason, in everything you do regarding the sales team. When you go out of your way to reward the salespeople, they will reward you with more sales. It's not just about handing out more money; generosity is more than that.

Sometimes the motivation of salespeople comes from their receiving accolades in front of peers, or a fun trophy for closing the most customers, or a reward trip to somewhere unique, etc.

TRUE STORY: At one company, everyone who shared leads that came to them but weren't in their territory got fake dollar bills with the CEO's face on them. At the end of the quarter those dollars were redeemable for rewards. It was a simple solution to reward teamwork and helped create a sense of community.

"Giving 'til you get" also means having the entire sales team go out of its way for customers when the selling process is long or a salesperson missed a selling window with a customer. Continue to sell the customer, provide market information, and build the relationship. Just because the sale didn't happen this time around doesn't mean that a potential customer is lost forever.

TOP TIP: Give *Full* Credit to the Sales Team:

As a sales manager, it's tempting to take all the credit for sales successes. You certainly deserved it when you were a salesperson. But now it's a different ballgame. Give full credit where credit is due—to the sales team.

This is especially true when you are in the presence of executive management. Initially your ego might demand that *you* get all or part of the credit for the accomplishments of the sales team. You might have jumped in at the end of the sale to help rescue or close it, or you might have been the hiring manager of the key salesperson who worked hard on the deal. Resist the temptation to boast about it! Get over it! Your senior managers know that you are in charge and they will see that your efforts are making things happen in your department.

If a salesperson closes a big deal, make a big deal of it inside the company. Reward the salesperson in every way you can for the effort and creativity exerted. You will ultimately get credit for a smart hire and for making the numbers, but don't take credit for the big deal. Let the indirect credit accrue to you without demanding it. Otherwise, it will just cheapen the accolades you are giving to the salesperson by creating the perception that the acknowledgement is only a way of showcasing your own personal selling skills.

TOP TIP: Develop Natural Leadership Skills and Personality:

In the midst of fierce competition for key sales management positions, it's often those with personality and natural leadership skills who get the job and then excel, but it takes time to develop into being a natural leader. Personality and leadership skills develop over time as personal experiences grow.

If you have ever wondered why the person who has the best sales numbers or makes the biggest sales often doesn't get the better sales management job, you can often look no further than their personality. Someone who is a good all-around sales performer and who gets along well with most peers in a non-threatening way is more likely to be trusted and get promoted into sales management. Such an individual is often more successful than your best-performing, solo sales star. (NOTE: Not promoting that star may require some special ego handling.)

Sometimes it truly is a personality contest. Upper-level sales executives want managers who will be well respected by their customers and peers, good-natured, and who can get the job done. That requires personality.

One of the sure signs that people can be promoted (although not a guarantee) is to hear from their peers and customers that they:

- Have a great personality,
- Are easy to do business with,
- Are fair-minded,
- Can get the job done under pressure,
- Keep a smile on their face, and
- Are well liked.

In other words, a senior manager won't have to worry about them.

TOP TIP: Give the Sales Team Your Next Raise:

No, this is not as crazy as it sounds. Plenty of people work on sales teams and don't make much money in the early part of their career—at least not as much compared to what their sales manager makes.

Want to make a lasting impression on them? Give them part of your next pay raise. Seriously! A small, base salary pay raise for a sales manager may not seem like much to the sales manager, but for a salesperson it is often quite a lot. However, it's more than just the money that matters. The gesture alone matters more.

TRUE STORY: Money for salary increases was tight so a sales manager gave up his raise so that he could distribute it across the sales team where it was needed most and would be more effective. The sales manager's boss and the HR manager were astounded. Was the manager crazy? Yep, crazy like a fox!

Giving the raise away to the sales team was more important to the sales manager than getting the raise personally. This was especially helpful to the salespeople in times where the big bosses were holding rank and file pay raises to a minimum. The sales team had been working its hardest to make sales happen and was gaining momentum. Getting minimal raises would have destroyed that momentum, and sent a message to the salespeople that they weren't all that important in the big scheme of things. Salespeople always like to feel important.

The gesture helped rally the sales team around the sales manager and the team had great successes, beating its quota for the year. The salespeople felt taken care of. The sales manager had calculated what he was giving up in the raise and compared it to the increase in sales that would be needed to make up the difference in his bonus and commission checks. Ultimately, it was worth the risk to give the raise away and recover it on the back-end, but there were no guarantees. Even if the raise hadn't been recovered by immediate sales successes, the loyalty and momentum that were created would carry on for more than a year and were worth more than the raise.

Thoughts about "giving" your raise away:

- Tell the sales team that you are doing it. This will put the emphasis back on doing a great job selling and less on trying to become a manager because of the perception that a sales manager makes more money (often they don't).

- Even if you don't think you can recoup what is being given away it doesn't really matter. The value of the gesture alone is worth even more to you over time.

- Giving the raise away is highly motivational to salespeople because the boss is giving something to them that is perceived as "near and dear," and belonging to the manager. This helps build tremendous loyalty.

- Doing this sends a message to the sales manager's bosses and other sales managers in the company that, sometimes, doing whatever you can for your team is more important than a short-term personal gain.

TOP TIP: Sizing Up a New (to You) Sales Team:

Don't rush to change salespeople until you know what's going on in the sales organization. Some current employees will be very good in helping you understand the hidden processes of other departments and where the skeletons are. They can be a huge assist during a transitional period. When inheriting a new sales team, try to not listen to gossip about the team members. Let the numbers speak for themselves initially unless you immediately see that there are personnel problems or, poorly defined or out-of-balance territories.

Be cautious in the early going. Those who are most eager to meet you early in your tenure and spill their guts are usually the ones with an axe to grind, the most to lose, or the weakest links looking for protection. The consummate sales pros will give you feedback about what they need to sell better and they will keep their heads down, keep selling and keep hitting their numbers.

During this time you will need to continue to motivate the entire team. Take the best performers and acknowledge their efforts. Make sure that the top salespeople are genuine performers and have not been merely "lucky" with territory selection or are "one-hit" wonders on closing big deals because the rest of the sales team will know it. Using such salespeople as an example of smart, motivated selling will not ring true.

TOP TIP: Stopping the "New Boss" Negotiations:

Some salespeople will often use the fact that you are new to the team to trigger a renegotiation of their compensation package. The timing is usually inopportune and the motivation selfish. Salespeople most likely to do this are the ones with the most at-risk financially. It may be the most marginal on the team or a top salesperson who has reached his peak, is feeling a sense of entitlement or insecurity, or who sees some of his top business slipping away and wants to continue making the same kind of money as in the past—at the company's expense.

Hear these people out, but rarely should you make immediate changes to their compensation package. Be clear that you are not changing any salaries immediately and that the best way to make more money as a salesperson is always to sell more. That strategy has never failed.

So what is the motivational point here? As it turns out, laying the law down early and letting people know that the new sales management won't be letting things get out of hand is a motivator. It provides a set of rules and expectations to work with and sends the highly motivational message that the success of the salespeople will be based on their own efforts (i.e., hitting their numbers).

Take time to evaluate the compensation plans carefully to see that everyone has an opportunity to earn their fair share. If you don't think that the plans are fair, work to change them. This can mean increasing or decreasing them.

TOP TIP: No Public Condescension:

Never, ever, berate salespeople in public. Save corrective discussions for a one-on-one feedback meeting. It
could be a few minutes later—or a week later. If a major
faux pas is made in a customer meeting, simply be polite
and firmly state the company's position if it's different
from what the salesperson says it is. Don't make it appear
as a public correction. You can usually massage this by
saying: "Maybe another way to look at this is to…"

Salespeople are usually very sensitive about being
corrected in public. Wouldn't you be? This is not at all
surprising since their egos are so heavily invested in their
work. They will view any public correction as a public
humiliation and maybe as an unofficial demotion. It's the
silent momentum killer, because if it continues to happen, it will lead to demoralization and increased attrition.
You might be thinking, "Hey, that's great, I was trying to
get rid of that person anyway." Well, in the long run, it
will reflect poorly on you. Why? Salespeople will trash
you publicly (since it was apparently OK for you to do
the same in front of the customer).

EXCEPTION: One of the few exceptions to this
rule is the classic "Good Cop, Bad Cop" routine. This
is usually displayed when a car salesperson gets publicly yelled at by the sales manager for coming in too
low on a car deal for a customer. This is usually an act,
worthy of an award from the Academy. In other
words, if it's all rehearsed, does that make it public
condescension? Probably not.

TOP TIP: Taking "Bullets" for the Team:

Want to earn instant respect from a sales team? Go with them on the "bad" sales calls as well as the "good" ones. Don't just be there for the big marquee deals. Going on "bad" calls will give you a deeper perspective on how the product is being sold, what the objections are, what tools you'll need to put in the hands of the sales organization, and how to fix serious problems. Everyone wins.

TOP TIP: The "First Hit" Theory:

Every once in a while there will be that salesperson who think that dinner with a significant other should be expensed as a treat because they are so good at their job and so overworked. Or they take other liberties that they shouldn't. You probably know the type. (It's OK, however, if you've approved it in advance.) There is a strategy you can use to keep that from happening a second time. It's called the "First Hit" theory.

TRUE STORY: An aspiring young sales manager once played YMCA football in grade school. He hated having to hit the opposing players over and over again. After all, he might hurt himself! Instead, he would always try to level the opposing player with the hardest hit he could on the first play (usually during the kick-off). He magically controlled the field after that "first hit."

The competitor really didn't want to keep getting hit over and over at that intensity. Truth be told, the aspiring young manager probably couldn't have hit the competitor that hard the second time anyway, but sometimes image (and perceived possible pain) is everything.

You can use the "first hit" theory with the sales team on an individual basis. Violence isn't being suggested here! While you certainly don't have to rough up anyone on the sales team verbally, you do want to let them know who the boss is.

PRACTICAL EXAMPLE: When a new salesperson, or one who is new to you, turns in their expenses, examine them very carefully the first few times. Put a "first-hit" on anything that looks odd and call them on the carpet for it (privately and politely). This lets them know you are watching closely. Chances are they will always think you are watching, and from then on will manage expenses more carefully. Check in with reinforcement "hits" whenever necessary.

TOP TIP: The "Need to Know" Rule:

Salespeople and customers receive reams of information every day. It is constant and can be overwhelming. Make it a practice to give your sales team and your customer base key information on a "need to know" basis. That is, give them *just* what they need to know to sell or buy the product/service. No more, less. That's harder than it might sound.

It really involves knowing the salespeople and what customers really need to know to buy the product or service. The mistaken tendency is to overwhelm people with information every step of the way. If you overwhelm salespeople with information, they, in turn, will probably overwhelm the customers, and that could slow the sales process. This is not to say that you should keep the product a mystery in the minds of the people who buy and sell it.

Countless sales presentations, proposals, and brochures, while great looking, are filled with either too much information, or not enough. The trick is in balancing the amount of information. It should be your call as to what is enough. Use that decision-making power carefully. Sometimes a selling concept is simple, but salespeople want to add a degree of difficulty to make it seem as though they're working hard to earn the customer's business. And they end up confusing everyone.

Sometimes too much information gives customers an opportunity to question things that may not be material to closing the deal—and that wastes time. Because you've put that information out there, you have potentially created additional questions in someone's mind that slows the process. That's a sales liability that no one can afford to have. This is not to suggest that you practice not disclosing material facts or misrepresenting critical information. On the contrary, doling out correct information carefully will speed up the sale. The two most important pieces of information a salesperson can have in the arsenal are the overall brochure and fact sheets specific to the product that the customer is considering. These are followed by practical examples of how the products are used and testimonials that the products do indeed work.

TOP TIP: Stealth Planning:

When you get a new sales management assignment, whether it's your first or your twenty-first, do yourself a favor: Go underground. Don't take on day-to-day responsibilities or get caught up in other details until you have a big picture of what's been transpiring at the company.

Do these things initially:

- Find out how things work internally.

- Determine what the sales process is.

- Figure out how your efforts will need to be fine-tuned. Take in all the data you can.

- Go out and see how your product is being sold. Ask people who are buying it what they think of the people who are selling it.

- Get copies of sales presentations and customer proposals from multiple salespeople around the country (or world).

- Lay it all out in front of you to start assembling a bigger picture of what's really happening out there.

Once you have the bigger picture, you can get a sense of how you can make the changes necessary to turn things around or at least improve them that much faster.

TOP TIP: Earn Respect by Resolving Issues Immediately:

The fastest way to cripple a sales team is to expect them to do their job when you aren't doing yours. Some sales managers just don't care about responding to their sales team. For some reason, they think they are invisible to the selling process and just there to occupy a position and get paid. Presumably it's because they've made it to the top and don't have to deal with any of the details any longer.

Sometimes, certain decisions have to go "up the flagpole" to get resolved. It's understandable when that happens and another manager can't respond quickly. That's not the point here. This is really about understanding that those below a sales manager will need support and, when they ask for help, they should get it in a timely manner.

To rule out any ambiguity here, make some rules for yourself on how to resolve issues:

- Set a time limit for responding.

- Keep whomever you owe an answer to in the loop while the answer is being determined. You'll know how much attention to devote, depending on the severity of the problem.

- Always think about how you would like to be taken care of if you had a problem.

- Try to filter out any predisposition that you might have to thinking that a quick response isn't important to you. Sometimes it's not the answer that counts as much as the response being made in a timely manner.

TOP TIP: Fear vs. Support-Based Management Styles:

There are two basic sales management styles: fear-based and support-based. No salesperson wants to be fearful of a sales manager. (No one wants to be fearful of any manager, period!) Salespeople want to be loved and helped. They want to feel that they have an open door to their manager when necessary. Not all sales managers (even the supposedly successful ones) see it this way. You can probably guess which style most people prefer.

Fear is not a motivator. Let's repeat that: FEAR IS NOT A MOTIVATOR. Think about this. Sales managers who have to engender fear to get something done usually haven't done a very good job of picking and training their teams well. The last resort is for them to manage salespeople as though they are slave labor.

When you think about how to manage salespeople, consider this question: *How would you like to be managed?* Probably not in a way that makes you live in constant fear of your job and your financial well-being. So why would *you* manage that way?

Generally, sales managers who employ the "fear" mode of selling are highly insecure people in their own right. They feel that they are adding value to the sales management process only by threatening their "lazy" salespeople with dire consequences if they don't make their numbers. How pathetic! Come on, now: Does anyone really think that professional salespeople don't know they need to make their numbers to keep their jobs?

Support is what salespeople need. They are *your* internal customers, so you have to ask yourself: *"Would I treat a customer like this?"* They need you to be there for them, helping them make the number that they (and you) signed up for with the company. They shouldn't expect you to do their job for them, but they should expect you to help pave the way for them to be successful.

You can do this by helping them:

- Get over internal hurdles,

- Gain access to tools they need to do their job, and

- Have a great product or service to sell.

Do the above with the thought in mind that you are all on the same team and need to help each other to win. If you do, you will win big.

There Are No Keys to the Executive Washroom:

Some salespeople think it's a good career-enhancing move to be included in high-level company meetings. They think it's a badge of honor to have a key to the executive washroom (if they still have such places), or an opportunity to get into the inner circle. It's the "grass is greener" perception when it comes to being in management.

Real salespeople hate wasting time in internal meetings. Although it is tempting to think that you could be making a wad of money sitting in meetings all day—if only that were true. The truth is: It's boring! Great salespeople don't make good bureaucrats, and vice versa.

How do you destroy the myth that executive-level meetings are some sort of a hip place to hang out?

Consider these ideas:

- Preface your comments with: "I would have much rather been out selling than sitting in that meeting." That will set the tone of how unexciting these meetings typically are to attend.

- Whatever affects the sales team (that you can openly discuss) should be shared with them, by you, shortly after these management meetings occur.

- Summarize the details for the sales team and down-play (or exclude) any controversial materials before you deliver the goods. This is a good communication skill to have so that everything that should be out in the open actually is.

You would be amazed at the number of points that good communication scores with a sales team, and how it cuts down on undue curiosity.

Dealing with Sales Bullies:

Bullying is becoming a more common problem in business today. It's typically happening where certain levels of success have been achieved and odd behavior has been previously tolerated. In reality, bullies can be anyone—those who have others reporting to them or who rely on others. It's usually a well-kept secret from the company's skeleton closet. With the press putting more attention on the upper management of companies these days, former and current employees are more than willing to talk. And more should.

The scenario is typically this: A manager in a position of power feels it is a given right to treat people brutally and unfairly in the name of getting the job done. This type of behavior is usually an indication that the person in power has some personality or organizational issues.

We all have our quirks but pushing people over the edge isn't one that should be tolerated.

CLASSIC EXAMPLE: A bully might wait until the last minute to delegate a particular project and then go totally berserk when it can't be completed in the abbreviated timeframe. Bullies hound and push people rather than jumping in and helping. They have no concept of time or effort, or maybe they forgot all the hard work that they once did and just assume that everyone can accomplish things at a superhuman level for unending periods. Typically that's not the case.

It's perfectly acceptable to request that things be done quickly and efficiently but if a manager sets-up people who are actually doing the work for potential failure by being unrealistic, then no one wins.

Bullying by anyone in a company shouldn't be tolerated. In elementary school, bullying usually starts with taunting followed by a physical attack. In business it's usually a verbal and psychological attack. No matter how high up in the company the bully sits, such behavior shouldn't be tolerated. This is especially true in a sales organization.

Salespeople and sales managers can be especially prone to bullying because of their ego drive and the stress of their jobs. Bullies are relentless when others don't deliver to the bully's timeframe, as unacceptable as that timeframe might be.

The warning sign that a bully is present is a disinclination of others to do projects for them. Staffers cringe when a bully asks them to do something, anything. Why? Because they rarely get praise when completing a project. They are not willing to re-up for another project because it was a painful and unfulfilling experience. The staffer taking on the project feels that the bully was irrational or unreasonable, and is demoralized by having to work on the bully's projects.

If you sense that bullying is occurring in your area of responsibility, take steps to stop it.

Try these steps:

- Have a conversation with the bully and say that you are experiencing difficulty in finding anyone who is excited about working on this person's projects. Explain that the bully is being unreasonable and too demanding. Ask them to work on that behavior.

- If it continues: Ask the bully to submit job requests with clearly delineated requirements and completion dates for your review. You will want to review them before jobs are assigned to a staffer to see if the timeframe is reasonable and if the proper tone for managing the project is set. Over time, you can manage the bully back into being a more compatible member of the team.

- If none of the above works, start documenting the issues and prepare for a reassignment or termination.

Personal Expense Agendas:

Some salespeople seem to have a personal agenda going. Not only will they try to maximize their sales revenue, they will often try to maximize their personal perks. If it saves the company money, that's a good thing, but sometimes it's done at the company's expense. That could include anything from scheduling vacations that happen to coincide with the end of sales meetings (acceptable) to charging food on their lunch tabs that they will be cooking for dinner at home that night (not acceptable). Always try to set the tone that if it helps save money, then you are for it. Within that limit is the understanding that it's not appropriate to schedule useless trips to some location for one "iffy" meeting in order to spend a week on a family re-union vacation nearby, partly on company money. That won't cut it. Being smart about the company's money and planning ahead are values that you might want to reward.

When you see abuses of trust, you should quickly and quietly rein in the problem person. Make it clear, in no uncertain terms, that "once" is the only time that it will happen and that you will be keeping an eye on future activities. Saving money for the company is one thing, making money off your expense account is entirely another.

Frequent Flyer Miles and Hotel Points:

Miles and points should accrue to the salespeople and sales managers that generated them, unless the company has negotiated ticket pricing to not include miles. Very few companies consider miles "theirs" these days. With travel becoming more difficult and delayed, it's the sales team members that are putting themselves on the line. They deserve the perks.

Teach Product Usage:

There is nothing like the actual use of a product to help understand it better and discover unique applications for it. Teaching usage is a way of helping the salesperson and customer find creative uses for the products or services the company sells. You can only sell people something they truly need. Sometimes they just need to know why they need it.

Additional thoughts:

- If you put the sales team in the shoes of the customer who is using your product, you gain a totally different level of understanding.

- Encourage salespeople (as well as yourself) to use the company's products, if appropriate. They will get a whole new appreciation for what the final customer's experience is like.

- Salespeople should spend time with new customers counseling them on unique and creative ways to use the product or service.

- If a customer has found a unique way to use the product, then share that at a sales meeting. Be careful about violating any confidentiality agreements regarding the customer's use of the product.

Typecasting Salespeople:

Sales managers will sometimes miss a nuance that can lead to sales success: Put your salespeople in sales territories that best match their personalities and skill sets.

You wouldn't ask an accountant to do brain surgery,

so why would you put a brash personality in a hand-holding, Kumbayaa-singing territory if it would set him up to fail and create problems with your customers?

TRUE STORY: Company A filled its new San Francisco sales office with salespeople fresh from New York. These were exceptional salespeople in their home market. It seemed that you couldn't get good NY bagels in San Francisco at the time and the transplanted New Yorkers let their customers know it! Company A's sales team was perceived as being abrasive to customers. It was a total culture clash and hurt the company's reputation.

The customers who did business with Company A referred to the NY-based sales team as "those jerks from New York!" Other customers refused to do business with them. (No offense to all of those New Yorkers who aren't jerks!) This didn't necessarily keep all the customers from buying from Company A but they probably weren't getting all the revenue they could out of those customers.

The poor planning on the part of Company A opened a door for Company B's sales team to get customers to split their buying and just try them. The strategy worked. Once the customer did try the product, Company B's sales team worked even harder to grow their market share. That strategy also worked. Company A's sales management never quite figured it out and continued to suffer.

Don't Just Tell Them – Show Them:

Sales knowledge is cumulative. Share your successful

selling style with the sales team out in the field. Do some presentations with them. Give them a chance to see you in action.

The salespeople will be eager to learn from you and then apply their own spin to suit their selling style. Just giving them a script of what to say or some sales materials is no substitute for hearing the real deal from the boss in a live scenario.

After you have shown them how and trained them, have them do the pitch in front of a few customers and give them positive, constructive feedback on how it worked for you and them. Always start with a compliment on something they did right and ask how they felt they did.

Next, ask for permission to give them coaching ideas to better their delivery. It may be anything from pointing out small inaccuracies in their facts or major derailments in the way the product was presented. Just keep in mind that any error can be fixed and that generally no mistake is ever fatal.

When to Help, When to Yell:

Calling the salespeople just to yell about something won't make them very responsive to taking your calls most of the time. If you know that you might need to ding them on something in the near future then do a positive check-in call in advance. Do something good for them when you call them, so they can be in a position to return the favor later by listening to your constructive criticism. This will help them understand that you aren't just constantly calling to yell at them.

Avoiding Lowest Common Denominator Management:

Don't allow the most difficult salesperson you manage to lower the bar for acceptable sales behavior in the company, unless there is an extenuating circumstance. As soon as you start accepting the sales pace of your weakest salesperson, then the sales team is in trouble. The top performers can be scared away when standards aren't held high. They will feel the entire sales organization is becoming mediocre and that they are underutilized and under appreciated. They may ultimately leave.

Lowering your performance standards is equivalent to a teacher's allowing the poorest student to slow everyone else down in the classroom. Remember what *that* was like? Take an opposite approach. Have the expectation that everyone will want to emulate the top salesperson and that everyone will be a stellar performer unless they prove otherwise. Giving them the benefit of the doubt from the beginning, and telling them so, helps raise the bar to which the entire team will measure up. Use the top salesperson as your yardstick and a good example for others to follow. The rest will get with the program or find the exit door.

Salespeople who are underperforming will need to be put on a remedial program. This could include monitoring them more closely, documenting all their prep work, call levels, closure on their projected accounts, creation of new business, etc. Not only is this necessary for providing a measuring stick, it will be important documentation if you have to let them go.

Late Bloomers:

Sometimes salespeople or sales managers want to give/get more out of a career but just aren't capable of it yet. This doesn't mean that they aren't valuable contributors to the company in some way. They might be late bloomers. Even though they aren't growing at the same pace as their peers they still feel compelled to ask for the same increases in responsibility and pay as the overachievers. That's a pretty human response and has to be dealt with carefully.

Late bloomers are people who need to be given a more clearly defined career path and to be handheld to some degree down that path. If they stay focused on achieving a set of short-term goals and know the rewards for those goals, they can be highly motivated.

The problem is that it might just take them a bit longer to get to the same level as others. That doesn't make them bad salespeople or sales managers. It's almost like being held back a grade in elementary school. It doesn't always feel good so it has to be handled carefully and with dignity. If you make their career track clear to them (if possible) and tell them that it's not about how they compare to their peers as much as how they relate to your expectations you can help keep their focus off being competitive with others, and focusing on the company's needs.

Full Customer Contact:

If a customer wants to elevate a problem with sales management directly, then take it on and get it fixed. Try to work out the problem quickly and have the salesperson do the majority of the follow-up. Make sure the salesperson actually does the follow-up and check in with the customer to make sure it happens. (After you've spoken to your salesperson, of course.) Don't do anything that will undermine the credibility of the salespeople other than taking full responsibility if "the company" made a mistake.

Ideas on handling customer problems:

- When something gets screwed up, have a path so it can be elevated to the highest level (usually you). That often takes the heat off the salesperson who is freed up to work on the solution.

- Respond to the problem fairly, quickly, and thoughtfully.

- Try to put yourself in the shoes of the customer. This will do more to turn a customer around in the long term than anything else you could do.

- Make sure, though, that the problem is resolved through your salespeople (via a joint conference call or other means) so that they continue to own the relationship with the customer.

Balancing Out-of-Control Sales Types:

Sometimes salespeople will just be too committed to their job. It's not only possible, but detrimental. They will work for what seems like 24 hours a day. They are living in their offices, hotels, or in their cars. You might think that's great, but it's usually a short-term situation that can be followed by severe burn-out.

There are usually deeper circumstances at play. Maybe the salesperson doesn't have much of a life outside of work, or is using work as an excuse to avoid a bad marriage or relationship, or any kind of a social life. Be aware of these things because they can throw some of the most talented salespeople out of balance. If a job becomes a personal life, then watch out. You might think you want to hire a whole team of these people, but they often burn out too fast, become a smudge mark on the road to success, and create staffing problems for you.

Then there is the flip-side of the situation: Just because the salespeople are at work doesn't mean that they are always working. Don't assume that because they appear to be working all the time that this "dedication" is a good thing. They may be hiding out and just using their office to do their personal work. Find out.

No matter what the situation, salespeople will burn out faster than anyone else if you don't jump in and manage them to a more even-keeled lifestyle.

TRUE STORY: A high-level sales operations manager was extremely valuable to the company but was approaching burn-out and starting to be disruptive. The Sales VP insisted she take time off and offered to pay for a plane ticket to Hawaii for a week to re-calibrate. The cost of replacing this manager would have been huge. The manager probably needed the excuse that the Sales VP was making her take the time off in order to go and enjoy herself. The Sales VP also told her to leave her laptop at home. When she got back from holiday the Sales VP worked to reset the ground rules, so she could continue to be a valued part of the sales team and put some much needed balance into her life.

Attending Trade Shows:

Attending trade shows can be an advantageous way to grow the business or a huge waste of time and resources.

Here are tips to help you manage your sales team's effectiveness at these events:

- Have the salespeople attending the trade show book appointments in advance. Start that process at least four to six weeks before hand. They (and you) should be busy at breakfast, lunch and dinner, and in-between. There have been countless trade shows where unprepared salespeople wander the exhibit aisles aimlessly in search of a customer, any customer, to talk to. They didn't plan ahead, and their competition booked meetings with the customers before they did.

- Have the salespeople save some time later during the trade show to prospect for new customers—or assign one of your more junior salespeople to scour the tradeshow floor in search of new customers for your sales team and distribute these leads to the senior salespeople each night.

- Have meeting rooms available (with sign-up schedules) so that salespeople can enjoy a quiet place to meet. *Quiet* is the operative word here. Companies spend hundreds of thousands of dollars on trade show booths and have well-appointed meeting rooms on top of the booth. The meeting rooms are typically roofless so every noise (and at trade shows there can be plenty) echoes right in. Murphy's Law usually is in play here: The quieter the meeting space needs to be, the louder the exhibitor's booth adjacent to yours will be.

- Hold a pre-show sales meeting the day before the show starts.

Consider the following:

- Recap current selling information,

- Review show promotions, and any competitive information,

- Train the salespeople on how to interact with customers in a trade show environment,

- Establish a "booth duty" schedule. Put your "party-hearty" types in the first slot so they will think twice about staying out until 3 a.m., boozing it up on the company expense account. Make sure you are there on a random basis to see that everyone is present. Make it painful when people don't show up. Encourage salespeople to trade their booth duty times if schedule conflicts arise.

- If you are having a customer appreciation party at the trade show, lay out rules for participating with the sales team in advance.

  - Figure out which key customers will need to be schmoozed by the top execs. Give the execs some background information on them.

  - Establish a one-drink rule for the sales staff, (possibly after the customers have gone).

- Remind them that they are representatives of the company, and at trade shows that means twenty-four hours a day.

- If the industry event you are attending is primarily seminar-based, then a different strategy may apply. It's best to network during coffee breaks while people are transitioning to different speaker sessions, or before/during cocktail parties.

TRUE STORY: A resourceful sales manager required all salespeople working a trade show to leave her a two-minute voice mail at the end of each day to recap their meetings. The message would recap successes and failures for the day and any exciting calls planned for the next day. This kept a laser-like focus on why the salespeople were there. It is impossible for a salesperson to hide from this level of accountability. As a sales manager, "high-fiving" the salespeople for a job well done each day shows that you are listening to their phone messages and that you appreciate their efforts.

Ego Management:

Insecure people have fragile yet resilient egos, which is why they usually make great salespeople. It's better to be calmly confident in your abilities, not obnoxious.

Salespeople tend to absorb the personality of their bosses (a subtle, but accepted, form of brown-nosing!). They figure that it'll make their bosses like them better. And that may actually be true in some cases.

Let's face it. Salespeople who have to constantly tell

you how great *they* are tend to be self-absorbed. They are tiresome. And chances are, they will be selling themselves better than your products or services.

Egos are a fact of life. Don't purposely try to deflate a salesperson's ego. Work with it. Manage it. In some respects people with big egos are the easiest to deal with because their ego-massaging needs are so obvious, which is fine as long as you can manage them.

Salespeople with big egos like to be acknowledged for their smart choices, which is why they are usually more into conspicuous consumption than salespeople with more manageable egos. At least you will know what type of gift to get them during the holidays!

Don't consider complimenting salespeople on their choices just to manipulate them. Most salespeople like to be noticed in some way. It's usually just the degree to which they get noticed that matters. When the compliment seems hollow and non-genuine that both parties would be better off if nothing had been said (i.e., more brown-nosing).

Efficient Selling:

Anything can affect the performance of a sales organization. Like a sailboat, even the slightest adjustment in the trim of the sails can affect boat speed. But trimming here doesn't meaning cutting. It just means monitoring and adjusting. Sometimes you let the sails out, sometimes you pull them in, and sometimes you take them down completely!

In a yacht race, every incremental increase in efficiency shortens your time to the finish line. It all adds up, especially in a long race where a few smart adjustments can be multiplied by hundreds or thousands of miles to win a race.

Everything you can do to fine-tune your sales "sails" to make the sales organization run more smoothly will get you to your goals that much faster. As a sales manager it's up to you to keep a constant eye out for possible improvements that can result in sales speed.

Some examples:

- Shortening the length of call reports or the time required to file them,

- Requiring less expense-report paperwork every month,

- Cutting down the number of internal meetings or conference calls,

- Actively minimizing bureaucratic BS,

- Monitoring and anticipating inventory shortages,

- Managing product changes and shortages,

- Reviewing shipping delays,

- Temporarily overstaffing to eliminate end-of-quarter bottlenecks within the legal department, and

- Lifting travel and entertainment expense limits.

Whatever you elect to do will need to be monitored (accountability!) so that you know you are meeting your goals.

Managing an Independent Rep Firm:

Independent rep firms can often lower your cost of sales if managed well. It's worth taking time to compare the "internal sales vs. rep firm" models before deciding which way to go.

Some things to consider when using an independent rep firm:

- Typically your products or services are not the only ones being sold by a rep firm and you will need to work to get face time for your products.

- Rep firms are often inadvertently removed from a significant flow of information inside companies they represent. That can hinder their ability to move quickly. This happens despite the best attempts by both parties to keep it from happening.

- Rep firms get fired for poor performance more often than inside sales teams. The reason is usually based on them not managing expectations well. Make it clear that you know what you are getting. Remember that you are being sold by the rep firm on why you need to pick them, so get any promises in writing and be sure that you deliver on yours.

- Some sales managers use a rep firm to create a convenient buffer in order to duck any personal responsibility for making sales numbers. Don't be that type of sales manager. You are responsible for hitting the numbers regardless of who is selling for you.

- Rep firms can be valuable up to the point where you will keep more overall dollars by doing the sales function yourself. Rep firms can help a company get to a certain level of sales but at some point they can make themselves unnecessary.

- Rep firms can provide tremendous up-front "selling value" to a company through their contact base.

- In some industries the companies that resell your product to the ultimate consumer will only do business with you if you use a rep firm. Typically these companies sell many products and cannot afford to staff buyers to deal with all the individual companies unless they represent a certain dollar volume to the reselling firm.

- Rep firms never assume full responsibility for selling, nor should they. They may lean on you for additional advertising and promotional materials over and above whatever has been contractually agreed to.

- If you use a rep firm, analyze the entire selling process and make sure that you understand who will be responsible for what.

There's a longer list of industry-specific things than we have time to cover here. But it pays to get everything very clearly defined, or the company may just get left holding the bag on certain responsibilities that you hadn't accounted for.

Transitioning Salespeople into Sales Management:

As mentioned earlier in this book, the classic problem that plagues most great salespeople is the initial transition into being sales managers. They can't keep their feet in both places for too long. Being the aircraft carrier captain is far different from being a solo fighter pilot. It requires changing a mindset while still being mindful of what it takes to close the sale. Remind them that, one never really stops selling.

For a new sales manager, giving the sales team credit for the successes and being humble about their contribution will be the hardest part. Mentor them on this. For them it will mean evolving from a tactical role into a more strategic and guiding role. That also means they will have to push more responsibility farther down among their direct reports. Otherwise, they will be dealing with small fires all day and never get their real job done.

12. QUOTAS AND COMMISSION PLANS

Quotas and commission plans will vary from market to market and company to company. This section isn't intended to be the end-all for creating commission plans. What is being stressed here is realism and simplicity. Here are some ideas on how to create the right plans:

MEGA TIP: Set Realistic Sales Goals:

This is one of the litmus tests of motivational sales management. Is what you are asking your salespeople to do realistic? Would you be able to reach these goals if you were a salesperson? This is not to advocate lightening up on goals or not having "stretch" numbers that a sales team has to work hard to reach. But it's quickly de-motivating if the goals you have agreed to become impossible to achieve, or better yet—to exceed.

IT HAPPENS: One trap to avoid is the "back of the napkin" quota-setting model imposed by some less-than-sales-savvy senior executives. They will take whatever number of salespeople you have and multiply that by how much they think an average salesperson should be able to sell. And that will be your budget—if you agree to it! When done at the 40,000-foot level, this all seems so simple.

Budgets assigned to territories should be realistic and appropriate, which means not just the *average*.

MEGA TIP: Be Analytical - Not *Anal*-ytical When Setting Budgets:

Many good managers (from the top down) can get caught up in analyzing the numbers of their job without looking around at what is actually happening in their marketplace. It's easy to do simple math and figure out average sales per salesperson and then look at those above the average as being good performers and those below as bad performers.

There's also the classic mistake of comparing all salespeople to the top salesperson or to some guesstimate as to the ideal quota that a salesperson should hit. This is all wrong. Sales managers all the way up to CEOs do this. If it were that easy to set budgets companies wouldn't need CEOs, Sales Executives, Sales Managers or top salespeople: We would just have a spreadsheet program manage by the averages!

When analyzing a sales team, take into consideration: The experience of the salespeople, the accounts they handle, the geography they work in, the products the company makes, the availability of these products, the competitive landscape, the territory history, local competitors' strengths and weaknesses, and the internal roadblocks that are put in the way of the sales goals. And despite all of that, there are still numbers to be made!

A process for determining reasonable budgets:

- Before any sales goals are agreed to, it's very important to review the available (read: sellable) inventory or future product availability.

- Project the availability of products over time and set conservative sell-through estimates to project reasonable revenue.

- Determine appropriate budgets for the sales team. The calculations may show that there are too many or too few salespeople. Or to look at it another way, too much or too little product for your team to sell.

TRUE STORY #1: A CEO was proud of her analytical skills. The sales team was doing very well against their numbers. The CEO and the sales manager wanted to increase sales. To increase sales by "X" amount the CEO felt that the sales manager simply needed to take the average sales per salesperson and divide that into the new sales goal. That would tell them how many additional salespeople they needed to hire.

It was as simple as that, right? *Wrong!*

The CEO insisted she knew the path to analytical nirvana so the sales manager hired additional salespeople. The new salespeople had to ramp up, and the entire sales team needed more inventory and products to sell to hit the new numbers. While funding the hiring of additional salespeople was a nice gesture (and no doubt perceived as the *easy* way to increase sales if everything else was in place), the CEO ultimately didn't create additional products or inventory needed to deliver those increased sales numbers. You probably already know how this story ended. The strategy failed.

TRUE STORY #2: The same analytical CEO then decided the following quarter that since average sales were heading down (based to some degree on having over-hired salespeople the previous quarter—go figure) the company would need to cut back on salespeople and then average sales would go up.

Most of the salespeople were maxed out already and adding additional accounts or territory to their work load would have been counter-productive. The CEO learned these lessons the hard way. Despite multiple warnings from all levels in the sales organization the strategy failed—again.

TOP TIP: Setting an Overall Sales Budget:

Setting up a sales budget can make or break your entire year, and possibly your career. In some cases there is a "cascade" effect to setting inaccurate sales budgets that can create potential company-wide problems.

Let's assume the Board tells the CEO that a certain sales number should be achieved. Let's index that budget number at 100%. The CEO wants to make that number, and possibly over deliver on it so she tells the Sales VP that the number is actually 105%. Chances are that the Sales VP wants to over deliver slightly so he tells the sales team the number is 110%. This continues to cascade down through the sales ranks until the entire sales organization has an overly bloated sales number to hit. Everyone wants to cushion their number at the expense of the people below them. This approach seems both selfish *and* smart. There's no telling which it really is.

The flip side of this scenario is that everyone knows what *the one single* number is from the top down and works towards achieving it. There is no covering at every level so the actual resources needed to make *the* number are readily identifiable and everyone is more focused on achieving the desired results.

Whichever the approach is, try to understand what the opportunities and pitfalls will be for the sales organization. If the company culture is to inflate the number then don't allow it to be over inflated at every level and skew all the resources necessary to make the number. If the company culture is to go with one number then make sure everyone is fully aware that there is no safety net.

Once you have *the* number start to proportionate it across the territories in a mutual effort with the senior sales staff. Make sure everyone knows what they are buying into and that the numbers are real. At any point in the budget delegation process you will need to know if your managers are "bumping up" the numbers to protect their commissions. Make adjustments accordingly. Get buy-in from everyone on the final plan.

TOP TIP: Understanding the Sales Ramp:

New salespeople (or existing salespeople who are new to a territory) often wonder how long they will have to be successful. It's a common question. Is there any science to it? A little, maybe.

TRUE STORY: The sales manager at a company did an analysis of all the salespeople the company ever had and how long it took them to hit their budget numbers. It wasn't overly scientific but the results kept replicating each other time and time again in subsequent companies for which the sales manager worked. So at least there was a pattern.

At a new company the same sales manager tracked the salespeople's budget progress quarter-to-quarter until they made their quota (or were terminated). For what it's worth, the sales manager found that the time of year in which the salespeople started selling didn't have much of an effect on the results of their "sales ramp."

THE RESULTS: On average a salesperson consistently attained:

- 30% of the average quarterly dollar quota for their territory in Q1;
- 70% in Q2;

- 90% in Q3; and

- 110% in Q4.

For the first year, the average was 80% of the average quarterly dollar quota for the sales person's territory. (And interestingly, most salespeople had started at the beginning of the fiscal year.)

When using the above sales ramp method, performance averages should be disclosed to the new salespeople as part of their plan. This gives them something to aim for, and exceed. Many salespeople will take it upon themselves to beat their Q1 and Q2 quotas by a wide margin. That's the attitude you want to see.

Progress should be monitored monthly for all salespeople, especially in the early part of their careers at the company. Use the six-month point as a "formal check-in" to see how new salespeople are doing. If they are close to the quota targets outlined above then keep them moving forward. Plan the revenue budgets accordingly. If they are significantly less than on schedule, it's time to take remedial action. If they are a lot higher, it's time to give them more responsibility.

TOP TIP: Setting a Salesperson's Budget:

The success or failure of a salesperson is often a function of how realistic and achievable the sales territory and budget are.

If there is any doubt about how achievable a budget can be, take the highroad. Set a short-term budget, and look at previous territorial successes to see if there are any comparables to work from. Take all the variables into consideration and do your best to model a reasonable plan. Make adjustments along the way. Give the salesperson who will be handling the territory high praise as a true "fighter pilot" (which is essentially what they are).

It's very important to involve salespeople in the planning process. Presumably, the best and brightest salespeople are chosen for projects like these. Have them help determine the size of the opportunity and the planning and time needed to make it happen.

Another Alternative to Sales Budgets for New Salespeople:

An innovative way to view the budgeting process for new salespeople is to try the "zero-plus-quota" six-month method. This works especially well when the selling ramp is bit longer for products and services. The concept is simple: All you do is give the salesperson zero budget in Q1 and a reasonable budget in Q2. That gives plenty of ramp room (maybe too much?) to work with. As with all good recipes, adjust the mix to whatever works best for you.

In Q3 and Q4 and beyond, the salespeople would have regular or slightly reduced quotas. At minimum, do a check-in in the middle and at the end of each quarter to see if they are on track.

Budgeting for BS:

Beware of salespeople and sales managers who will give you an over-inflated budget just to get resources for their own pet projects—or to extend their employment just a little longer. This is different than building a cushion into their budgets to protect commissions. Hold them to the budget numbers that they supply (assuming you agree with them) unless something happens that is completely out of their control. This is why budget estimates need to be realistic.

The only way to get to the truth from a sales projection is to ask a lot of hard questions. If projections seem too rosy to you, there is probably a reason why. Salespeople and sales managers at all levels seem to naturally overestimate their potential. They want good things to happen and that's understandable. You can attribute this to ego, bravado, unending optimism or whatever. At the end of the day there are only so many resources to go around and if you allow people to take advantage, the company loses.

Track changes to budgets whenever you do your budget reviews (weekly, monthly, or quarterly?) Take note of those salespeople and sales managers who vary the most from their initial projections and respond accordingly.

TOP TIP: Setting Up Commission Plans:

TRUE STORY: In one sales organization the sales team had no weekly goals, no quota and no incentive-based commission plan. And this team was supposed to be excited every day they came to work—to do what?

Things to consider with commission plans:

- Commission plans and sales quotas should be: simple and easily calculable, crystal clear, written down, and signed off on by the salesperson and sales manager. This way, there is no question at the end of the quota period just what the expectations were.

- You can add additional bonus plans or incentives depending on short-term corporate goals. These include bonuses for: total units sold, number of new customers created, and incremental sales to existing customers, hitting quota for each month or quarter, market share growth, etc. But these additional incentives should be just as clear and concise as the main commission plan. They should complement each other and not compete.

Sample Commission Plans:

There are multiple approaches to commission plans. If your company already has an approved commission plan and it's not negotiable, just do what you can to make it easy to understand.

Here are some basic plans that have been effective. (There are many others.):

PLAN A: Salespeople get a flat commission on everything they sell, from the first dollar sold, until they hit their quota. On anything over quota, they get higher and higher commission rates depending on what incremental levels they reach.

PLAN B: Salespeople get paid commission back to the first dollar sold, but only after they attain a certain percentage of their overall quota (30-50%).

PLAN C: Variable commission rates depending on level of quota achieved.

- 0-50% of quota—no commission.

- 50-75% of quota—W%, retroactive to the first dollar sold (back to 0% of quota).

- 75-100% of quota—X%, retro to the first dollar sold (back 0% of quota).

- 101-110% of quota—Y%, only on the amount in this range.

- 111%+ of quota—Z%, for anything sold over 110% of quota.

- W, X, Y & Z are commission percentages of your choice. Generally these percentages go up as a higher percentage of the quota is achieved.

Here's an example of a really confusing, if not overly complicated, commission plan:

TRUE STORY: A CEO once thought this was a brilliant plan:

The salesperson earns 70% of commission dollars upon achieving up to 79% of their sales budget. Once the 80% level is obtained the commission goes retroactive (from dollar one) to the full commission rate. (Say that fast 10 times…) Huh?

It sounded simple but was ultimately confusing to the salespeople. Some non-sales commission genius decided that this would more motivational if the salespeople were paid "short commissions" until hitting a certain point. And the finance-focused CEO thought it was a good idea. That will depend on what you consider motivational.

As it turned out—hitting 81% of quota earned an

increase in sales commission (a higher rate was paid back to the "first dollar" sold) which was substantially more than the incremental sales increase (from 79% to 81%). Hardly an advantage to the company.

BASIC RULE: Try to determine what the desired revenue outcome of a sales plan should be and create the commission plan based on that. If the sales team needs to make 80% of its overall budget for the company to break even, or whatever the internal "executive level" metric needs to be, then add in a mid-range motivational bonus for hitting 80% of quota. (This could mean a higher commission rate—retroactive—once they hit 80% of their quota.) That's much easier to understand and the sales team doesn't need to know that this is a break-even point: It's just a point at which they make more money! You can make the math work out any way that you like... you just want to have a plan that makes sense to the sales team without exposing any unnecessary internal metrics.

Avoiding Discriminatory Commission Plans:

Creating discriminatory commission rates is a common mistake. It's done by paying different commission rates to salespeople who are at the same job level and selling the same product, with the same sales goals. Yes, it happens, and when it's discovered by salespeople (they *do* talk about these things among themselves), all hell can break loose.

There are many causes for discriminatory commission rates. As a rule, commission plans should be blind to gender, territory size, sales goals, or experience. Salespeople hired from inside the company may be on different commission plans (= lower) than those hired later from outside the company. For some reason, there is a mentality that often exists with sales managers that a salesperson from outside the company is "better" or "more effective" (read: worth more) than someone from inside the company. This is generally a perception and not a reality, except in very rare cases where a sales team is being upgraded.

Here's how a discriminatory commission rate plan could happen:

EXAMPLE: Assume that Salesperson A, who was hired from outside the company, has a commission plan of $70,000 (in addition to base salary) and the sales goal is $2 million. That's a 3.5% commission rate at 100% of goal. Salesperson B, who is already a salesperson inside the company, has a commission plan of $60,000 and a sales goal also of $2 million (this happens frequently depending on experience levels, etc.). That equals a 3% commission rate.

The problem is obvious: The commission rates aren't uniform. Note that both salespeople A and B are selling the same product/service, and the assumption is that since quotas are the same, sales opportunities are the same in each territory. The disparity of commission rates in percentage and gross commission dollars to a salesperson just doesn't seem all that fair.

There are plenty of reasons why these disparities exist. Salesperson A might have a lower base salary. Or Salesperson B might be just a bit junior and/or it simply took less to hire them. (That's the free market at work.) Either way, these disparities exist, but shouldn't.

One solution might be to set the standard commission rate at 2.5% and then take the remainder of their commission plan and pay that as a bonus if, or when, the salespeople hit quota. At least that keeps the commission percentage uniform and the conversations among the salespeople on a different topic.

In the above example, Salesperson A would earn $50,000 in commissions a year on a $2 million budget and get a $20,000 bonus check for hitting annual quota. Salesperson B would also earn $50,000 in commissions for the year at quota, but would get a $10,000 annual bonus check. That's still not completely fair but it does tend to "fly under the scrutiny radar" a little more easily. As Salesperson B becomes more experienced the end-of-year bonus could be increased. Such bonuses could also be paid quarterly or monthly depending on the sales plan. Bonuses can also be set based on some set of objectives that aren't measured solely in terms of revenue created.

Other ways to handle the inequities of commissions for similar quotas:

- Keep commission rates and bonuses the same and raise the base salary of people who are more experienced.

- Give your star players higher budgets and expectations.

- Set territory budgets more accurately. This may require taking the geographical size of the territory and the customer base into more careful consideration. (Consider travel time to, from, and within a territory as part of the equation.)

- Don't allow your salespeople to low-ball you on what their territory can do. If one does it, they all probably will. (One way to keep this from happening is to tell the sales team you may have to hire more salespeople and cut down the size of the territories—this may help them get some "religion" regarding the sales that can come out of their territory.)

- Make the budget-setting process a mutual task.

- Be open about rewarding bonuses for bringing in particularly difficult business.

- Create different commission rates for different product lines and create specific quotas for each category.

- Set up bonus plans based on certain measurable objectives that are indirectly linked to revenue creation (market share, new customers, new categories, product mix sold, etc.)

Other Commission Plan Thoughts:

Commission Draws: Let's hope you have hired smart salespeople. If so, you don't need to use "commission draws" to motivate them. Basically you are lending them money until they sell something. They will feel bad enough if they are consistently under quota and they won't be around long. There are very few examples where the company and the salesperson aren't better off with a combination of base salary and commission, unless someone is an independent sales rep.

Straight Commissions: Some salespeople do prefer straight commission plans. This works well when the business is solid and increasing but offers very little downside protection for a loyal salesperson in a market that is in start-up mode or experiencing seasonal ups and downs. Usually straight commission plans are more appropriate for independent sales reps. Independent reps typically cover all their own expenses. That commission is usually at a higher rate than what an "inside the company" salesperson would earn because the independents cover their own expenses.

TOP TIP: Knowing When to Divide a Territory

If sales have been so good that all the accounts can't be covered appropriately, it's probably time to hire more salespeople and start dividing territories.

Knowing when it's time to split a territory:

- The sales team can barely keep up with the demands of the customers.

- They are working late at night just to keep their heads above water.

- New business starts to fall off because no one can get to it.

- Existing customers start to complain that they aren't getting enough attention or details aren't being attended to.

TRUE STORY: A top salesperson was exceeding her goals, and putting in long hours. Yet complaints in the territory were at an all-time high, and coming from customers whose calls weren't being returned. That was a problem. There wasn't enough time in the day to get to all the potential accounts.

The decision was made to divide the territory. The salesperson went nuclear and wanted to know why her territory was being "decimated" and her income "reduced". The sales manager explained that there was no way that the salesperson could physically cover the territory and offered two thoughts to help the salesperson understand why the decision was made:

- The sales rep would be better able to service her accounts if the territory was cut down geographically. More accounts could be focused on.

- The sales rep would make more money in the months ahead than before because she could get deeper into each key account and find more revenue opportunities.

The sales manager asked the salesperson to take a leap of faith that the sales manager was going to be right on this one. The salesperson agreed and the territory was split. Within a year, the salesperson was the top salesperson in the company, had bigger commission checks, and received awards at the annual sales meeting.

TOP TIP: Sharing Split Accounts:

Having multiple salespeople work on the same account is often a fact of life. Sometimes the split is among product lines or geographies and it's not possible to have one salesperson cover all the bases. The bigger the customer's company is, the more complicated it all becomes, and typically more salespeople are involved.

There are some fairly simple rules for dealing with split commissions. A general rule of thumb is to split commissions evenly among the primary salespeople working on the particular piece of business. So, if two people are working the account, they each get half of the commission.

EXAMPLE: A magazine sales staff has a car manufacturing customer in Detroit. The car manufacturer's advertising agency is in Southern California. There are local magazine sales offices in both locations. The advertising agency has made it clear that the magazine should focus the majority of its selling attention on the agency and not the car manufacturer. But the magazine's management feels that it's the car manufacturer that ultimately pays the bills to the magazine, and if the agency goes "into review" (meaning, they have to re-compete for the business and could lose it), the magazine should always have a relationship with the car manufacturer. In this scenario, two salespeople call on the business: one at the agency and one at the car manufacturer. And the commissions are split equally, providing both reps are servicing the account properly.

Generally it's best to not split an account further than

two salespeople. It is more acceptable to split commissions down the middle than to make a value judgment regarding which salesperson should get more. If there are a large number of split accounts across the company, the math tends to average out anyway.

On some pieces of very important business, salespeople can be double-commissioned. This means that they each receive 100% of their earned commission dollars. This can be done when there is a tremendous amount of work done on the part of both salespeople and the account represents a large amount of revenue.

Communication on split accounts is the key and often very difficult to make happen unless mandated via a compensation model. There is a way of handling split accounts that will increase communication. Believe it or not, some salespeople have been known to keep a split account a secret to get the entire commission. It's often easy to determine, after the fact, through billing addresses or the involvement of third-party vendors that an account is actually a split. But you shouldn't have to find out about it that way.

If it does happen, you can have a very simple rule:

In the case of an "unshared" split account (the other salesperson involved isn't covering their side of the account because they didn't know about it) *all* the commission goes to the salesperson who should have been working the split account for the period of time that the account was being held "hostage" by the other salesperson.

Violating that rule can cost some very big money if a

salesperson isn't honest. Reiterating this rule at least once or twice a year, especially when there are new salespeople, is a good idea.

Underwater Quotas:

There is nothing more un-motivating than the feeling a salesperson can get of being "underwater" in his or her quota. This means being so far behind in hitting numbers that he or she gets discouraged and drowns in a sea of pity. This can happen when quotas are given annually or quarterly and roll over each month. Which is to say, if you don't make your quota this month it rolls over to next month, and the month after that, and the month after that, etc., and the salesperson just gets deeper and deeper underwater.

Some people would rather quit than face the daily, and long-term, humiliation of being underwater on their goals. This doesn't only affect under-performing salespeople, so picking and implementing a reasonable sales goal is important for the entire team.

External factors can affect product sales, but it's more likely that most problems are internal. If product marketing people or sales executives had an overly enthusiastic expectation of the sales potential of the products, then good salespeople shouldn't bear the brunt of that.

To solve quota issues, try things like setting monthly/quarterly quota numbers that don't roll over into the next period. Once the period is over, you move on. And if the numbers aren't met, the salesperson doesn't make a ton of money but the impact to the company is in small, measured increments rather than a big annual surprise. Try slowly ramping up quotas so that they are more reasonably achievable period after period.

SIDE NOTE: Interestingly, when sales are going through the roof and quotas are being blown away everyone thinks the sales guys are geniuses (except the CEO or the COO who will ask why the numbers weren't set higher!). But, when the numbers aren't being made it's only the salespeople who are at fault. Damned if you do, damned if you don't!

Lowering Quotas:

One particular consideration during particularly slow economic times is to lower the sales team's quota. This should only be done under very unique (= dire) circumstances. Once quotas are lowered it is hard to raise them again. Once salespeople know that their quotas could be lowered that will be an ongoing talking point. In general, lowering quotas should be avoided whenever possible. If they were created with smart thinking, there should be no need to change them.

13. MANAGING EVERYONE ELSE

Managing salespeople is one thing, managing everyone else is another, especially if they don't report to you. We all "manage" others to help companies make their goals. Here are some ideas on how to do it:

MEGA TIP: Treat People Below You Like Kings and Queens:

There are many managers who pride themselves on managing "up" the corporate ladder often they don't realize that sometimes the real support or resistance to someone's management success comes from below them, not above them.

Here are simple rules for managing people whom you work with in an organization (even if they don't report to you):

- Treat everyone the way that you would like to be treated.

- Treat the people who are below you in the organization like Kings and Queens,

- Treat those above you like regular everyday people.

- Treat everyone as a peer.

MEGA TIP: Treat Everyone the Way *They* Need to Be Treated:

Some managers have only enough bandwidth to treat everyone who works for them the same way. By treating everyone the same "average" way you treat no one the way they need to be treated. Some may call that *being consistent* or *fair*. In reality, it is a waste of your sales management time. Each salesperson is unique, so manage uniquely, when possible.

It's OK to be consistent and fair and you should be, but the approach you take to achieve that consistency should be as unique as the individuals whom you are dealing with. Different people are motivated based on their own individual set of experiences and expectations. By getting to know the salespeople whom you work with, you will know how to better motivate them.

It pays to take into consideration here, that men

and women might have different views of the world regarding what is fair treatment and what isn't. When you are working closely with men and women in a sales environment you are, in many respects, in a "relationship" with them. This is, of course, a general consideration. Even well accepted gender differences (women will cry at work, men will almost never cry at work) cannot be applied to everyone. Ultimately you are dealing with individuals.

There has been plenty written on what motivates men and women and just how different they are in relationships. Much of this logic can and should be extended to business relationships. While most people might not make the connection of why this is important, as a manager you deal with people of different temperaments, talents, and convictions, as well as different sexes. Money and power are some of the biggest reasons that people have difficulty in their personal relationships, and that also applies to business relationships. Any emotional intelligence you can bring to understanding how these differences affect someone's motivation will help you better manage your team.

TOP TIP: Nothing Gets in the Way of a Sale:

Nothing should get in the way of making a profitable sale. Not a legal department, not a marketing department, not a finance department, and certainly not anyone in upper management who doesn't understand the concept of creating profitable revenue. There is often a lot of lip service paid to doing this—but nothing makes change happen faster than blowing a huge deal.

One of the best strategies to keep the sales pipeline humming is to constantly look for bottlenecks in the system and fix them quickly. Start work on this before the end of the month or the quarter, or you will probably be accused of just trying to make excuses for not hitting the numbers. Lobby to get a supporting department additional help if you think it's going to help business. It's your job to get the selling job done.

TRUE STORY: A new sales manager had just missed the first quarterly revenue numbers by a few percentage points. The sales team had sold nearly every piece of sellable inventory that was available to them. In the end-of-quarter revenue review meeting, the sales manager confirmed what the sales team had suspected: total inventory was off by a wide margin. In this case it was over 10%.

The sales manager did a quick calculation and determined that if inventory had been available as projected by the product-marketing team, the sales team (and the company) would have exceeded the sales goal.

The sales manager then asked the chair of the meeting, the CEO, who in product-marketing was responsible for delivering the inventory numbers. The CEO returned a blank stare. As it turned out, no one in product-marketing (or anywhere else in the company) was tasked with being accountable for delivering on what the sales team was selling. How this happened was unclear. That didn't matter. What was clear was that, outside the sales team, the company wasn't revenue-focused. This was preventing sales from happening. Needless to say, an immediate search was started to staff this particular job while members of the product-marketing team covered in the interim.

TOP TIP: Sincere Praise:

Have you ever noticed how much more helpful people are when you simply thank them for a job well done? It's one of the easiest things to do. Yet some sales managers don't do it because they think that people should just do their jobs and be happy with their internal satisfaction and motivation. Telling someone how nice a job they did takes almost zero effort on your part and burns no calories. It does, however, require thinking effort. You have to learn how to deliver it in a genuine way. People can see right through insincerity.

POSITIVELY SPEAKING: Many sales managers know how to show gratitude and thankfulness when appropriate and needed. The results are simply amazing. It's motivational and energizing. It makes people want to work that much harder, especially during "crunch" time. Appreciation should be given in limited quantities or it will lose its effectiveness. Be careful to not encourage the "teacher's pet" syndrome where salespeople will only do things to be noticed, and get that "gold star" next to their name.

LESS THAN POSITIVELY SPEAKING: There are top executives who rarely, if ever, thank anyone (especially salespeople) for even trying. This can be the case even if the salesperson failed at something extremely difficult, such as a high-risk initiative in an emerging market.

There are executives who ridicule salespeople who close nice deals by asking why they didn't ask for a bigger deal. Executives like this tend not to be particularly well liked or have command of many social graces. Not that they had to be gracious, but a typical reaction from salespeople could be: "Why should we go out of our way to make this #@%$!!&%#$! rich?"

Being a "hard ass" is often mistaken as a sign of shrewd, hard-driving, business sense. In reality it's a sign of insecurity, lack of confidence, social malad-justment, and quite possibly just being an "ass."

TOP TIP: Appropriate Praise:

How do you praise someone for a job done well, but not overdo it? Look at the level of the task that was accomplished. Was it done with flair and creativity? Would it have taken you or others realistically as long or longer to accomplish the same task? Praise in direct pro-portion to a job well done plus ten to twenty percent. Go a little overboard!

If the work is incredibly stellar, make sure the praise is given more publicly. In-person and in front of a group is best. E-mail alone is not really a great vehicle for sin-cerity because it seems like an overly effortless way to communicate, but one advantage to e-mail is that it can reach a wider audience.

Remember that *you are praising the job that was done, not necessarily the person doing the job.* This is a key con-cept and there is a substantial difference. The company moves forward because the *task* was done well, not necessarily because of *who* did it. Maybe anyone could have done the job well, but this was the person who happened to be in the right place at the right time to do it. Don't give the impression that only one person could have done the job well. Do give the impression that doing the job (every job) well is what matters for the company. Instead of saying: "*You* did a good job," try saying, "*That* was a job well done. Thank you!" This will help keep people focused on doing the work, then getting praise for the work that is done, and not because of being the one who did it.

TOP TIP: Making Mission Statements Work:

Building mission statements isn't easy. They only work if the people in a company believe what they stand for and live by them every day. Get involved in building the mission statement. Its creation is generally driven by the CEO. If your company doesn't have a mission statement, raising the need for it and getting the process started can't hurt.

After the company has a mission statement, the stage is set to establish mutual goals across departments or divisions on how to work together to make the mission happen. This is where managing others becomes extremely important. When it comes to "enforcing" these mutual goals, the potential combustion chamber between sales and other departments can't be ignored. Sales sells products and services, they typically make promises, and sometimes (most of the time) the company has to live up to those promises. So it pays for all departments to know what has been agreed to and to support it. And it pays for the sales team to be realistic in its promises in order to get a sale.

TOP TIP: Creating Reciprocal Departmental Goals:

All departments should have the same goal: Get a great product to market, get it sold, and get the money in the bank. That helps a company create more customers and more profits. You can start a successful implementation of the company's mission statement by establishing reciprocal goals with each department the sales team touches. This *quid pro quo* thinking gives both parties a vested interest in success.

EXAMPLES OF RECIPROCAL DEPARTMENTAL GOALS:

- *Shipping* agrees to ship all orders in 48 hours if *Sales* agrees to have a policy of closing daily orders by 3 p.m.

- Another might be: If *Sales* agrees to orchestrate a fax-based sales blitz to the customer base, then *Marketing* agrees to redesign all sales materials into single-sided, easily faxable sell sheets.

- And, another might be: *Product Marketing* agrees to seek input from the top ten company customers if *Sales* agrees to take marketing teams on the road to meet with their top buyers.

These shared goals get departments talking to each other and helping each other solve mutual problems.

TOP TIP: Managing with R-E-S-P-E-C-T!:

A lot of effort is required to manage expectations, communicate, and coordinate mutual goals. It's not always easy. The first step to success as a company with a common goal is for sales managers to have respect not just for departments that sales touch directly, but for everyone in the company from the CEO to the night janitor.

All employees have a challenging job, no matter which department they work in. When working with people across multiple departments make sure they understand how important they are in the process. When appropriate, communicate the key issues to all who are affected and update them as appropriate. Thank them for what they do.

TOP TIP: Face-to-Face Problem Resolution:

It's always better to have an eye-to-eye discussion when solving a significant problem, especially a people problem. Hiding behind an e-mail is usually perceived as a cowardly move. At a minimum, have a phone conversation regarding a problem. Show the sales team that you care. The point here is that you will want to face the problem issues head-on and do it quickly and professionally. It's less stressful and allows you to move on to other issues.

Gather as much information as you can about the problem at hand, and be as fair as possible in resolving it. It's OK to take some time to think over the issues, assess the available information, and craft a fair and amicable solution.

Explain your position clearly and then get feedback. Be open-minded to the feedback. Someone may have thought of things differently than you did. Most of the time, changing your solution based on more updated facts will be well received by everyone. Sticking to your guns when presented with new and illuminating facts shows a level of inflexibility.

Ask the salespeople what they would do if they were in your position. Try to teach them a little about what it's like to have a broader view of a problem and its solution from a manager's perspective. Make it more of a discussion than a dictate. They will appreciate the learning experience and what it means to be in sales management. Once you've made your decision then stand by it.

TOP TIP: When Non-Salespeople Want to Sell:

For those who think selling might be for them, a good strategy would be to recommend that they go into sales support or marketing first. They should take the time to learn how the product is marketed or how current customers react to the product and how it is sold and serviced. Once they think that sales will be right for them, they should jump in with both feet! Marketing people who have had some sort of selling experience are simply better marketers and salespeople who have marketed are better salespeople.

TAKING A SELLING TEST DRIVE: When a non-salesperson expresses interest in sales suggest that they take a personal day off and go on sales calls with one of the top salespeople. Make sure that the salesperson is OK with this and that the day selected will be representative of a moderately intense schedule. This can be very eye-opening to a future salesperson. Make sure to follow-up with them in a few days to see what they thought about the experience.

Marketing Department Alliances:

One of the best alliances you can strike outside of the sales team is with the marketing department. Marketing people who have sales experience are to be cherished. They often better realize the direct relationship between sales-driven marketing tools and a sale. Marketing materials by themselves don't often kill a sale, but their absence can. When created properly, and used effectively, marketing tools can certainly *help* make a sale.

Be an Intra-departmental Diplomat:

During intra-departmental meetings, take on the role of diplomat whenever possible. When different departments meet, there is often some built-in animosity between groups. Be the one who smoothes over differences and promotes working together to solve problems and meet goals. Take the high road.

TRUE STORY:

The Problem: The head of a department was running an interdepartmental meeting and was consistently late or wasted time talking about things unrelated to the meeting.

The Facts: The person running the meeting shows up late to a multi-person meeting and makes a comment like: "Gosh, I didn't know how long it took to get here from our offices!" This is the second time he is late for the same reason, so the excuse is obviously wearing thin. You draw your own conclusions as to how bright this person is, or if he has ever run a group meeting before. He then proceeds to talk about the virtues of potting plants for five minutes with one other individual in the room. This wastes everyone's time.

You Have Four Options:

1) You can go nuclear on him in front of the group and say he is wasting people's time (mainly the time of people in *your* department) and that talking about potted plants is completely idiotic.

2) You can pull him aside after the meeting and tell him "as a friend" that being late for the same reason twice is making him look really bad in front of the group, and he is losing the respect of the team.

3) You can turn the potted plant scenario into something funny by noting that you don't see a potted plant topic on the agenda and humorously suggest that you aren't prepared to talk about it, so could the group move on to the first topic of the agenda?

4) You can choose to have no one from the sales team attend the next meeting. While this might sound like an immature approach, if the sales team's time is being wasted, they could be doing something better, like making sales.

WHAT'S THE RIGHT ANSWER? It's probably a combination of all of them, but will depend on your relationship with the person and how you choose to discuss it with them. It's best to try the light-hearted approach first and pull out the heavy artillery later—if they simply don't get it.

Brown-Nosing:

Who hasn't tried brown-nosing in their career? When it's done for real, it's ugly. Why? It's a sleazy, disingenuous attempt at trying to politically suck-up to someone else by working their ego. There's nothing wrong with a nice genuine compliment. Most people are astute and when they are getting the brown-nose treatment; they don't appreciate it.

When brown-nosing is done in jest, it works wonders for enhancing the sales culture and the corporate sense of humor—especially if it's done for fun and sport. Though, there is a fine line between good and bad brown-nosing.

Real brown-nosers are the scourge of the universe. They generally aren't good at it and all their peers think they are idiots for being so obvious about it. Brown-nosers are like people who wear bad toupees: everyone *knows!* Take control of any real "brown-nosing" situation. The best way to stop it is to call it when you see it and mock it in such an exaggerated and humorous way that everyone is aware that you don't think its career-enhancing. Say something to the offender like: "Do you think you could be any more obvious with your brown-nosing?" You can also try brown-nosing the brown-noser. This is typically a crowd pleaser and provides comedic relief in certain situations.

TRUE STORY: A sales manager once put a

brown-noser on the spot in a meeting after he had just sucked-up to the CEO by complimenting the brand of the CEOs sport coat. (Sure, it was a nice coat, but...)

The sales manager said saying something like: "My, my (Mr. Brown-noser), you too are looking exceedingly well-dressed today. And I know that you of all people would appreciate my hollow, brown-nosing, suck-up compliments more than anyone else in the room!" (This was followed by group laughter!) The brown-noser blushed, laughed and cut way back on the brown-nosing.

At the annual sales award dinner, make sure that the most egregious brown-nose event in the company is fully acknowledged in a humorous way. Make a special award of it. This will become an unofficial badge of honor and will mitigate any advantage of doing it for real. Any future attempts to get ahead politically through brown-nosing will be greatly diminished.

Managing in the Real World:

Have any of these scenarios touched you?:

- CEOs that have no respect for salespeople or the sales function.

- Companies with imperfect products that may not be completely competitive, but you still have to sell them anyway.

- Salespeople who think they make the world go round because they can sell something while engineers or product marketers can't.

- Engineers and product marketers who are so methodical that they have no concept of market timing, much less getting a product to market fast.

- Salespeople who make promises to customers that can't be met.

- Product marketing people who conceive products without first asking customers or salespeople their opinions.

- Salespeople who think any revenue is good revenue.

- Senior executives who think the company's "brand" does all the selling and that salespeople are stupid and a necessary evil.

- Product marketing people who think salespeople ought to have no role in the product development process even though these salespeople are often closest to the customer.

- Salespeople who think the only job of the marketing department is to make pretty brochures and fact sheets. (There are marketing departments that think this, too!)

If all this sounds familiar at some level, it's because it happens every day. This "silo" mentality is what can cause companies more problems than their competitors. What a circus this can be!

While it's doubtful that *all* these things happen in the same company at the same, they do happen now and then. There is usually a legitimate reason: lack of communication and respect for other functions within the company. By virtue of a heavy workload alone, people can get so parochial in their day-to-day work that they only communicate outside their group and area of responsibility when forced to. They rarely know what's going on in the entire company and how all the pieces should work together. They can also operate in their own universe and rarely come up for air to show respect for colleagues outside of their own department.

When attitudes like the above start forming within a company, you will need to do something to promote open and honest communication, and to appreciate what other departments do, as well as thanking them for their contributions.

14. MANAGING YOURSELF

Learning to lead others is a key part of going from successful salesperson to equally successful sales manager. One of the less obvious management assignments you will take on is managing yourself. Some of the tips below may apply to you, and some may apply to managing others. Here are some ideas to think about for your own personal success:

MEGA TIP: Always Maintain Personal Integrity:

The most important asset that a salesperson or sales manager has is integrity. It has to be protected at all costs. It's the single most important skill that moves with you from job to job in your career.

Integrity can be defined as doing the right thing for the company and the customer while maintaining high ethical standards. If you are asked to do something that just doesn't feel right or doesn't seem fair to all parties involved, then your integrity is being compromised. If you feel uncomfortable your integrity "trigger" is working properly and you should call it as you see it (and possibly refuse to compromise).

A short-term compromise might not seem like much but could have a long-term effect on your career. It might come back to haunt you at a future date. The unfortunate thing is that what we see as being completely ethical today may not be viewed as being completely ethical in five or ten years. If you are in doubt, and the issue is high-level enough, consult your peers, accountants, lawyers, or someone else you trust, and get their opinion. Don't assume that because others are doing something, 1) it's legal, and 2) that you should be doing it, too.

Some people can get very creative in the gray areas that surround integrity. If you are comfortable pushing the envelope without having to rationalize why, then by all means go for it. Just remember that it is generally true that "what goes around comes around."

MEGA TIP: Be Your "Genuine Self"—It's Easier:

Always be your genuine self in a selling and sales management situation. That's no doubt easier said than done. That means saying what you think and feel and always trying to do the right thing for the company and the customers. It also means being as polite as you can about it without being political.

Plenty of new sales managers "suck up" to their superiors by acting just like them instead of just being themselves. It's a short-term solution that isn't going to get anyone very far. The downside of acting like your superiors is that when they are gone, you have to do a lot of soul-searching as to what the real you is all about.

The same "genuine self" approach applies when contemplating lying to others. It's too complicated trying to remember what was said to whom and how it differs from what you said elsewhere. By always telling the truth you don't have to worry about "back-tracking."

TOP TIP: Ask for Forgiveness Instead of Permission:

When you are convinced that you are doing the right thing for the company but are receiving resistance from those around you who don't share your vision, then sometimes it's just best to do it—and ask for forgiveness later. It's your call to decide if asking for forgiveness after the fact fits into your personal risk profile.

Sometimes You Need a "Little" Frustration in Your Life:

There may be a point where you can't take the frustrations of sales management, but try to keep your sense of humor, no matter what happens. In the end that's all you have. As they say: "What doesn't kill you, will make you stronger." Being able to laugh and shake your head while calmly walking away is much better than losing it.

Time Is Your Best Friend, and Your Worst Enemy:

Over time we develop our own sense of what works best for us (i.e., we become our own person). We are a mix of our personality, sales skills, what we learn from those who have mentored us, our observations of the world around us, seeing people being treated well or poorly, a strong sense of right and wrong, and an even stronger sense of how we would like to be treated.

Along whatever path that brings you to being a sales manager or sales executive, you will make choices and judgment calls. You will observe and decide if what you experience should be part of your way of doing things. The trick is to always make an honest decision that you can be proud of and that is true to your own style. There is no short-cut for the time it will take to develop your own sensibilities.

TOP TIP: Under-Promise, Over-Deliver:

This is a fundamental rule of sales. Never over-commit personally to anything if you don't believe it's possible, based on all the data you have. Don't be "rah-rahed" into it. Your life will be miserable from the second you start the job. That's true with an inherited goal or when you are getting direction from above you. You will ultimately own these numbers, so you have to be comfortable with them. Be realistic, then surpass the goal.

This is not to suggest that you don't have a set of goals to "stretch" for. You should. And if you hit them you should be compensated aggressively. But being realistic when setting sales goals is what sets the tone for successful selling.

Are you a "sand bagger"? It's often said that over-achieving your goals can be as bad for business as missing them by a mile. A company would certainly rather be oversold than undersold on their products, but the problem that's created has everything to do with inventory. If you oversell that's great, but you can create a cascade of problems for purchasing, production, and shipping by selling way more than what you agreed to in your plan.

Top sales managers can be quickly viewed as "sand baggers" if they keep coming in way over quota. So, communication is everything. Nothing will annoy the rest of the company faster than unexpectedly having to scramble to find the resources to help you exceed your numbers. (And the assumption will be that they are making you filthy rich in the process because of your sand bagging!)

TOP TIP: **Change Policies That Aren't Good for the Company:**

Isn't it interesting that companies will set policies and just run with them with little change over time, even though the world is changing so quickly around them? Sometimes those policies make sense when instituted but fail to stand the test of time. Yet they are bureaucratically defended by people who often don't have the common sense to see the big picture. (Or perhaps they just don't have the vision—and maybe they aren't expected to.) If policies have a negative effect on your ability to make revenue, then change them! Nothing about bad policies makes them set in stone.

TRUE STORY: A sales manager worked for a company that had an antiquated policy regarding its approval process for pricing and selling a certain product line. The person who controlled the product was simply doing his job and unwilling to change any of the rules. It wasn't in his realm of responsibility to do so. He was the perfect bureaucrat! Making a change might have cost him his job, after all. The sales manager did an analysis that showed the company's inability to revise the policy was costing upwards of $8 million a year in profitable, legitimate revenue. Ouch! So the sales manager pushed hard to have the policy changed at a higher level.

TOP TIP: Extract the Ego:

Becoming the top sales manager usually carries with it an accumulated ego. It took years to build your sales reputation, so you are going to show off and take credit for it! Right? Well, not so fast!

In reality, when you reach the top, it's time to take your ego in the other direction. Park it. Be proud of personal accomplishments that made you a top salesperson, but remember that from here on out it's the work of others that will make and keep you a successful manager. It's time to get rid of your ego. Put it back in its cage. If people can see or feel your ego in public, it's not a good thing. It should be an internal motivator only.

TOP TIP: Face Your Weaknesses:

Not everyone can do everything well all the time. If you don't do something well, make a point of acknowledging (without dwelling on) it, and then work on it. When you get feedback from your team or your customers that you could have handled something better, accept it, try to fix the way that you did it, internalize it, and try to make sure that it never happens again. This is a really key point. Wanting to fix the problem is the only way it will happen. *Rationalization doesn't fix problems.*

TOP TIP: Listen to *Your* Customers:

As the head of a sales team, it's always in your best interest to listen to your own internal customers—*your* salespeople. When what they are telling you makes sense, acknowledge it and incorporate it. Give credit where it's due. They will follow your lead, and the amount of time spent covering tracks will be minimized. Salespeople follow their leaders. Make sure they are following the right example. This "egoless" way of contributing to the greater good of the sales team will be noticed and you'll receive more power and respect than you ever expected.

TOP TIP: Staying Healthy:

Being busy all the time can take its toll on your health. Balance is everything, so exercise frequently. You need the energy to run a sales organization! Try to run or walk or do sit-ups and push-ups every day. Exercise DVDs that you can pop into your laptop when you are on the road and just hit "PLAY" are helpful too.

Getting exercise doesn't just include walking into the building where you work! Make a concerted effort to carve out at least 30-45 minutes a day for exercise. It is well worth the time invested. It keeps you sane. It helps you deal with stress better. You don't have to be a fitness freak, just keep your body trim. People like being managed and sold to by people who have their physical and health acts together.

Exercising, like selling, is a never-ending process. You keep selling to make money and you keep exercising to stay healthy. There are plenty of ways to get exercise and not have to go to elaborate lengths (or distances) to get it. Take as little time as necessary to get to your exercise destination. Sometimes the best place to go exercising is right out your front door.

When exercising, just stick with the basics. Doing initial stretching, sit-ups, abdomen crunches, and push-ups on the floor of your hotel room along with taking a brisk 30 minute walk or run will make all the difference in the world. It will clear your head and get you prepared for the day (or the next day). Do whatever it takes to get some exercise daily. Start slow by exercising three times during the week and one day during the weekend. (Discuss all exercise plans with your doctor first.)

There are plenty of daily opportunities to turn something that isn't exercise into something that is. Park your car farther away from any building you visit. Take the stairs instead of the elevator. Walk to lunch. Better yet, walk and eat lunch at the same time. Encourage others to join you. When you add up all your activity at the end of the week, you will find that you have used a lot of energy and worked your body physically. You'll feel better and perform better.

Forget dieting, if you keep realistic about your food intake—type and quantity—and add some exercise, you will start losing weight and start to become more healthy, happy and trim. It's all about choosing the pattern that works best for you.

TOP TIP: Use Your Vacation or Lose It (Along with Your Mind):

Take your vacations regularly. Everyone else does, why not you? If the company culture is to work hard and give up your vacation time, don't do it. You are entitled to a vacation, so take it! It will recharge your batteries and increase the quality of your work.

More and more companies have created vacation policies that cap accrued vacation time. That's a big message that you should use it or lose it.

TOP TIP: Know When to Turn Technology Off:

Higher-level executives are often required to have pagers or two-way interactive devices so they are always accessible. These are great tools as long as access to them isn't abused.

Some salespeople and sales managers complain about being constantly called or paged on their devices. They say things like: "It just never stops buzzing or ringing! Arrrgh!"

The solution to this is simpler than it seems. It's up to you to take control of the device. Here's how it works: Place it (cell phone, pager, or whatever!) firmly in your hand and then hit the "OFF" button until you are available again. James Bond was an early innovator in not being a slave to technology. If he didn't want to be bothered he just turned the bloody devices off! He had better things to do.

TOP TIP: Like Your Peers:

This is probably one of the most important things to know and understand: Salespeople are your peers. You are helping them help the company make its goals. If you aren't a people person or don't genuinely like the people whom you work with or for, it will be all the more difficult to motivate and manage them in a sales environment. Find something to like about everyone you work with. Take a real interest in the things they are interested in. With trust, and a more common bond, more can be accomplished.

It's a two-way street, however. While it can be easier to get positive things done with people you are close to, it may be harder to deal with negative issues. If you have constant communication, with positive and negative feedback, the chances of there being long-term bad feelings to deal with (like reprimands, firings, etc.) will be minimized.

Ninety percent of the time your salespeople will be doing a great job. Tell them so, but remember that you might have to occasionally put their "head in a vise" over their most recent knuckle-headed maneuver. While getting a point across about negative behavior, keep the tone light and your sense of humor. Be firm but fair.

TOP TIP: Be Humble:

Don't take yourself too seriously. People will think you are full of yourself and you'll throw up walls around you that will keep others out. No one will want to deal with you. They might *have* to, but they won't *want* to.

Things to be humble about:

- Your successes,

- Your interaction with your peers,

- The car you drive,

- The clothes you wear,

- The way you treat people,

- The places you vacation, and

- Talking about your investments.

One of the best self-deprecating "I'm humble" lines ever heard from a salesperson is: "Aw shucks, I'm just a Florida boy trying to help my customers be successful." (Fill in the blanks for your state and gender.) That comment was used by a very direct and driven salesperson who was trying to still get the company's product in the door once a decision was made to buy another competitor's product. It helped to disarm a group of people who were feeling intimidated by that person's presence (the salesperson was the only one in the room wearing a suit, and he was selling for a very high-powered company).

Only be humble if you are, and you mean it. You should always feel that way anyhow. People are quick to see through insincerity. Being humble always works best. People who aren't humble are no fun to be around, anyway. No one really wants to spend his life listening to others boast how great they are and then, of course, having to agree with them.

TOP TIP: Time Management:

Whenever you have multiple people reporting to you, your time will be scarce. You have to manage it well like everything else.

Here are some general guidelines:

- Try to touch any issue only once. Get your facts together and make a fair decision. Be clear and upfront about your decision and you won't have to do a lot of re-explaining later.

- Have a trusted group that you consult for feedback when you are problem-solving.

- Try to respond to minor issues the same day and major issues within twenty-four hours. If you can't respond immediately because of delays from others involved, keep in communication with the person you owe the answer to, so it's clear that you are still on top of the issue.

- Use face-to-face, phone, cell phone, snail mail, and e-mail, as appropriate, when dealing with a specific issue. Block off time to respond after business hours, when you can be more thoughtful and clear-headed.

- Delegate when possible, but don't lose touch with the issues.

- Realize that you are only one person and that you can only respond to so much in one day. Exert every effort to make responding to others' issues a priority.

- Leave "anytime" filler projects for downtime when you can't communicate with others (late at night, on trains, in tunnels, on airplanes).

- Always be doing something with your time that "adds value." That includes taking power breaks to tend to your personal projects, or just catching up with your personal reading. None of this should occur at work, however.

• If you *must* work while on vacation, set a limit and specific period of time (one to two hours a day), but make sure that your vacation is a vacation and not just a change of venue from which to work.

TOP TIP: Take Risks:

If you aren't making mistakes, then you aren't taking risks—and therefore you aren't learning. The core lesson of risk-taking is to learn from your mistakes and move forward with brilliant new ideas.

Do you remember learning to ride a bicycle? If you weren't falling down, you weren't learning how to ride! Remember how scary it seemed at first and then the sense of freedom it gave you once you learned how? Even at an early age people learn to take risks. The same is true in your business life. You have to take risks to succeed, to learn. They don't have to be huge risks at first (although they might feel huge), but pushing out of your comfort zone from time to time will keep you moving forward.

TRUE STORY: A CEO once implored his senior managers to take more risks. Everyone tried. The CEO wasn't an inherent risk-taker, but actually very conservative, so it seemed odd he would be imploring the management team to take risks. The biggest risk the CEO took all day was deciding what to have for lunch in the company cafe. Yet he wanted everyone in the company to push out of their comfort zone and take a risk that would move the company forward, and quickly.

The sales team came up with a range of ideas that would push the company's comfort zone. They weren't too dramatic under the circumstances and were geared to not put the company in any excessive jeopardy. In the end, the CEO said "No" to everything that was suggested. The ideas were too risky for the CEO, so nothing happened.

The lesson learned here is that risk-taking makes sense, and it should happen, but only if it's going to be supported from the top down.

It later came to light that this particular CEO had recently read a trendy management book that encouraged risk-taking. His request for the management team to take risks was coming from the author of the book and not from the CEO's own heart, and it ultimately showed.

For risk-taking to work, the desire to do it has to be genuine, and the acceptance follow-through and support have to be there, as well.

TOP TIP: Be Flexible:

Every day that you are managing salespeople requires some level of flexibility. You never know what will happen. You may have an irate customer problem, or a huge deal may start developing or start unraveling. You may have annual review paperwork due by close of business. The great thing about sales management is that nothing is ever routine. Always think in terms of being flexible and adjusting to what comes your way.

TRUE STORY: Peter Ueberroth, who ran the Los Angeles Olympic Organizing Committee for the 1984 Olympics, once said that you should be flexible every day that you come to work. Some days you might be showing a politician around town. The next day you might be stuffing envelopes. The day after that you might be picking up fast-food for some international dignitary's children. Every day presents a different set of challenges and opportunities. To be successful you will need to be flexible.

Be the Sales Architect:

The best way to be a successful sales manager is to approach your job the way a good architect would. Design a strong foundation and build the sales structure on top, one solid salesperson and sales manager at a time.

Of course bad hires will be made along the way. But a little bit of due diligence before making each and every hire will do a world of good. Even one bad hire out of every twenty still means you are doing a stellar job as a hiring manager. Assembling the best team possible is ultimately the most important thing a sales manager can do. Success is all about the "people inventory" that make the business run day-to-day.

This is similar to what a strong CEO would do: Surround herself with the smartest people she can find and let them do their jobs. Then the CEO has time to do her job more effectively.

Attending Trade Shows:

Attending trade shows is a great way to meet a large number of customers in a compact amount of time, especially key industry or consumer trade shows.

Attending panel discussions at these trade shows isn't often as rewarding. Honestly speaking, panel discussions can be a waste of time: Usually it's "important" people in the industry talking to other "important" people in the industry. And they usually talk about the same thing over and over again. There are occasional jewels of wisdom but they are often few and far between.

It's often difficult to attend this type of event because usually a degree of self-promotional hype is going on. It's probably better to read the recaps in the daily trade show papers, if available. Exceptions are the keynote speeches. These are often very interesting, help spot key trends, and set the tone of the trade show, or sometimes they are just the world's biggest sales pitch. You be the judge!

As a rule of thumb, it's better to be on the trade show floor selling during panel discussions. Chances are that your most important customers won't be hanging out at these sessions. They are probably too busy for that.

Speaking on Panels:

Attending trade show panel discussions as a salesperson is one thing (and a bad one at that!), but being on the panel is great for getting exposure for your company, if the right audience is there. But usually, more can be accomplished by taking your customer to lunch and having an in-depth conversation.

Some sales executives are known to hog a stage and relentlessly pitch their product or service when that wasn't the purpose of the panel. Moderators and audiences squirm when this happens and the reputation of the executive gets flushed right down the drain. These executives think they are doing the right thing and carrying the sword for their company. What they are really doing is enjoying listening to themselves speak while falling on that sword.

If you can get on a group panel discussion, it will usually have most of your competitors there, too. Try not to be quick to give away too much information in situations like these. While you might think it will help sell your audience by giving a lot of the latest details, you are actually giving your pitch directly to your competitors. You should assume that the competition will take the opportunity to misrepresent your pitch at their earliest convenience.

If you are on a panel or doing a sole presentation, consider populating the audience with your own salespeople to meet potential customers or ask questions of you or about your competitors.

Asking That Memorable Question:

Suppose that you can't get on a panel discussion or be a primary speaker at a trade show. There's always a guerrilla marketing way to get noticed. Be the one who asks a memorable, insightful question or makes an intelligent comment in front of the entire crowd. That could enhance your reputation and your company's.

Avoid making gratuitous, self-serving, promotional

comments, as people will figure that out immediately. Be sure to clearly identify yourself, and your company, so that you get some free "branding" along the way.

It's hard to know what questions are best to ask for a specific industry, but generally they should:

- Play to the positive,

- Be topical and fairly uncomplicated,

- Show your level of understanding of the market,

- Not be an opportunity to get on a soapbox and blather about something,

- Be brief and to the point, and

- Not be "set-up questions" that you think have one specific answer that helps make your company or product look good. This can backfire.

Write questions down while you hear the speakers talking. Sometimes you have to be fast enough to ask the question before someone else does, or before someone on the panel addresses it. Sometimes the questions will be obvious, other times they will be harder to uncover.

Practice the question in your head before you actually say it. When you are ready for your moment of glory, approach the microphone and fire away!

Industry Associations and Committees:

Every industry has its own industry association. While they may help move an industry forward (albeit at an often slow pace) try to be involved in them only peripherally. Have your company join and have your marketing people represent you at the meetings. Your job is to keep your team selling.

If membership in an association doesn't help the company directly (or even indirectly) sell anything, it's hard to want to be there. The exception is being involved in the standards committee. That's where the participation of your company will matter the most. If you think that a powerful player in the industry wants to change a standard to benefit only their company, someone from your company needs to be there to call BS on it.

Be happy when your competitors get involved in industry associations. They will now be so busy being political that they won't have time to fully manage their salespeople or sell anything themselves. For the most part, when looking at résumés that have industry association involvement written all over them, don't rank them as highly as those that show positive sales results.

Without sounding too two-faced here, you should make every effort to join in the industry association's social events. These are great places to network for future salespeople or your next job. They are usually "after hours" events so they won't prohibit you from your real selling and sales management career.

Dealing with Demanding Behavior:

Demanding behavior is very different from irrational behavior. A sales executive may come in contact with many peers and higher level executives who have a constant stream of demands of you that seem to keep you from doing your job. These are not necessarily irrational demands, just frequent, or many and different. You may often wonder why other people cannot handle them on their own.

The frequency and detail of the requests are usually what lead to the perception of someone being demanding.

Demanding people can raise these questions in your mind:

- Am I being taken advantage of?

- Couldn't they be doing these things themselves?

- Why are they asking for so much, so often? Or,

- Why are they asking me for this stuff at all?

How do you deal with demanding people? If you feel that someone is making a lot of demands on your time for no apparently good reason, it might be a good idea to just ask, in a non-defensive manner, why, and what is the information for. Then you can better understand their motivations. You may determine that someone is just neurotic and has to constantly be busy managing "lucky you," or maybe because you are so accessible, they feel that they can make demands whenever.

One way to manage multiple requests is to let the requester know that you might not be able to get to everything on their list within a certain period of time. Have the person prioritize requests. This will set the tone that you can't jump every time, and say "How high?"

Dealing with demanding behavior can often come down to a simple communication issue. Opening the communications link between you and a peer or an executive above you may help you both to understand the impact of the requests and the time available to fill them.

TOP TIP: Your Personal 30/60/90-Day and Annual Goals:

Whether you are new to sales management, or a seasoned sales executive in a new company, or just starting a new fiscal year, you should map out a strategy as to what you expect to accomplish personally and quickly during the first thirty, sixty, and ninety days, and then annually. Have a set of stretch goals that you want to accomplish if all your stars line up properly.

Call your plan an "expectations plan" with clearly defined goals. Then work like crazy to beat your timeframes. Review an appropriate summary version of these goals with your boss and staff frequently so that everyone knows what you are focused on. Take their input. Make revisions whenever necessary. Move things up on the list when you can accomplish them sooner. Be very self-critical about moving anything farther down the list. Nothing should be set in stone such that you can't make an on-the-fly adjustment. Always keep your list accessible. Check against your list frequently to see how you are doing.

Personal Balance:

Getting personal balance is hard to do unless you are really focused on it. Your job shouldn't be your life. Try to make it fit into your overall life. Compromise is important, but if you don't purposely strive for balance it won't just happen. When you finally do start making the job fit your life better, your career will start to take off. You may not think that's the way it's supposed to work, but it does.

People like working with and for interesting people. You won't be too interesting if all you do is work all the time. Work reasonable hours and force yourself to get a job done in the allotted time. Don't let a job linger into the late evening, unless you are on a short deadline or an emergency has come up.

On the flip side of the coin, striving for balance can only be a successful strategy as long as your extracurricular activities don't take away from the time you devote to your sales team. Be careful about the perception you create here. If your employees sense that your out-of-office activities are more important than your work, they will become resentful and feel as if they are left holding the bag and doing all your work. If they have no balance in their lives, they will be even more resentful.

Are You Open 24 Hours a Day?:

Don't stay open or be accessible 24 hours a day. You need time to sleep, re-energize, and do other things. You have a hard job, so take care of yourself. Having the cell phone, pager, and e-mail on constantly can often disrupt your personal time. If you don't want to be contacted, then temporarily disconnect and take some time for yourself.

Be Accessible when Necessary:

Once you're the big dog, don't hide from your puppies! Keep an open door and open e-mail policy. Make yourself available. This may sound counter to what was said above that you shouldn't be open 24 hours a day. You shouldn't. But during working hours (and a little extra on either side of the day) you should be available. You are in demand! You have the answers. People want your guidance and opinion.

Walk around the sales area when you can and say hello to people. See how they are doing. Ask what they are focused on. Simple interaction like this means a lot to a sales team. They are on the front line all day and need to know that they have a sales manager who cares about them and their job.

Get a Real Life:

Do more than just hang out in the office. Plant roses in your garden and smell them (literally). Do something that you want to do with your family or friends. Get involved in something outside of work that means something to you. Some of the best experiences you will ever have are in the form of giving back to others. Volunteer for something. Help others who are less fortunate than you are—they will give an added perspective to your job and personal life that you won't appreciate until you try it.

Be Adventurous:

Once a quarter try something new. Take a class on a new subject that you think you might be interesting but that you've never been able to get around to. See what your local community college has to offer. You may decide that you won't be a long-term wall climber or kick-boxer but at least you've tried it. Some people never get that far!

You might think that these types of adventures won't help you in your job, but they will. If you only have your job to do, that's all you will *ever* do and you'll be in your office constantly. If you have other responsibilities and other places to be, you will learn better time management and have a better perspective on how work fits into your life.

Maintain a Laser-Like Focus:

Whether you are in a selling or managing situation, don't waste time with mundane administrative projects. Get to whatever your pre-determined goal is as quickly as possible. This could be getting your expenses done, doing annual reviews, disciplining a salesperson, setting up meetings, etc.

Getting as much done as possible will require laser-like focus and preparation on your part. Don't loaf around or put something off—even the distasteful stuff. Get all the issues aligned in your mind for the day and start executing. Make a list.

Drill right in on whatever issues you have to face, dissect them, prioritize them, work on them, solve them, and then move on. People will come to respect the attention you bring to resolving issues and your team will start to follow your example.

TOP TIP: Embrace Change:

Always embrace change with a positive attitude. Change keeps you in the center of the action, builds confidence within your team, and earns major points with your peers and superiors. It's true: Change is constant, get used to it. The sales team of most companies is where that change is magnified the most.

Change often puts salespeople's reputations on the line with customers and needs to be well managed. There will always be negative situations that arise out of a dynamic selling environment and they need to be dealt with on a case by case basis. Then there is the mainstream set of customers whose response will be more predictable. Be ready for all of these scenarios. Tell your more negative-type customers what is happening a little before you tell others, but just a little. Give them a bit more time to internalize it.

Different people respond differently to change. Some will go with the flow. Some will take it personally, as "life threatening," and spin out of control. Some will take it as an opportunity to hold the company in contempt for being badly run. The best strategy seems to be to work individually with others and graciously accept whatever change happens.

Leadership in Problem-Solving:

Most problems can be solved once you find out where the core difficulty exists. Getting to that core problem is the hard part. If you can help salespeople be self-sufficient with problem solving, you will free up more of your time to deal with bigger issues.

Some salespeople find it difficult to prioritize the facts surrounding a problem, which keeps them from narrowing down the issues quickly to what really matters. They will have to relate the story to you in its entirety and often be unable to discern what is important to solving the problem.

It's not a hard process to uncover the significant facts if you practice a few times. You begin by asking a lot of questions. Be the facilitator. This creates a process of elimination of extraneous information in order to get to the core. By continuing to ask questions, you may actually learn that the solution to the problem isn't what you originally thought it would be. Avoid the tendency to try to solve the problem quickly with too little information. Help salespeople prioritize the information and figure out what is material to the solution. Teach them a process so they can be more self-reliant in the problem-solving process.

Managing E-mail:

Checking your e-mail all day can be time-wasting. Constant beeps announcing new e-mails can be annoying to you and everyone around you. Just check every couple of hours. Scanning to see what's come in is OK, but sitting down and responding to all of it in a non-prioritized way isn't the best use of your time. Don't forget that your job is sales management, not being an e-mail routing service.

Managing *by* E-mail:

Sometimes managing by e-mail works, sometimes it doesn't. It will depend on the severity of issues to be resolved. Resist the temptation to become holed up somewhere and control your entire sales universe via e-mail.

Trying to have in-depth discussions on e-mail across a wide group of people can become a multi-conversational disaster. No conclusions are drawn and people may be responding to previous parts of a discussion. Sometimes it's best to take an e-mail discussion off line and set up a meeting to discuss the issues. How do you know?

Call a meeting rather than use e-mail to resolve a problem when these things start happening:

- The discussion has many contributors with no distinct solution coming through.

- People are still responding to previous points when the discussion has already moved on.

- The e-mail thread (responses to the original) become too long and confusing.

- The discussion becomes heated.

- Only a few people are responding, or they stop responding altogether.

- It is taking too long to get resolution (assuming there is any resolution).

Follow up any mass-mailed e-mails with personal notes attached, along with the original, to anyone who you think might have had trouble understanding what you meant. People are more likely to respond to one-on-one e-mails if they have been confused.

Always Ask: Can We Sell This?:

When you are given a new product to sell, even before you present it to the sales team, it never hurts to ask "Can we sell this?" and "Does this product make sense?" Salespeople are the biggest supporters of new products and also the toughest critics because they have to sell the product to demanding customers and create new markets. They usually know what the customers want. Never let a product be developed without some sort of input from the sales team.

This isn't to suggest that the sales team become the product planning group or be the "go" or "no-go" decision makers on a product. People outside the sales group may view the concept of sales input as absurd because salespeople are perceived as only wanting products that are easy to sell. That's a hard perception to get over, but it's rarely true. Salespeople want products their customers will buy. At a minimum, salespeople should be able to give input (accepted or not) to the process. In some cases, it could help make a product a huge success or avert a total failure. Why? They are closer to the customer than anyone else in the company and know what the true needs are.

TOP TIP: Blocking the Icarus Effect:

If the person running the company you work for is caustic, then a portion of your job may be spent saving your salespeople from exposure to the top. You are protecting them from what is known as the "Icarus Effect." That is to say, if your salespeople get too close to the heat of upper management their "wings" will melt and fall off, and they will come crashing to earth. That's a euphemism for their being exposed to the craziness at the top and becoming alarmed and disillusioned. Be a buffer for them. You can take the heat while they may not understand that this type of thing goes on in most companies. If upper management is irrational, doesn't understand the selling process, is overly emotional, has general contempt for salespeople, or are just mean, you will need to swing into control mode and keep your salespeople away from them. How? Keep the salespeople out in the field where they belong—selling.

Communicating Globally:

In a global economy you may be called on to communicate, any time of day. Respond as immediately as you humanly can, in whatever way is most appropriate. Nothing slows a sales team faster than time zone driven unresponsiveness. Clarity is also key here. Before you communicate anything, be sure it makes sense to all involved.

Consider these issues:

- Will everyone understand your colloquialisms?

- Will they understand your humor?

- Try to understand fully that you are communicating across multiple time zones and cultures.

- Are the concepts simple?

- Will the audience understand acronyms that you might be using? (It never hurts to define a term so that everyone is clear.)

TOP TIP: The "No Surprises" Mentality:

If you are in constant communication with the sales team and always ask to know the good and the bad from them, then you won't have any surprises. Surprises are bad. Even good surprises can be bad, like sales being way over budget and putting additional stress on manufacturing and shipping departments at the last minute.

Don't kill the messenger when the news is bad or you'll never hear what the problems are again. Be deep enough into your team's selling effort so that you can anticipate when problems are about to surface.

Encourage people to tell you about the good *and* the bad. You'll need multiple sets of eyes to help you do your job effectively.

Dealing with Plastic People:

There is nothing worse than fake people who make it up the corporate ladder, especially if you have to deal with them. They are annoyingly plastic, and seemingly perfect, and you will swear that they have something to hide from the world because they act so Teflon-coated. They rarely express emotion or passion for what they do and it's very difficult to get to know the "real" them.

To be most effective in your work you have to be able to roll up your sleeves around others and just be real. If you are in direct working contact with fake people like this then try to get to know them, but it will be hard. Fakes they don't want you to know anything about them. But keep trying anyway. There is probably a good person underneath it all, and once you can find something to be friendly about you can start slowly to win them over and have a better working relationship. Over time you can get everything on a more solid footing.

15. CAREER MANAGEMENT

Managing your career is just as important as managing everything else in your life. It's probably the one thing you think about the least as life goes on. Here are some ideas on how to manage your career more effectively:

MEGA TIP: View Your Career as a Series of Projects:

Think of your career as a series of projects, with each one giving you cumulative knowledge to take you to the next level. Think about how each successive job can move you forward. Even a lateral job may actually help expand your horizons more than taking a job at the next level. You may want to hone your skills managing sales-people who sell something different or to a different type of customer at some point in your career to help round out your expertise.

MEGA TIP: Establish a Measurable Track Record:

When it comes time to upgrade your career, the success you have helped create for your team and the company as a sales manager is one of your most sellable products. So no matter what you do (as long as it's ethical), do it to the max—it will come back to help you later. Keep track of all the successes.

When it's time to sell yourself into another job, be visible (but not boastful) with the success of your team. No one believes a sales manager who swaggers in and says that he single-handedly made their previous team what it was. As it's been said, there is no "I" in "Team."

Here's how to record a track record:

TRY THIS: Map out the goals that you and your teams have had and how you mutually accomplished them. Find the key success metrics that resonate in your industry and compare how your team did against them. Look for common themes from job to job.

If the universal metric you have been judged on is increasing sales by X-XXXX%, the number of X's that your team accomplished is what will make you a star in the eyes of your next boss. It's your ability to get others to do what you need them to do that says it all. Make sure you track it for future use. Be accurate.

If your successes came at an unusual time in the market, make sure that you are clear about that when selling yourself. This was especially true when companies were spending money hand over fist in the late 90s as a result of the dot-com bubble. Don't let a potential new boss think that your sales team was only riding up on a high tide like everyone else. Many sales teams with mediocre products did well in the boom years, because they did a stellar job of selling and servicing their accounts. Even in highly competitive markets, plenty of options are available to buyers, good and bad. Make sure that you clearly define what you did to set your sales team's efforts apart from other companies.

TOP TIP: Always Be Asking: Is This Job Really for You?:

If you are new to sales management, or looking to move up the ladder, make sure that you are up to the task before you accept the job. Check your motivations before committing to this type of career move.

Make sure that it's something that *you* want to do. Seems obvious, doesn't it? It really isn't always that clear. Many people want to be in sales management because they think they will make more money or be shielded from the day-to-day requirements of hitting a sales goal.

That's not always the case. Stress is multiplied, not divided, when you go into sales management, and the rewards are different, more often indirect.

Some people are pushed into sales management—by their bosses, peers, family, finances, significant others, and/or their own ego. Only you will know if you are really up for the task. This is not the time to lie to yourself. It takes tremendous humility to determine whether you think you are right for sales management, now or later.

TRUE STORY: A salesperson had done well in the sales ranks and as a regional sales manager for years. The company she worked for was fast-paced and constantly launching successful new projects. The CEO of the company came to the aspiring sales manager one day and asked if she would be run a new project. It was a great project with a solid future. As much as the sales manager's ego wanted her to say yes, she ultimately thought that ego alone was the wrong motivation to take the job.

The sales manager did a lot of soul searching and decided that if her career was going to continue to progress successfully, she should take a pass on this particular opportunity until she had more experience. She simply wasn't ready... by her own admission. It was a complete exercise in soul searching and self-assessment that drove the decision, not ego. Usually it's the company that doesn't think someone has enough experience. In this case it was an individual who made the call. The sales manager took the time to get to know herself better and spent the next year getting experience at the pace she felt comfortable with.

Ultimately the sales manager took a Vice President of Sales job with a new division in the same company, when she was ready, and had a higher degree of self confidence than she would have in the other position. That segment of the business became highly successful and so did the sales teams that she managed. She was able to move forward and be even more successful than she would have been in the opportunity that she originally turned down. Timing is everything!

Seek as much input as you can when you are considering a senior sales management career. Ask people in sales management what they like and dislike about their jobs. Get the real scoop. Be an investigative reporter of sorts—try to get an un-biased opinion of what the job is like. Opinions of others are one thing, but remember that they are filtered through other skill sets. Not yours. Make the appropriate adjustments when you compare how you would do with respect to others.

This advice is equally good to give when your direct reports come to you with interest in advancing to the next level.

Some questions to ask other sales managers or senior sales executives:

- What is their typical work week like?
- What do they like and not like about their jobs?
- What is it like, managing other people's headaches?
- How much do they travel?
- How did they get their first sales management job?

- How did they get their current sales management job?

- Did they have to change companies to get a sales management job?

- How much time do they continue to devote to selling?

- How do they interact with customers?

- How often are they in the field?

- How much responsibility do they have?

- What management style do they use with their salespeople?

- How much personal free time do they have?

- What's the hardest part of their job?

- What's the most fulfilling part of their job?

- Does upper management support them? How?

- How do they work with the product, marketing and finance groups?

- What is the single most important thing they have learned in the role of sales manager?

There is no end to the questions you could ask. It's really a function of the amount of time your contacts have to answer, and how deep they will let you get. What you are trying to uncover are learning points to help you evaluate your skill set. You might also learn tips to tuck away later and use in your own way. Asking multiple sales management contacts an entire range of questions will help you understand how they have adapted to their jobs. Treat them like informational interviews.

Some people hate what they do but continue to do it. You don't want to be one of them. Be sure that the job is one that you want and that you are ready. And then be ready for a great journey with unique twists and turns.

TOP TIP: Avoid the Golden Knight Syndrome:

Sales managers are often hired to be the "Golden Knight" who rescues a company's flagging sales. That's not an atypical situation to be put in, but expectations can be off the "deep end."

Make sure that you know what you are getting into when you a join a turnaround situation. In some cases, expectations of the executive team don't match market realities.

Sometimes:

- The product has a longer sell cycle than expected (or longer than anyone is willing to admit).

- The product is outdated.

- The product just sucks!

Dig deeply into situations like these *before* you take the job. Being on the hook for "the number" when the cards are stacked against you isn't a good feeling.

If you are there to do a turnaround ascertain that your CEO is clear on that and that you communicate effectively regarding just what will be needed to get the job done and what the expectations are. Make sure that you get the support you need to be successful, and get it in writing if there is a chance the support offer is flimsy.

Build in some contingencies to your contract in the

event that situations change the likeliness of making the sales goals. Possible contingencies include:

- Guaranteed one-year employment contract, and six-month to one-year commission plan.

- Part of bonus compensation tied to meeting "turn-around" objectives, not just revenue goals.

- Alternative compensation plan for meeting sales goals despite other departments not meeting their goals.

TOP TIP: Analyzing Your Next Job Opportunity:

Having the opportunity to accept more responsibility in a new job is always a compliment. Sometimes executives have no idea what type of person they are trying to hire and what the right balance of responsibilities should be. Many are looking for a Swiss Army Knife, and finding that sales manager who is a jack-of-all-trades is often an impossible task. You may need to look at the offer and suggest a better job description and set of responsibilities that are mutually agreeable.

Assuming that your next potential employer has a great future and a great product, here are key questions to ask:

- What revenue will you control?

- What's your realm of responsibility? Does it extend to the product or marketing side of the company?

- Who determines the budget levels?

- Who or what do you have override authority over?

- What level of support do you get inside the company?

- PLUS: See all the "How to test your CEO for revenue-focus" related questions on page seven.

TOP TIP: Take That Recruiter's Call!:

Always take recruiters' phone calls and, when possible, try to refer them to the appropriate people to fill their positions. There are two reasons for this. They may help you find a new job one day, or they may be able to help you realistically analyze a job that you may be considering.

TRUE STORY: A sales manager was offered a high-level job with a company that was in the midst of a turnaround. The company had a seemingly good CEO who checked out well and the sales team seemed great. An offer came soon thereafter. The salary and commission package seemed fine. The stock options seemed very low despite hints to the CEO that lack of upside, in lieu of increased salary, would be a deal killer.

The company's recruiter said that the options were appropriate given the current market conditions. The sales manager candidate didn't have a good feeling about it, and to get feedback on the offer, made a few calls to recruiters who had called on him over the years.

What many people don't know is that the information flow goes both ways.

After speaking with four recruiting friends (and

reading related company financial documents and talking to two CFO friends), the sales manager candidate found out that the stock option package was indeed very low and just a fraction of industry averages. This provided the information necessary to negotiate, which led to a more favorable option package.

Selling Yourself When Necessary:

At some point in your career you might have to make a move to another job. When it's time to sell yourself again, you have to be prepared. Some people never think they will be in that position, but we all are at the crossroads at some point in our careers.

In every job you have, strive to excel in the most visible and appropriate ways possible. That builds up your "resale" value. Not only will you get better at what you do, you will build a strong résumé and reputation as a good person to work for. Take note of your accomplishments. Always have your résumé polished up and ready to roll. Update it every six months. It helps you keep track of your accomplishments and a proper perspective about each job.

Look Before Leaping (to Another Company):

Be smart about jumping from one company to another. If the company with a potential new job is offering more money than industry averages, there is often a very good reason why. The company might be a complete and utter hell-hole to work in and has to pay more to lure good people away.

Or, the company may be leading a new technology initiative and need to lure sales executives out of their comfort zones and into theirs. Weigh these issues carefully. Try to assign percentages to what is important personally. In addition to the material things like compensation, options, bonuses and perks it's often the intangibles that matter most, like: work environment, culture, commute, location, people, etc.

Looking Out for Hell-Hole Companies:

How can you tell from the outside if the company you are talking to is a hell-hole? The first place to look is at management turnover. Read the press, do search-engine searches on the company, talk to people who do business with the company and see what the experience is like. Try talking to people inside the company to see what the real scoop is. Typical signs could be unusually high salaries that are needed to draw people in, but this isn't always an accurate measure. In some cases the hell-hole company may offer lower-than-industry averages because the CEO thinks that people should consider themselves fortunate enough to work there.

The Tell-Tale Stock Option Plan:

An indicator of whether a company might be a difficult place to work could be found in its stock option plan. Look at the company's first vesting cliff (the initial time period that must pass before you can start exercising your options). Longer initial vesting schedules for stock options might signal that executives in the company set them up to keep people as long as possible, before they quit. The rule of thumb would be that the longer the vesting cliff, the higher the potential risk employees will not last a long time, most likely due to issues internal to the company.

A good personnel retention strategy is to give stock option ownership earlier in the process, as long as people are working hard to earn it. Having a piece of the company earlier makes employees feel more a part of the action. If the industry-average, initial vesting cliff is one year, then an eighteen- or twenty-four-month, initial vesting cliff is usually a sign that there might be huge trouble ahead. Always ask why the initial vesting period is longer than industry averages, assuming it is, and look deep into the answers. While a stock option plan might sound good in terms of number of shares it could deliver, this will only matter if someone is there to vest and exercise them.

If you sense that a potential employer has any of the above traits, feel free to ask how long the person who held the job before you lasted and what the average tenure of a senior executive in the company is. Scrutinize the answer carefully for "spin" (like suggesting the employees were responsible for their own departure, and not the company, etc.). If you feel that something is being hidden, then immediately start digging (or stop digging and look elsewhere). Use your intuition and you will probably be right.

Timing, Timing, Timing:

Some people get lucky, while others plan their good fortune. Some people have a plan and still get lucky anyway. Make career moves that you like and seem interesting and take on new, unproven opportunities whenever they are offered.

TRUE STORY: A new sales manager was hired from outside the industry for his first job and did *zero* due diligence on the new company. He ended up unknowingly going to work for a bottom-tier company. No one inside the company or industry wanted the job, but this aspiring sales manager wanted to break into a new industry, so it was a good match at the time. Timing *can be* part of a good personal success strategy.

As you grow older, and hopefully wiser, you learn to pick your opportunities more carefully. This involves looking at SEC filing documents, doing Web searches, looking at independent, industrial relations websites, talking to investors and board members, consulting friends in the industry, and speaking to people who used to work for companies that you are interested in—all *before* pulling the trigger on a new opportunity.

Luck vs. Hard Work vs. Smarts:

Salespeople and sales managers can sometimes strike it rich by making a very good job choice. They go to work for the right company, have the right product to sell, and/or have good market timing. They make it look easy, right? Often they will *feel* they are more lucky than smart. Luck is perceived as a random experience but you can make your own luck by working smart.

Often, the feeling of "only being lucky" impedes any desire to change jobs or move up the corporate ladder.

Insecure salespeople think it's the product or the company that is bringing the success, and not their efforts. Some senior sales managers like this kind of thinking. It allows them to keep salespeople who are otherwise highly valuable to other companies.

A different point of view, one that gets more value out of your salespeople, is to reinforce that *they* are the reason for the successes, not just the products. Good timing is not a bad thing. It's not luck, it's simply making a smart decision at the exact right time. It is borderline brilliant. This is a confidence-builder. Products don't generally sell themselves (despite what non-sales types might think). Competition is fierce these days and sometimes good (but humble) salespeople will think that they aren't adding to the value chain when they are adding more value than they can ever know.

Salespeople who don't feel that they are adding value when they actually are need a little bit of extra "tender loving care." They need to know that the work they are doing is as important as the product they are selling. The more confidence they build, the better salespeople they will be. There's always a risk that they will wake up some morning and figure this out on their own. It's better for you to let them know along the way, so that when they do wake up to it, they will understand that their successes are real. They will also appreciate the fact that you helped them identify this in themselves.

Salary Negotiations: Is It the Money? Yes, It Is!:

Negotiating business deals all day long on behalf of whichever CEO and company you work for can be a lot of fun. Negotiating your own compensation package can be the exact opposite. Why? It's a lot more personal.

This may sound odd, but if you've had the right conversations about your compensation-package expectations all through the negotiation process, then the actual offer should be subject to only a few minor adjustments.

If it takes numerous back-and-forth gyrations on your package or multiple pages in an offer letter to spell out the specifics of your deal, then be afraid; be very afraid. Your goal should be to walk into a company from day one and be happy with the opportunity, compensation, and upside that is being presented to you, period. Having a tense negotiation about your package only creates potentially unrealistic expectations and attitudes from the beginning. It should also send you a clear message regarding the type of senior management team that you are dealing with.

Every salary negotiation you do will give you cumulative knowledge on how to do better the next time. When you took your first sales job you probably got paid average market rates. As you got better at selling, you could do better and better in your compensation negotiations. The same will be true in the sales management ranks.

All along the way, you get smarter and realize that getting the right deal makes all the difference in the world in your motivation to do the job. There is never a standard set deal, no matter what the HR department tells you. The best deal for you is up to you to craft. You may be willing to give up some things to get other things, but a word to the wise here: Be realistic. If you ask for 120% of everything that you want, you will be the one creating the tense negotiation.

You should get paid what equivalent "stars" in your category get paid. Aim to get what you are worth. Check out S-1 IPO and 10K documents and other financial filings, if available, to see what your peers at publicly-traded companies are earning. Look at salary, commission, options, bonus and perks. Don't settle for less than industry averages. Check with other CEOs whom you might know, and HR people from recent companies whom you worked for. CFOs you trust are also helpful sources. Work your network. They can give you a good idea of what the position you are considering is really worth.

How Many Stock Options?:

Determining the correct number of stock options to ask for as part of a compensation package always seems to be more art than science. To feel that you are getting the most appropriate number of options consider the following ideas:

- Look at readily available public documents to determine what the appropriate percentage ranges are for option awards in your company.

- Ask your potential employer to provide a brief spreadsheet that shows what percentage of the company you would be allocated.

- Or, do the math yourself by taking the number of outstanding shares and divide your potential options by that number. If the percentage doesn't fit in the range for your position and the size/age of the company then negotiate for more.

- If the company is in the early stages of development make sure that future investment rounds won't dilute your percentage ownership as the company grows.

- Determine how additional option awards are tied to performance reviews, promotions, or other types of goal achievement.

Low Ball Job Offers:

When a company makes you a verbal offer and the actual offer comes in lower in the offer letter, think twice about taking it! Ask why it's lower. And if you don't like the answer, walk away. You don't want to work for a company that is unethical with its senior management before you even get there.

TRUE STORY: A sales executive was negotiating a VP of Sales job, and the HR director of their future employer gave a trial balloon offer. The question was: Would the sales executive come to work for a certain base and certain number of stock options? The sales executive said, "Yes."

When the offer letter came in, it was for 80% of the salary and options. The sales executive asked the HR Director why and was told that was what the CEO was now willing to pay. It was a classic "bait and switch," and later found to be typical behavior for the CEO of the company. The lesson was learned the hard way. In the end, it worked out OK. The stock was worth a lot after an IPO but 20% more of it would have been even better.

Are You a Survivor?:

Believe it or not, most senior sales executives last about eighteen months in their jobs. That's pretty typical in high-pressure markets. After that, they are either promoted, fired or choose to move on.

Sometimes what you were promised by the executives above you just doesn't pan out, sometimes companies change strategies, or products don't appear as planned, or the chemistry between you and others just isn't there, or expectations are unobtainable, or people are just unreasonable, and sometimes you might just suck at your job.

Whatever the facts in your personal situation, be realistic about what you contributed overall and learn from it. If you are the one who needs to let people go, let them know why. If you are let go, make sure that you are clear as to why. Don't ever take anything as a step backwards—only as a cumulative learning experience to help move you forward into something better suited to your unique talents.

TOP TIP: Knowing When It's Time to Go:

In companies with well established products, coherent business plans, and a respected sales organization, the tenure of a sales executive may be longer than in more dynamic industries.

Failure can usually be predicted when there is a big disconnect between sales, upper level executives and the rest of the company regarding the expectations placed on the sales organization. Good sales executives that don't recognize this may have themselves to blame or may have unknowingly been set up to fail based on the culture of the company. It's usually a mutually responsible situation that causes personnel changes.

There are a series of questions that you should review for yourself if you or someone you manage needs to leave a sales management position:

- Were you managed as well as you could have been?
- Did you know what your goals were (business and revenues)? Did you meet them?
- Did you have a well-defined and detailed job description?
- Did you have the resources you needed?
- Did you manage others as well as you could have?
- Did you endear yourself to those whom you worked with?
- Did you manage expectations properly?
- Did you communicate up and down the chain so that there were no surprises?
- Did you sign up for reasonable numbers?
- Did you make your numbers? If not, why not?
- Did you hire the right team?
- Were you there for the team during the good or the bad?

- Where you ethical in your behavior?

- Were you honest and open with those around you?

- Did you resolve issues promptly?

- Did your team respect you?

- Did your peers and manager's respect you?

- Did your customers respect you?

These are just some of the many questions that can be explored. If the answers point a finger *away* from you, then ask yourself why. Sales managers are rarely fired when they do everything well. It's a tough issue to deal with. Ineffective salespeople and sales managers are the absolute best at rationalizing why they failed. The *worst* thing you can do is blame what happens to you entirely on something or someone else. It happens all the time. It's always the other person's fault, the company sucks, or some executives didn't like you—whatever! It's always something, isn't it?

Denial-o-philes run rampant in the sales business. Don't be one of them. If you are asked to leave a company, take stock of why it happened and accept more than your share of personal responsibility for its happening. Write out your feelings in a journal or speak with a career coach.

Get yourself to the next level by always reassessing your skills and making the proper changes. As the old saying goes: If you aren't making mistakes you aren't learning. Once you have figured out what happened, take time to recalibrate. It might be time to rethink the type of job that you excel at. Be honest with yourself; that will be the hard part.

Setting the Record Straight:

It's often very frustrating to leave a company when you know that things could have gone better but were out of your control. One initial instinct might be to write a letter to the CEO of the company (if they aren't your direct boss) or to the board of directors to outline all the issues that you believe aren't being addressed.

If you do take this route, be as factual as possible. Don't point fingers in a malicious way. Once you have written the letter, put it in an envelope and let it sit for a few days. Take time to calm down. Don't react out of anger. Being right is one thing, being angry and right is another. The "I'm angry, but I'm right" attitude won't have the desired corrective effect, so avoid it. Otherwise you will be viewed as a psycho.

If you still feel the same way a week after you write the letter and you believe that what you have written is constructive and will help the company and its shareholders, then by all means consider sending it. Just make sure that your severance check has already been cashed!

16. PERSONAL SELLING

You never stop selling. And you shouldn't now. You learn a lot about selling from customers and salespeople by listening to them. Here are some ideas to keep your personal selling skills sharp:

MEGA TIP: Help Create More Customers for Your Customers:

It has been said a few times in this book that at the end of the day, sales is all about helping your customers create more of their customers. If this is your focus, it will also create better customers for you.

Here's why this makes sense:

- No business-to-business customers will come back tomorrow if you haven't helped them create more of their customers today.

- Or, in the case of business-to-consumer sales, if you haven't made the ultimate "retail" customers happy, they won't be back either, and they will tell all their friends multiple times over if they weren't treated well.

Sometimes, the link between your involvement as a sales manager in the process, and how it helps your customers create more of their customers might not be visible inside your organization. Take the time to help people in the company understand this.

If the way you are managing the sales organization doesn't support adding value in customer creation for your customers, you will have an uphill battle trying to be successful. This is true even if you are selling parts to another company that are hidden away somewhere inside a bigger product. If those parts fail your customer, you could cause them to lose their customers, and you could, in turn, lose yours.

MEGA TIP: Simplify Complexity for the Customers:

The concept of simplifying complexity is missed by many companies in the selling process. A publishing executive and exceptional editor once said that explaining a complex idea was simple, as long as the audience could understand those complexities. Since most customers don't understand the complexities of a product like salespeople do, the real selling talent is in being able to take something complex and making it appear simple and straightforward. The more that people can understand and grasp about how ingenious a product really is, the more they will buy of it. It's the old "better mousetrap" concept, which is to say that it's a product that can be sold without a salesperson! Just because there is a technically better mousetrap doesn't mean that anyone can understand it or will buy it.

TOP TIP: Sell Value:

Selling is not just about being the low-cost provider. It's about providing the best value, no matter how expensive or luxurious the product. Low-cost providers often go out of business. Why? They can't afford to provide good service. Customers don't stick around long if their cost per customer and the lifetime value of that customer don't hit the mark. The better trained a sales team is in helping customers create more of their customers, the more successful everyone is.

You might be thinking: "Huh? We build car seats based on a very specific requirement from a car company, how can this apply to us? How can we help them create more customers?" You can, in more ways than you might think. When potential car buyers open the car door, they see the seat, then they sit on it. They can be turned off on the entire car very quickly if the seat trim is poorly stitched, if the seat is uncomfortable, if it squeaks, if the reclining mechanism doesn't work smoothly, if it wears out too quickly, if it doesn't slide forward and backward effortlessly, etc., etc. By working closely with the appropriate seat manufacturer the car builder can effectively create a better customer experience and more customers. You aren't just building a car seat—you are part of the overall brand experience. And if you fail at delivering that, you can't help your customer create more of their customers.

TOP TIP: Selling Up the Food Chain:

The higher up in a company you try to sell a product the more benefits-focused (and less technically-focused) you should be. Always try to sell your products as high up into a company as possible. If you get a high-level audience in a company and immediately start selling deep on your technical capabilities, you will typically see eyes glaze over. The customers won't get it, and why should they? It isn't their job to be hyper-technical experts in what your company has to offer. At a high level they want to know how your product will make their company more productive, and in the long run (either directly or indirectly) help them create more customers. Take that approach and you will be closer to a sale.

Sell and Tell:

If you operate in a selling environment that requires you to call on a customer as well as the company that buys products on behalf of this customer, that can put you in an awkward position. Whom do you sell and who do you take direction from? Don't assume it's always the one who buys. In the end sometimes it's the one who ultimately *pays* that matters most. Having to hear "No Sale" from the company that "buys," even though you have a relationship with the company that "pays," is tough.

The rule of thumb here is: "Sell the Customer, Tell the Buyer" (if the buyer is a third party). The primary customer always has a vested interest in getting the best value. The buyer has a vested interest in getting the best price. There is a difference.

TOP TIP: Service Matters:

Customers never forget when you go out of your way for them. Even little things can make a difference. Remembering a birthday or other event can go far in differentiating you or your salesperson from the competition.

TRUE STORY: An airline customer was about to miss his plane. The airline's customer service manager saw what was happening and logged-off his ticketing terminal and ran with the customer to the gate so he wouldn't miss the flight. This happened post 9/11/2001. It was true dedication to helping the customer.

Things to consider:

- Do you think that customer will ever forget the extra step that customer service manager took?

- How many people do you think that customer will tell about that good experience?

- How many people do you think that customer will tell about a potentially bad experience?

Going out of your way for a customer will help create a bond of trust. That bond works both ways.

Some customers might be jerks and you won't want to help them, but try to make an effort to break through personality differences, even to let your toughest customers know that you care about them. A little kindness may be all that it takes to win them over.

TOP TIP: Always Follow Up:

Following up is rare in sales, unless you are a fantastic salesperson. Then it's second nature. These stories say it all.

TRUE STORIES:

DROPPING THE BALL: A potential customer went to a motorcycle show to view the latest bikes. He found one he liked but it wouldn't arrive at the dealer for a month. The customer made a simple request to the salesperson: Call him when the bike comes in and he would come down for a test drive. The salesperson *never* called. The customer never bought the bike. No Sale! Enough said.

RUNNING WITH THE BALL: A customer was looking for a particular type of pre-owned SUV. The customer knew exactly what he wanted. Unfortunately these models were few and far between, but they were out there. The customer gave the salesperson a list of requirements for their dream SUV but didn't hold much hope, having worked with car salespeople in the past to find particular vehicles.

No one had ever called back. Much to the customer's surprise, this particular salesperson called not just once or twice, but three times, each with a different vehicle that met the customer's needs. The customer now recommends this salesperson to everyone who needs an SUV.

TOP TIP: **Sell As You Would Like to Be Sold:**

This is a basic rule: Don't attempt to sell anyone anything in a way other than the way in which you'd like to be sold to, if you were in the market to buy. If you aren't enthusiastic and committed to your product, it will show. Sell what you believe in. Whether you are managing the process or selling on the front line, if you are asked to sell something to your customers just to make a number, reconsider which is more important: your career, your company, or your customer. In the end it's your reputation that's on the line. Your reputation is what gets you your next job. It's not just your reputation inside the company as a salesperson—but what the customers think that matters, too. Being customer-focused is always the winning strategy.

TOP TIP: **Head Games:**

Knowing what motivates the customers to buy from a salesperson will make your job easier. To learn what motivates them, spend some time with them. Be observant. See what pictures or toys they might keep in their offices. If you've got a point of commonality between you, use it to your mutual advantage. You don't have to manufacture one, but if you have a broad range of interests you will probably be able to find something in common that you both can relate to outside the selling process. A friendship makes the job of selling that much more effective.

Try to know and understand why your customers might act the way they do, both good and bad. The better you understand their motivations, the better equipped you will be to react to their actions. You may even be able to anticipate their reactions and keep problems from happening in the first place.

TOP TIP: Losing Gracefully:

You won't win every sale. You won't lose every sale either unless you are doing something really wrong. Take the time to find out why you won a sale. What made everything click for the customer? See if you can continue to repeat that process for as long as it works to your advantage. Whenever possible, have the top salespeople tell the rest of the sales team the nuances of what worked for them when they closed their sales.

When you lose, also take it as a learning opportunity to find out why.

Ask questions like:

- What could the salesperson or company have done better?

- Was it the product? The marketing? The return policy? The salesperson?

- Was it the selling process?

Find out what isn't working. Fix it so that it doesn't become an issue again. Fixing it once will usually fix it throughout the sales team. Use what is learned as a "real-life" case study and take it upon yourself to explain to the team why the sale didn't go as planned.

If the problem was a personnel issue, then address it behind closed doors. Don't take it as an opportunity to publicly humiliate someone.

Out and About:

Being out in the field and listening to customers first-hand is very important to overall sales success. You will learn more about how to make the companies you work with more successful in a day of sales calls than a week of sitting in internal meetings. Listen to customers *and* salespeople out in the field. See what works, or doesn't, for both of them. Report back and make changes.

Make sales calls with members of the sales team whenever you can. Be careful not to do their selling job for them, unless you're out on calls to make a company announcement, introduce a product, handle a big problem, or personally solicit feedback. Situations like these can be tricky, though. If you develop too close a bond with customers, they may want to deal directly with you, not their designated salesperson. Avoid that, unless you are actively looking to replace the salesperson and need to cover the account until it is covered by a new salesperson.

Dealing with the Top Guy:

Customers usually want to deal with the person they perceive as being able to help them the most or the one who has the highest title. So do the salesperson a favor and make it clear who will do the follow-up after the call (the salesperson will!). If you do get a customer who wants to deal with you directly, that might raise the issue of quality in the salesperson you have calling on that customer. Make sure you are listening to any signals your customers give you, regarding this. Make corrections quickly if you need to. Reinforce the power and responsibility of the salesperson on the account.

FOLLOW UP TIP: When the customer requests something, make sure that it is clear that the salesperson will do the follow-up and when. And that you will be keeping an eye on things.

Selling through a Channel:

If the product is sold through a channel, spend ample time knowing how that channel works—with not only the channel customers but the "end-user" or "retail" customers as well. The customers are the experts at every level. They shop the competition constantly and sometimes they buy from the competition and not from you. They know what they want and will be happy to tell you so. Ask them what competitors are doing or what it will take to buy more product from the company you work for. Huge improvements in design, marketing and selling of products can be made by listening to customers.

Customers As Friends:

You rely on customers for your livelihood. So treat them well. A good rule of thumb is to treat them no differently than you would your friends. It's much easier that way. Having a split personality is too complicated! Treat everyone as though they matter to you. It's a question of to what degree they matter. You don't have to spend a ton of time with *all* your various customer friends. But you need to make them a part of your life in some way, because they *are* a part of your life, directly or indirectly.

Customers can make you happy or sad or angry—just like anyone else in your life. The difference is that you have a business relationship with them. So you'll need to make sure that your professionalism stands above everything else. The key is to treat the customer with respect. Respect their opinions, their needs, and the pressures they face in their jobs. Help them when you can, and when you can't, tell them why.

Just Looking?:

How many times have you seen a potential customer tell a salesperson that they are "just looking" and not ready to buy anything just yet? And the salesperson just continues selling and ultimately upsets the customer.

Customers are getting smarter all the time and have greater access to information than ever before. You can thank the Internet for that. They often know more than the salespeople do. That's pitiful, but true. Most of us are always "just looking" until we are ready to buy something. And when we are ready, look out! Not listening when customers say they are just looking can create long-term ill will and create a multiple of ill will with all the people that the *potential* customer knows (or would the word *former* be more appropriate?).

TRUE STORY: A guy and his friend go to check out a new pick-up truck at the local car/truck dealership. They make it clear to the salesperson who greets them that they are just looking and absolutely won't be buying anything that day. They are being upfront because they don't want to waste the salesperson's time. He understands. This particular salesperson only specializes in used cars so he passes the guys off to a new truck salesperson along the "They're just looking" message.

The new truck salesperson immediately starts following the two guys asking classic "trial close" questions like: Which one do you like? What color are you looking for? Are you trading anything in? The guy and his friend made it clear *again* that they were just looking and absolutely weren't going to be buying anything, but the salesperson kept pressing. The two guys asked the salesperson *again* just to let them look at the trucks without trying to sell them. Then a stunning admission: The salesperson said that he had to follow them around because his sales manager demanded it. One of the two guys says, "Hey, who is the customer here—us or your boss?" All the salesperson could say was: "Oh, good point," and then he left.

But the story isn't over. A second new truck salesperson shows up with similar trial closing questions. At this point, the two guys were *furious*. The salespeople were simply not listening and just having fun at their expense. The second new truck salesperson went so far as to tell the guys that the engine in the new pick-up truck was built by Ferrari (um, it wasn't).

Then an amazing thing happened. A third new truck salesperson showed up and actually started to further hassle the two guys. At that point the two guys left the lot—quickly. Not only did all the salespeople upset the two guys who were just looking, they also made sure that anyone who knew these two guys and was browsing for a new truck would be told to steer clear of this particular dealership.

A customer's saying that he is "just looking" is a great defense mechanism, telling a salesperson that they aren't ready to buy yet and please don't put the heat on him. Salespeople should respect that. Make sure you, and the sales team, are listening. As long as both parties are communicating openly a successful exchange of information can take place.

If customers are "just looking," that's an opportunity to get an idea of what they are looking for, to give them some pertinent information, to tell them about any time-sensitive deals that may be out there, to give them tips on what's hot about the product, or discuss what other people have been buying (but not all of these at once, and certainly not in a way that "hassles" the potential customer).

Ready to Buy...Yet?:

If you think that you will not make a sale during a "just looking" phase of the customer's buying process, think again. Leave at least one subtle benefit statement in the mind of the potential buyer. More than that will just confuse the issue. The next time you talk to her the chances are that she will be much more receptive because you didn't overload her. The smartest salespeople know that in reality you can't sell people something they don't truly want to buy. The trick is in helping them understand why they want to buy something sooner rather than later.

You should always part ways with customers with an understanding of when they might be ready to buy and make it easy to get in touch with you. Give them a business card. If you happened to miss the selling opportunity this time around, take note of the next opportunity, keep in touch, and be the first one there with the selling doors open again.

Changing Sides Selling Keeps You Sharp:

Being on the receiving end of a selling situation is good practice every once in a while. Think of it as a refresher course on how you'd like to be treated as a customer. Whether it's in your field or not (depending on the products that you sell) try to buy something new sometime. Buy it online, over the phone, in person, or through a catalog. Try all the various ways to buy things. Remind yourself what it's like to be a customer. See if you can improve your selling skills as you experiment with different ways to buy products.

Learn from the Best:

Find the best salesperson you can and see how they sell to you. Ask for the top salespeople wherever you go. See how comfortable they are with what they do. See if there is anything you might be able to pick up from them. If it works for you, make it part of your own selling style, and teach it to others on your team.

NOTE: When most salespeople buy from other salespeople there is some ridiculous code of honor that dictates that they must immediately fall all over themselves and admit that they too are in sales. Don't do it while you are observing how others sell. Just be quiet and learn.

See How Others Handle Objections:

When you are being sold to, throw the same buying objections at the seller that you get. See how they handle them.

Other questions to ask:

- What are the competitive products?

- Is their product moving well now, or are things slow?

- What is the best kind of customer for them?

- What else are their best customers buying?

- What type of changes would they make to their own product to make it better?

- What are the popular options for the product?

- What would they buy with *their* money?

- What would they buy with *your* money?

That's Entertainment:

Entertain your customers. Get to know them better. Don't do anything illegal, of course, and be aware of company or government requirements for limits on gifts or entertainment (this has to be said).

When entertaining (this is obvious but often forgotten), don't take advantage of your company.

TRUE STORY ONE: A sales executive lined up a golf workshop for his "customers" and when they couldn't make it (hmmmmm...) he got a personal $40,000 golf lesson with a famous golf professional, for free.

TRUE STORY TWO: Another sales executive used to take customers to a seafood restaurant for lunch and then put additional fresh seafood on his tab for his personal dinner. The guy was making a good six-figure salary plus commissions and just felt he was "entitled,"—until he got called on it.

TRUE STORY THREE: Yet another sales executive felt that she was entitled to expensive personal spa treatments on the company's dime. And she used an unsuspecting salesperson's credit card to cover the costs! How's that for bad form?

None of these people lasted long in their careers. Their continued bad judgment finally caught up with them and their reputations became legend in their respective markets.

17. PERSONAL FINANCE

Not having your financial house in order can really add to the stress levels of any job, especially sales management. With the late hours, tending to customer and salesperson issues, and travel that is often involved you'll want to minimize the stress levels in your personal financial life.

Make sure that you discuss any changes to your current finances with an investment counselor and possible tax implications with your accountant. Talking it over with your significant other is also a must.

Here are some "common sense" financial management ideas that have worked over the years for many salespeople and sales managers:

At the end of each section there are some keywords you can search on through your favorite search engine, to get the most current information.

MEGA TIP: Live Below Your Paycheck:

Treat your paycheck like it's the only check you get. And then live below it. Live an uncomplicated life. Look at all the stuff you have and see if it makes you happy; if it doesn't, get rid of it.

Some sales managers get used to having their pay go up each year. If it does, then great, but what if it doesn't? Smart people know that what goes up can come down again (the personal computer and Internet bubbles are proof of this) and they plan for it. The best contingency plan, in addition to having an emergency savings account, is to live below whatever standard of living the "Joneses" have. You can't get hurt financially that way.

Take everything over and above your paycheck and put it to good use creating real wealth. Then you will control your own destiny all the sooner. Buy bigger or better things that you think you "need" with cash only. Using cash will not add to your recurring monthly bills.

MEGA TIP: Act As If You Already Have a Million Bucks in the Bank:

Have you ever wondered why wealthy people seem to make smarter business decisions? They just seem to do it with grace and confidence that mere mortals don't have. Why? They don't have to make business decisions based on how they will pay their monthly bills. They aren't stressed about this kind of stuff because they have money in the bank. It's not about spending money as if you have a million bucks. It's about projecting the confidence of having that money available if you need it.

One way to start changing your attitude is to act as though you already have money in the bank and that you are only making decisions for the good of the company. And mean it. That may seem like a stretch if you don't have money in the bank, but behaving this way is the right approach to take. Ultimately that attitude will put more money in your bank account over time because you will always strive to "do the right" thing instead of the "gotta pay my bills" thing.

Remember that it's not always about how much you *make*, it's about how much you *keep*. The average millionaire doesn't fit a flashy profile. He or she is typically low-key, enjoys what they do, and lives within their means. They don't maintain a "conspicuous consumption" lifestyle. They are more confident because they already have the confidence of money in the bank. They have nothing to prove to anyone and can be clear-headed when it comes to making business decisions. There is minimal risk if they lose their job doing the right thing, because if they do get fired they have plenty to fall back on.

Those paranoid sales execs who constantly worry about their wallets, their monthly payments, and their reputations when it comes to making decisions, will never be able to move their companies forward and get to the next level of their careers if they don't change their attitudes.

KEYWORD SEARCHES: *Millionaire mind, think like a millionaire, millionaire mindset, and millionaire thinking.*

To Be in Debt, or Not to Be in Debt:

Sales managers love it when their salespeople are in debt with mortgages and expensive car payments. Senior executives love it when their Sales VPs, Senior and Executive VPs are in debt up to their ears, too. Why? Pressure! You gotta pay those bills each month and live that big *nouveau riche* lifestyle, so you have to produce!

You are now locked into the "system" of earning more and wanting more and then needing more to pay for it, and it never seems to end! You have to produce sales to cover the cost of your lifestyle. It's the American way! The heat is now fully on *you!* (Doesn't feel too good, does it?)

If confronted publicly, most senior executives won't admit that debt is often a motivator they consider valuable. But many have certainly snickered about how generally greedy people make great salespeople: These salespeople always want the next cool thing and will work their butts off to get it. Some senior executives perceive your massive debt as a way of having control over you, that you will work that much harder to cover your debts, that you will sell whatever they ask you to sell. And you might just have a heart attack in the process.

This is an obviously cynical approach to make a point here. Not all senior executives think this way and not all salespeople act this way, either. But there's a simple rule that many salespeople and sales managers have finally caught on to: Don't spend past your means and you will be much happier. This wisdom isn't limited to sales types, but it does seem to affect them more than others.

Being more in control of your finances means that you won't have to act under pressure. You'll have more control over your own destiny in terms of jobs you take and when you decide to take them. You can't do that if you are mortgaged to the hilt. You are free to do things with your money like create a "time off" fund (also known by other names) so that you have a cushion when you are ready to move on to other opportunities, or make exciting new investments.

TRUE STORY: During the late 90s-dot-com boom, a fair number of salespeople (and their managers) thought that their sales and commissions would continue to grow and grow…forever. We know how that story ended for most people.

Seasoned salespeople who have weathered cyclical markets could have guessed what was coming, but even some of them were surprised. Many salespeople had never faced a massive downturn. When it hit them, they were ill prepared to deal with it.

One salesperson was so excited about scoring big in the stock market he even wanted to take out a second mortgage to cover exercising his stock options. He sought advice from his sales manager and ultimately decided not to do it, and a good thing it was, as the company's stock price went down 98% in one year.

During boom times, people continue to buy more and more stuff. They buy things they think they need just because they can now afford to, even though they didn't seem to need these things just a year before. And for many people it will all catch up with them. The lesson to be learned here is: Buy only what you truly need, and can afford.

Time will prove that being in control of your finances will make you a better salesperson or sales manager. If you can manage your own financial situation smarter, that's a sign that you can help manage others better as well. Salespeople are happier when they are seemingly in control of their own destiny. Some people go into sales so that they can simply make money or keep up with the Joneses. They think selling is the fastest way to make money.

Having a large house, taking elaborate trips, driving expensive cars, having fancy watches and all the latest toys (or any combination of the above) will generally cause people to have excessive debt. This is not to say that you need to live a Spartan lifestyle, just that people who live comfortably and simply will have less stress and be happier. You can ultimately choke on your own debt if you aren't careful—and no one in sales is immune. Moderation is the key. Spend as much as you feel you need to, but not more than you have.

KEYWORD SEARCHES: *Debt counseling, staying out of debt, out of debt, debt free, debt management, and debt reduction.*

TOP TIP: Treat Commissions Like a Bonus:

If you are on salary plus commission, then view your commission check as "icing on the cake." Don't consider it part of your annual salary (unless you are 100% commission-based!). The concept here is to never live past your base salary for your day-to-day expenses. Initially this may not feel right with everyone around you buying expensive stuff with their commission checks, but when sales or the economy in general takes a downturn, you will always come out on top! Even if the economy keeps moving up you will have more flexibility.

Bank or invest your annual bonuses and commissions. After you do this once or twice in a row, you will not get in the habit of blowing your commission on "stupid stuff" that you *think* you need. Your money will grow and you will be able to do more interesting things with it later on.

How you put your money away is up to you. Some people like to roll into conservative investments, while others are willing to take more of a risk. Whatever your approach, just make sure that you at least have a strategy that you are comfortable with, and stick with it.

KEYWORD SEARCHES: *Balanced financial planning, estate planning, financial independence, financial planner, retirement planning, investing, and investments.*

TOP TIP: Drive a "New" Used Car:

What's more important to salespeople or sales managers than their "ride"? It's often their office and second home! Consider buying low-mileage cars that are three years old for business use.

Why? Here are some good reasons:

- If you are driving a brand-new expensive car you may create a perception in the mind of your customer that you are overpaid or gouging them. You might think it's a sign of success, but these days people are very sensitive to overpaying for just about anything. They won't say it, yet they will think it. It's not always a fair perception...but people can be that way. Consider this: When you buy used, why not tell your customers so? (Unless your customer is a new car dealer!) Let them know that you are being smart about *your* money (which they will see as *their* money!).

- With all the new-car financing deals out there, three-year-old cars are taking a beating on depreciation. People are drawn to the shiny newer models. But the slightly used versions are still great cars (and often the *same* car). Lease returns are always a good bet. Banks and car companies don't want these vehicles sitting around for too long. You can usually upgrade to the kind of car that you want to be driving and, after three years, most cars will have depreciated 40-60%, depending on the model. Consider tracking the lease deals that manufacturers are offering today and keeping an eye out as these cars come off lease in 2, 3 or 4 years.

- Let someone else take the depreciation hit. Most people wouldn't buy a new $70,000 car for business purposes (unless their company leased it for them), so why not buy that same car with low mileage just three years later for $35,000 and drive it for 5 years?

- Other than zero percent financing, most new car and used car rates aren't that far apart. If you take the difference between interest rates for a new car (slightly lower than a used one) or a used car and you take the difference between the overall cost of a new car compared to a three year-old-used car (at nearly half off!), the difference is still far in favor of the used car.

- In many cases you can lease a used car with low mileage. This will save you a lot on monthly payments or allow you to upgrade substantially because you are only paying for use of the car for a specified period. Keep in mind that you won't get free maintenance or a bumper-to-bumper, new-car warranty. If the car has had a reliable history, this may be the most cost-effective way to go.

KEYWORD SEARCHES: *Pre-owned vehicles, lease swapping, consumer guide used cars, consumer reports used cars, car leasing, and buying a used car.*

Used Car Extended Warranties:

Most new cars have the bugs out of them after three years of ownership. Look at Consumer Reports to see what the historical reliability is on the car you are interested in. If it's average or worse, and you still crave the car, then consider buying an extended warranty.

Shop around for the best pricing and warranty features. See what your dealer recommends and compare it to what warranty providers on the Internet will offer. It's not just about getting a good deal on the sale price of a car that matters... it's the total cost of ownership over time.

An extended warranty can help lower your costs if you keep the car for the entire, extended-warranty period. That's what makes an extended warranty worthwhile. In other words, the warranty company makes almost no money off you if you use the full value of the warranty over the warranty period. This is the most efficient way to make use this type of warranty.

Here are some basics on what to look for in an extended warranty:

- Partially refundable if the car is sold.

- Transferable to another private party at least once if the car is sold (helps resale value).

- A short list of "excluded items" that won't be covered under warranty.

- Strong insurance companies backing the company in case of financial difficulties.

- Bumper-to-bumper coverage on non-listed items is a plus.

- Can be used anywhere if the repairing mechanic is industry-certified.

- The warranty company will pay the repair facility directly.

- Quick turn around when you file a claim.

- Refund of unused value if the car is totaled.

- Look for rental car, towing and travel protection; they may be add-ons already covered by your car insurance. (Most car insurance companies cover you if you have an accident but not necessarily if you have a mechanical breakdown—ask your agent.)

- Avoid companies that offer "perks" that might be covered under your car insurance (like windshield "ding" fixes, etc.). You may be paying for them twice.

KEYWORD SEARCHES: *Extended car warranty, used car warranty.*

TOP TIP: **Drive a Leased Car:**

If you always want a car that is under warranty to minimize your costs, consider leasing a new car. Leasing takes the worry out of a car depreciating faster than you anticipated, which might leave you "underwater" if you bought the car. (This means that the car's market price is worth less than what you owe on it when you go to trade it in.)

A general rule of thumb is that to get the best value out of a car, buy it and drive it until the wheels are about to fall off. That isn't always the best strategy for someone in sales who relies on a car and can't take the time to keep fixing whatever breaks as the car gets older. Leasing might make more sense. Especially if you have a car allowance or you can write off the majority of the lease payment.

Whether you lease or buy, many car companies include maintenance for specified periods, and some even include replacement of "wear and tear" items in warranties. Don't think that you aren't paying a little extra for these perks. Sometimes you are, but with the car market being so hypercompetitive these days, it's not uncommon to see these value-added programs thrown in for a minimal increase in sticker price.

Most car companies today (as always) are striving to beat their previous year's sales numbers. One way to move a car quickly without giving the perception that they are offering huge discounts off the sticker price is to offer a great lease payment. Don't take the bait. The car dealer is going to sell the car to a leasing company (often an in-house company) on your behalf, so get the best price that you can before you say that you want to lease it.

Some advantages of leasing:

- You only pay for the value of the car that you use.

- You pay sales taxes on the lease payment only.

- If leased for the appropriate time period, the car is always under warranty.

- In some cases, car maintenance is included.

- You can buy the car at the end of the lease for a pre-determined price.

- You don't have the risk of that trendy "cool blue" color you selected being an unpopular trade-in four years later.

Things to keep in mind:

- Avoid having to put a large amount of cash down to lower the cost of the lease payments (this effectively keeps you from being able to use that money for something else). It's "cleaner" to just have a slightly larger lease payment that you can write off each month for business.

- Compare "zero-interest-rate financing" to leasing. Remember that when you buy the car, you are still buying the entire car, not just for the time that you are using it. Chances are that the lease will still be a much better deal if you only want the car for a 2-4 year period.

- Negotiate the price on the leasing deal in much the same way as you would if you were buying the car. The negotiated price of the car will have an impact on your monthly lease payment.

- Know what the interest rate is that you are being charged. Negotiate that too. Consumer protection laws have made the "lease factor" less of a well kept secret these days.

- Make sure you know what all the fees are when setting up a lease, and when you end it.

- Determine the sales price on the car at the end of the lease. Compare that to the trade-in value for the car. The car may be worth more or less than the agreed-to price. Estimating the price of a car at the end of four years isn't a science. If it's worth less and you still want to buy it, negotiate a better price, or walk away. If the car is worth more, it could have value as a trade-in or be a great buy because it has some built-in equity.

NOTE: When determining the value of the car at the end of the lease, it is a good idea to call around and ask dealers what "market based" trade-in values are. Do not use the price you get from online car sites. For numerous reasons, car dealers rarely accept these numbers (unless the online prices say your trade-in is worth less, or the car you want to buy from them will cost more).

- Wear and tear or excess mileage charges can be painful at the end of a lease. When you pick an annual mileage you are placing a bet that you will be close to that at lease end. If you come in substantially under the agreed-to mileage, you have probably overpaid for the lease (but the car may be worth more as a trade-in). If you come in over mileage, you may pay a mileage penalty, or not.

EXAMPLE: You lease a car for 4 years at 10,000 miles per year. Lease payments are $400 a month. At the end of the lease you have paid $19,200 and driven 40,000 miles. The 'car' cost per mile is $.48. If your lease contract charges you less per mile for miles over the agreed to mileage, you have effectively paid less per mile for the overage. Make sure that you know what the additional charges are per mile and compare them to what you are paying per mile on your lease.

KEYWORD SEARCHES: *Car leasing, vehicle leasing, and lease vs. buy.*

TOP TIP: Buy Only As Much House As You Really Need:

This may sound counterintuitive, but as you earn more and more money, resist the temptation to keep buying a bigger and bigger home, which typically gives you a bigger mortgage. Some of the biggest millionaires in the world have opted for this strategy—and what do they have to prove to the neighbors?

Those who "play" the real estate markets or relocate from a high-cost real estate market to a low-cost one can greatly increase the size of their house and keep their mortgage payment approximately the same. Just buy the size home that suits you the best and feels comfortable. If you can get a house that's the same size as the one you have now and pay a lot less, why wouldn't you? You can always do something else with the extra money.

Often it's not the size of the home that matters, it's how useful it is. Some people prefer smaller homes that are in city, some prefer condos with minimal maintenance, some prefer lots of land with a view of the country. You can buy whatever you want, but be mindful about getting your money back some day. The key is that you should view a home as an investment only if you plan to sell it in the future. Be forward-thinking about what the market might be like down the road.

As you make ongoing real-estate investments, remember that as more baby-boomers downsize their bigger homes there will be a glut of these on the market. Will the market be able to absorb them? Time will tell. Don't get stuck with real estate that might go down in value. It's not a given that real estate (or any investment) will always go up, although real estate has traditionally done well.

KEYWORD SEARCH: *Home buying guide.*

How Much Should You Spend on a Home?

There is a rule of thumb (mostly perpetuated by mortgage banks and real estate agents) that people should spend 25%-30% of their disposable income on housing (it's a lot higher in some markets). Guess who benefits from that little rule? It's like the diamond marketers telling men for years that they need to spend two months salary on an engagement ring. Says who? In this case a rule of thumb seems to apply only to those that don't know better. These "rules" seem materialistic and self-serving. When it comes to your home, buy what makes you happy and works for your finances.

KEYWORD SEARCHES: *Home spending guidelines, shelter spending guidelines, home purchase guidelines, don't make yourself house poor, and What should I spend on my mortgage?*

TOP TIP: Accelerate Your Mortgage Payments:

You can pay off your mortgage sooner than later with very little extra effort. Even something as simple as making a half-payment every two weeks or one additional payment each year (the math is approximately the same) will reduce your mortgage payments by years. Yes, *years.*

The concept is simple. You can make a half-payment every two weeks and in 52 weeks you will have made 13 payments. Or you can take two other approaches: You can just make one extra payment each year (the sooner the better) or make an additional principle payment equal to 1/12th of your money payment each month and designate that it go to principle reduction. Any of these scenarios reduces your outstanding principle amount. The faster you pay down the principle amount, the less interest you pay over the life of the loan. If you look at the interest charges on a 15- or 30-year loan you will be astounded at how much you are paying. There are Web sites that can calculate the savings for you.

There are formal programs that will coordinate these payments for you. If you need that level of structure, by all means go for it. In the end it's a very simple concept that you could probably do on your own, thereby saving a set-up fee.

KEYWORD SEARCHES: *Mortgage accelerator, bi-weekly mortgage payments, mortgage calculators, mortgage payments, and home loan calculator.*

Do You Even Need a Mortgage Payment?

Paying off your mortgage is often the best strategy of all. The property will most likely continue appreciating while you hold it, but you no longer have to pay for the privilege of borrowing the money. By paying off your mortgage you can do something else with your money.

You also have the ability to have a home equity loan equal almost to the value of your home and which, in most cases, will have deductible interest. You can use this money to buy just about anything you need and often pay back only interest until the home is sold. Few of us will ever be able to pay off our mortgages in under fifteen or thirty years, but it should be a goal since it is the single largest expense (and investment) most of us will ever have.

It's widely known that when you have a mortgage, you are paying a significant sum of money just on the interest of the loan. These interest payments are generally tax deductible to a certain amount. At the beginning of a loan repayment is when interest payments are generally the highest (the bank makes sure they are getting their interest back as fast as possible). As everyone knows, you can deduct interest payments for your home loan on your taxes, which effectively lowers what you pay (think of it as a government funded homeowners subsidy). The *net* deduction, however, is not the amount of interest you paid, but your taxable rate applied to the interest. If you are in a 30% tax bracket, your net deduction will be 30% of the interest paid. Figure accordingly. The downside is that you are still parting with your money to someone else. You are either paying federal taxes on your income or interest on your loan when you own a home.

Mortgage payments can make sense in a few cases:

- In markets where real estate is appreciating rapidly, even if you can pay cash for your home, having a mortgage can help you leverage real estate in an up market. Not all real estate goes up, however, so be careful. A little spreadsheet modeling could help you understand the ramifications.

- If you have no mortgage, the money you make each month that would be going to your mortgage payment is taxed at your regular federal and state (if applicable) tax rate. Invest it and watch it grow.

- Owning a lower-priced second home is another way to take advantage of interest-expensed tax deductions. Using a home equity loan to cover the cost of this real estate can be a smart strategy as long as you are convinced that you will have upside in the second home and not put your primary home in jeopardy.

KEYWORD SEARCHES: *Why do I need a mortgage*

loan?, tax advantages of buying a home, and mortgage tax savings.

TOP TIP: Online Banking Is Your 24/7 Friend:

Use online banking whenever possible. If your bank doesn't have it, get a new bank. This is one of the greatest things to happen to banking since the days of getting a free toaster for opening an account.

With this service you can pay bills from anywhere in the country, or the world, you can schedule payments so that they get paid just in time and earn maximum interest, and you can schedule recurring payments to be paid automatically.

Online banking also allows you to transfer money between different accounts like checking, savings, and money market, etc. It's easy to set up and safe to use, and it's available 24 hours a day, 7 days a week.

KEYWORD SEARCHES: *Online banking comparison, online banking guide, internet banking, and online bill pay. Also: Check your bank's website for its online banking products.*

TOP TIP: Keeping Cell Phone Costs Low:

It seems that offers from cellular service providers keep getting more competitive. But if you are an existing customer, don't count on being informed on the latest and greatest deals. It's been said that the best customers are those whom you already have but that doesn't seem to ring true with cellular service providers, even though cellular phone numbers are now competitively portable across service providers in most major metropolitan areas.

Cellular service providers are offering great deals to new customers via massive advertising campaigns, but don't assume that you are being switched over to these deals automatically. You have to do your own research and ask for these deals. The problem is that usually people sign one- or two-year contracts that lock them into a certain arrangements, so there is no reason for the cellular provider to lower your bill by giving you a more competitive deal. These long-term offers are usually based on getting special pricing on the cell phone handset and/or special service features at introductory prices. Market dynamics are changing. Cell phone handsets no longer have to be purchased from the cell phone service provider. You can buy them from electronics stores and on eBay.

Every six months or so it's worth a call to the customer service folks at your friendly cellular service provider to discuss your current usage levels and determine what offers are available to you at that time. If you sense a better deal is available, ask what strings are attached. If there aren't any, see if your contract can be back-dated to the beginning of the month or the quarter.

KEYWORD SEARCHES: *Cell phone plans, wireless plans, wireless comparisons, and wireless phone service.*

TOP TIP: Max Out Your Retirement Program:

If you have a retirement option at your disposal (401k, IRA, Roth IRA, etc.) max it out each year. The money is taken off the top and you can get used to not having it be part of your take-home pay. With very little effort, you can grow your retirement fund. This is especially true with Social Security's questionable ability to help you retire comfortably in the future.

Retirement programs are an especially valuable option if your company has some sort of matching policy. Make sure that whatever your company matches goes into the account first so that you get full benefit of their contribution.

KEYWORD SEARCHES: *Retirement plans, retirement planning, 401k, IRA account, Roth IRA, individual retirement account, self directed IRA, traditional IRA, and retirement options.*

TOP TIP: Know All Your Credit Scores:

As a busy sales manager, you often need to move fast when you are working with your own personal finances. Being pre-emptive and having everything in place in advance of your needs is important. That means knowing your credit ratings and making sure they are accurate and up-to-date.

There are plenty of websites that make available credit reports from major reporting sources. Get the one that shows info from all three major credit reporting groups (Equifax, Experian, and TransUnion) and your FICO score. Your FICO score is your overall credit rating expressed as a number from 300 to 850, 850 being the highest score you can get, which is nearly impossible. A score in the range of 720-850 typically gets you the best interest rates. Do you know your FICO score?

Once you get your report(s), print them out and review them. You will find that typically each of the three credit reporting agencies will have different levels of accurate information on you. Sometimes a current or closed account will show up for one credit reporting agency but not another. You may find a lot of inaccuracies that you never knew existed, which may explain why you couldn't get a higher credit card limit or a better rate on a loan. You might find old credit card or loan accounts that were never closed and even though you haven't used them in years they may still be considered open lines of credit. Clean up all these discrepancies as quickly as possible.

The most efficient process is to write a letter to each company that granted you credit and request that your information be corrected. Supply them with a copy of the page from your credit report where the creditor is listed, the account number, closing date of account, and specifically request about the correction you want made. Request that a correction be sent to each credit reporting company that has incorrect information on you. Once inconsistencies are fixed, send a letter to each of the credit reporting companies explaining any inaccuracies that you have uncovered and that you have addressed them with each company that granted you credit. Attach the letters that you sent to the credit grantor. It will take some time for the process to take effect and for changes to be made. Allow at least 60-90 days for information to be updated. Whatever the state of your credit, get it as clean as possible.

TRUE STORY: A sales executive checked her FICO score via an online service that gives all three credit reports. She wanted her credit rating to be as clean as possible so that when she found the ideal home, she would be pre-approved. The FICO score came back at 798 out of 850, which was quite good.

Still, there were numerous mistakes that appeared on each of the three credit reports. While they appeared to be minor, they might have kept the sales exec from getting the absolute best mortgage rate. She corrected the mistakes through a series of letters and conversations with the credit grantors and the credit-reporting agencies.

No ideal home had been found and six months later the sales executive's credit score was checked again in anticipation of a home purchase. The assumption was that it would be higher than the last time because all the details had been cleaned up. The sales exec's credit rating actually went down to 750 (still quite good). Why? It appeared that her credit wasn't being used *enough*! She had plenty of credit available but her balances were kept to a minimum and there was no mortgage or car payment. The act of cleaning up any accounts which had not been shown as "closed" actually gave the impression that the sales exec wasn't using her credit capacity up to its full potential, therefore the score was lowered.

KEYWORD SEARCHES: *FICO scores, credit reports, credit history, credit rating, and credit scores.*

TOP TIP: Credit Card vs. Credit Cards:

Have only one personal credit card and get a high credit limit. Negotiate the Annual Percentage Rate. Pay the bill off every month, in advance, if possible. Most credit-rating agencies will look at the number of accounts you have open and the "potential for available credit to be used" as part of your overall credit assessment. They also look at the ratio of "outstanding balance" to "overall credit available" on your card. If you can get one card with a high credit limit and then only use a fraction of the available credit, you will have a lower ratio and be in better financial shape.

If you have to use a company credit card, turn in your expenses as quickly as possible or you will be the "bank" for your employer.

If you don't have to use a company credit card, then put all your expenses on a credit card that gives travel miles or some other perks that are most appropriate to your lifestyle. You could earn some nice free vacations this way (which makes them easier to take!).

KEYWORD SEARCHES: *Credit card management, debt management, credit card debt, debt reduction, credit card advisor, low APR credit cards, credit limits, credit card limits, credit card offers, and frequent- flyer credit card offers.*

Know Your Stock Options:

If you have stock options that are available to exercise, get an accountant and work out a strategy on how you will exercise them to meet your long-term financial needs, and what your vesting schedule will be.

As you vest your options consider the following:

- Make sure that you have exercised enough options to cover your *full* tax liability. Try to reserve an amount for taxes that covers the highest tax rate that you think you might achieve. This strategy is a little on the conservative side but there are a lot of people from the "Internet bubble" years who wish they had done this. They are still paying for their options.

- After you have covered taxes on exercising your options, decide how many shares you will keep and how many you will sell outright and diversify into cash or other investments. Only in very rare circumstances will one single stock do so exceedingly well that it's worth the risk of holding on to all your shares. You will have to fight the thought that the company you work for is the best investment you can make. Former Enron employees certainly don't think so and not even Bill Gates follows this strategy.

- An ideal model would be to allocate approximately the percentage equivalent of your combined federal and state tax rate to cover taxes, and split the remaining as exercised shares that you hold and would put into other diversified investments. Make adjustments according to your risk strategy. Realize that this plan could change as the tax laws change. That's why it's important to have your accountant involved.

KEYWORD SEARCHES: *Knowing stock options, incentive stock options, non-qualified stock options, understanding stock options, and stock option strategies.*

Online Payment Services:

These are different from online banking services, although they can be linked together. Like online banking these are protected services that allow you to pay for items offered on the Web in a quick and efficient manner. What makes them different is that you can select the most efficient way to make payments and do so directly to someone's e-mail address. You can set up these services to withdraw money from various bank accounts or charge your credit or debit card.

If you don't have an online payment service like PayPal or PayDirect, think about setting one up. More and more transactions are being done this way. Many people use it to make online donations, pay for entrance to charity events, or buy and sell just about anything.

KEYWORD SEARCHES: *PayPal, PayDirect, online payment services, payment services, and online payment tools.*

Bid Out Your Personal Insurance Business:

Bid out your car, renters or homeowners, and earthquake insurance out every year or two to take advantage of the best rates and services.

Switching insurance companies isn't all that difficult. You get insurance from a new carrier and then you cancel the old one. Having a clean record and multiple types of policies with the same company is what gets you discounts, not necessarily the length of time that you've been insured.

It's not always necessary to change carriers every few years just because rates are lower, but re-bidding your insurance does give you peace of mind that you aren't getting ripped off too badly year after year. Sometimes the savings can equal hundreds of dollars per year. It's almost always worth investigating.

Keep in mind that a multi-line discount for having different types of insurance with one insurance company can often be less expensive than bidding out each type of insurance to the lowest provider. There is also a convenience factor for having one company to call when it's time to file a claim.

KEYWORD SEARCHES: *Auto insurance, car insurance, homeowners insurance, liability insurance, life insurance, independent agents, multi-line insurance agency, and online insurance agency.*

Smart Use of Frequent-Flier Miles:

If you have frequent-flier miles try to use them before they expire. But be cautious here. Compare the cash cost of taking a trip somewhere to the number of miles you would need to expend. Sometimes you have better luck with paying for short trips and saving miles for a more elaborate, globe-hopping itinerary.

KEYWORD SEARCHES: *Frequent flyer programs, and compare frequent flyer programs. Also: Go to the airlines you have your frequent flyer miles with and review their programs.*

Clean Out Your Stuff:

If you have a lot of "stuff" that you never use, think about donating it to charity. Get a receipt. Donate as often as you can. Take the tax deduction.

If you aren't feeling particularly charitable, sell your excess stuff at a yard sale or on eBay and put the money in the bank. Consider giving some of the proceeds to charity.

KEYWORD SEARCHES: *eBay, charitable donations, and local donations (+ your city or state)*.

Maximize Your Write-Offs:

Make sure that you legally "write off" any expenses not reimbursed by your company, but that are still tax deductible. These are called "un-reimbursed employee business expenses" and can include: a DSL connection at home that is used for work; car license fees; additional work-related computer equipment used at home; a portion of your home office; car leases (work portion only… and don't forget the taxes on the lease); and work related cell phone bills over the company maximum, etc.). Keep all your receipts, you will be amazed at what you spend on small items that can be legitimately written off. Consult your accountant for the full details.

KEYWORD SEARCHES: *Un-reimbursed employee business expenses, form 2106-EZ, legal expense deductions, business deductions, and IRS business deductions*.

Seek Balance through Counseling:

No, not psychological counseling! Debt management and/or investment counseling!

Work towards minimizing your debts and establishing a balanced investment portfolio with stocks, CDs, real estate, cash, bonds, mutual funds, retirement, etc. That way you will be protected over the long term. If you are unsure, talk to debt and/or investment counselors or read a few books on the subject to get an array of opinions. In the end it's your decision, your willingness to accept risk and, it's your money! Do everything in your power to let it work for you.

KEYWORD SEARCHES: *Investment counseling, debt counseling, financial counseling, financial planning, financial advisor, and independent financial advisor.*

18. THE REALITIES OF BAD CEOS

Not all CEOs are bad. In fact, most aren't. When you get one who is bad, you will usually know quickly. Here are some ways to deal with the inevitable issues that arise from working with bad CEOs:

When the Bad CEO Won't Listen to You:

There are situations when you will try to communicate sales needs to your CEO and he or she just won't listen. Sound familiar? If he or she won't listen to you, maybe he or she will listen to your customers.

EXAMPLE: Suppose that there is a critical issue that isn't being addressed inside the company and it is costing the sales team profitable sales. The CEO has control of the budget that will solve the problem but won't address it, won't rally the right people, and won't put on the pressure on your behalf. It just isn't seemingly a priority, or he could be just too scared to make a decision.

How do you make it a priority?

One way to open the CEO's eyes to the problem is to involve his ego in the problem-solving. Internal involvement in the issue isn't enough, you already tried that. The CEO might also have to be put on the spot outside of the company to get something done.

It's a mildly devious, yet cunning plan, but it has worked in the past.

How?

Invite the CEO to go on a sales call to one of your key customers. Specifically, go to the customer who will benefit the most by your company's solving the internal problem that is blocking the creation of revenue. Make it a high-level call. Make sure that the CEO hears directly from the customer (at the highest level) that not solving the problem is keeping them from doing huge amounts of business with your company. Attach a dollar value to it if possible. If the CEO has any amount of ego, he will be embarrassed that the problem isn't being addressed and promise to resolve it immediately.

TRUE STORY: A CEO just wasn't helping the sales manager resolve a revenue opportunity. No matter how many people made a case regarding new enhancements to an order entry system, nothing was happening. So the sales team got creative. A resourceful salesperson picked a top customer who wanted to spend $100,000 *more* a month with the company if the company solved the internal system problem with a software fix. The salesperson was getting nowhere until she took the CEO to the customer and had one of their execs say that he would like to spend $100,000 *more* a month with the company but couldn't.

The CEO became magically focused on solving the problem, because he was now being personally associated with it. When the CEO returned from the sales call, his first comment to the sales manager was: "Did you know that we have a customer who wants to spend $100,000 *more* a month with us and we can't take their business?" B-I-N-G-O! (No kidding!) The sales manager had been telling the CEO that same thing for two months! Changes were then put into play.

When a Bad CEO Exhibits Irrational Behavior:

Irrational CEOs are one of the most difficult things to deal with. Why? Because, when irrational behavior comes from *above* the sales manager level, it is difficult to control. Coming from below sales management level, it's pretty easy to put a stop to, especially if it's from inside the sales team. Irrational behavior can come from inside or outside the company but an internal origin is often the most damaging.

Irrational CEO behavior accomplishes absolutely nothing. Sometimes it's done just as a control issue to prove a point. It seems to be more common today for irrational CEOs to have expectations that exceed possibility. Some execs think it's a rite-of-passage into CEO-dom to become demanding and forget what it takes to really get things done. Some irrational CEOs expect sales managers to constantly renegotiate deals with customers to gain an increasingly one-sided advantage to the company. This is rarely helpful and creates bad reputations. Customers aren't typically stupid.

In many cases it all boils down to the irrational CEO feeling he or she can be unreasonable because of the position, or because ego demands it. (This should *not* be confused with simply being demanding. When done the right way, that's OK.) Sometimes irrational CEOs are simply naive (or arrogant) when it comes to the ways that true sales professionals conduct business. They can't be faulted for wanting the best deal for their companies, but they can be faulted for not knowing when to stop pushing it.

Not knowing when to stop is the core of irrational behavior. The irrational CEO seems to forget that there are smart people on the other side of the table who will call BS if the deal becomes one-sided. Persistence here leaves bad feelings. Only when both parties win can everyone walk away with a done deal. As they say: If it's not a "win-win" deal it's a "lawyer" deal.

Irrational CEOs have no idea what it really takes to get something done. They probably haven't spoken to a customer in years and over that period of time have gotten a more and more jaded view of how sales should work. They fly at the 40,000 foot level and think that everything can be easily accomplished in a "big picture" kind of way. They've got no realistic idea how the negotiation process works, how details fit, or that the world below them is imperfect. But they continue to push—in an unreasonable way—and it's worse for sales managers than hearing fingernails scratching across a chalkboard.

How do you deal with irrational CEO behavior? Often you can't, fully. It's just an ugly fact of life. It takes a real pro to turn around an irrational situation, close the deal, and manage the bad behavior all at the same time. Do whatever you can to shield your salespeople from such situations.

Here is a problem scenario and possible solution:

HYPOTHETICAL CASE STUDY ONE: The XYZ company wants to do a deal with your company. You have done business with them before and have a good working relationship with the management on the other side of the table. Nothing should get in the way of a deal that works for both companies as long as both companies benefit. Both companies respect and need each other but the deal is at risk because the irrational CEO at the company you work for (or theirs) has just inserted himself into the sales process. He is in the background making demands that don't fit the scale of the deal. Every time that you think the deal is agreed to, your irrational CEO asks for more favorable terms. This is not a bad strategy as long as the demands are for less and less, the closer you get to doing the deal. But in this case, the demands are actually increasing!

What's the solution? It might be time to form an *ad hoc* alliance with executives at the other company. Yes, this sounds risky and disloyal, but sometimes irrational CEOs can work in ways that don't actually benefit their company. (This will be a surprise to them, no doubt!) You have to isolate them so they can't kill a great deal.

If they know you well enough, your counterparts on the other side of the table will probably be able to sense irrational behavior from your CEO that is being channeled through you.

At some point you might want to work with your counterpart at the other company to have XYZ's

CEO contact your irrational CEO to say the deal will be off if he continues to push for lopsided terms. The irrational CEO may look in the mirror, get some "religion" and back down; then again, maybe he won't.

As noted in other examples, sometimes it takes an outside party to intervene. Rather than fight it, work with it. Irrational CEOs will often take their own employees to task privately but are much more mild-mannered in a more public forum. When the irrational CEO sees that his or her behavior is being put on public display, they may be self-conscious (egotistical?) enough to temporarily stop. Don't expect that to last too long, though.

HYPOTHETICAL CASE STUDY TWO: Another approach to the above problem might be to sit down the irrational CEO and explain the concept of *quid pro quo* negotiating which essentially means that when you ask for more you need to be willing to give more to get it. The CEO probably won't get the concept and will have the attitude that the other company needs your company more than you need them. That's often the basis for most irrational behavior. You will want to continue to be the professional that you are and try to work toward a final deal.

If the CEO continues to be irrational, there may be a point where you will really have to ask yourself if this is the kind of company that you want to work for. If you like the money more than the abuse, then stick around.

MEGA TIP: **Don't Quit on a Bad CEO:**

Some companies have very anti-revenue environments where CEOs wouldn't lift a finger to help make sales happen. When sales don't happen according to expectations, it's not fun for anyone, especially people with big revenue numbers hanging over their heads (and usually with big neon arrows pointing at them!).

Don't compromise your integrity by quitting in a situation like this. Despite all the pressure you may have to endure you should rarely ever quit a job. That ability to "stick with it" alone should help you get your next job.

There are other benefits to the "don't quit" strategy:

- Your CEO will have to display the guts to fire you. If he or she is not revenue-focused, chances are that they are so introverted they will feel guilty and cut you a decent severance check. As well they should!

- Have a pre-negotiated termination agreement in advance to take care of situations like this. These are not bad things to have and at the highest levels of sales management, they are necessary. Think of it as having a short-term insurance policy for your integrity *and* income.

- Typical ranges for termination agreements are three months to a year in duration for base salary, and something additional related to commission. In many cases these variables are part of an employment contract.

- Resolving owed commissions is the sticky part. Everyone will have a different take on how to handle commissions. Some deals are prorated up through day you leave or will cover longer-term deals depending on what you are selling.

- Make sure that both parties agree to the terms (run it by your lawyer if necessary) and then when it's time to leave the company, triggering the agreement should just be *pro forma*.

Exit Interviews with a Bad CEO:

It's a natural reaction to consider using an exit interview as your soapbox to vent about what is wrong with the company you are about to depart. Especially if the CEO is the problem. It's best to weigh the long-term ramifications on your career before you go in for the final interview.

Chances are, if you have just been fired, your opinion won't be worth too much inside your company, so cool it. Just be professional and get out of there with a minimal amount of friction. Write a calm and thoughtful letter later if you feel the need. See *Setting the Record Straight* in Section 15, page 290.

If you are leaving the company on your own accord, the same thinking above would still apply. It might be good to offer a few general suggestions about what you'd change. Just avoid the tendency to point fingers and leave scorched earth behind you. This is especially true whether you are leaving or asked to leave because you may still need this company for a future job reference (in exchange for leaving quietly).

TRUE STORY: A CEO hauled the Sales VP into the corner office and told her it was time to go. It had been a long time coming. The CEO and Sales VP didn't get along. The CEO had a reputation for "falling out of love" with his direct reports just a few months after hiring them. The Sales VP needed the CEO's support to be successful. Needless to say, she was relieved it was over, but not happy since this was the first time she had ever been fired.

As part of the exit compensation package the CEO graciously allowed the Sales VP to receive stock options through the first vesting period. In reality, the CEO was cheap and this was a cost-effective way of terminating a high level employee without the cost of a salary severance package. (Smart!)

The Sales VP accepted the package and agreed to an exit interview a few days later. At the interview the CEO wasn't interested in hearing what could be done to improve the sales organization or the relationship between the CEO and the sales team. The Sales VP expressed displeasure that she was not being listened to and started to tell the CEO what she was really thinking. Then the Sales VP just stopped talking, took a deep breath and smiled, and thanked the CEO for the opportunity to work there, shook hands, and left. Why did she stop mid-sentence? She was thinking: "I had better shut-up. This #@&%$#! CEO is about to make me wealthy! Just shut up! Maybe it's time to smile and just go away… the CEO isn't listening to me anyway!"

The happy ending for the Sales VP was that by the time the options were exercised the shares were worth ten times more than on the day she was fired. She had just become *very* wealthy.

Chapter Five

Future Trends, Second Opinions, and the Emergence of the Chief Revenue Officer (CRO)

Future Trends:

You've just read over 300 tips to help mentor you through many of the issues that today's sales managers face. Some of them are common sense, some are new thinking, some can be morphed into ideas more appropriate to solving a specific problem that you might have, while others show the need for executives in companies to wake up and smell the coffee when it comes to modern selling. Many of these tips will stand the test of time, but what about tomorrow's sales management issues—how will companies deal with them?

In the future, sales teams will become more proactive and vocal about how they are managed. They will begin pulling coups to rid themselves of senior sales executives who add no overall value to the company or who hinder the sales team from doing its day-to-day job. In fact, it's already happening in some companies. I have watched sales teams refuse to work for ineffective Sales VPs, and they were right to do so.

Sales teams are no longer accepting the fact that they aren't being managed well, and/or the products aren't delivering what they promise. When asked directly, many honest sales teams have readily admitted that well over half of their selling problems are internal to the company and not market driven. They are asking for leadership not only in sales management but from the CEO and Board of Directors.

Smart CEOs and board members are beginning to view effective senior sales managers as more valued members of the executive team. They are the company's eyes and ears to the marketplace. Many companies are upgrading their senior sales positions and hiring talent accordingly. They are listening to and involving sales executives (and customers) earlier in the product development and marketing process to determine if future products can actually be sold and be profitable.

At the same time, smart sales executives are getting more focused on their jobs, finding mentors to be their sounding boards, listening more closely to internal and external customers, and placing the creation of profitable revenue at the top of the company's priority lists. If you are a part of this revolution, you will reap its rewards.

Investors and shareholders have returned to the old fashioned way of valuing companies. They too are very focused on the creation of profitable revenue, and in many cases, higher dividends. It's the "new old thing" and it's an increasingly important requirement in today's economy.

Great salespeople will always be in high demand. Keeping great salespeople will always be difficult.

Great sales managers will be in even greater demand. Growing great salespeople into great sales managers, and those sales managers into great sales leaders will be even more challenging.

There is not an automatic transition to management and leadership as many think. Not every natural salesperson is a natural sales manager. It takes a lot of training and hard work to develop these skills. It certainly takes the right attitude and commitment to build a sales team that does great things, plays for the entire game, and will be ready to go into overtime for the company, if necessary. Finding the right CEO and Board of Directors who support this type of sales leadership can also be an ongoing challenge. If you look at the turnover in CEOs these days, you can see that boards and shareholders clearly get the concept of accountability and creating more profitable revenue.

Second Opinions:

Board members, CEOs, and other senior executives are also getting more deeply involved in understanding how the sales process works. They are doing a better job of mentoring their sales executives—or finding someone who can. Sales executives are responding by doing a better job of mentoring their sales managers and salespeople. All involved are asking smarter questions and demanding more revenue accountability across the entire company. These executives refuse to take the 40,000 foot view of the sales organizations and are getting into the details of what specifically is happening with sales.

Bringing in a mentor to help make a sales organization run better is a common sense idea that more companies are utilizing today. Bringing in a mentor doesn't always mean that there is a weakness with sales management or salespeople. It's quite the contrary. Many healthy companies look for outside opinions to improve existing approaches to selling and sales leadership. These companies are constantly striving to do better. Often, the value of an external mentor can be found in uncovering weaknesses before they break a company or before the company grows to the next level.

Much of my mentoring business has come from board members or higher level executives in a company who have referred me to their sales executives. This allows those sales executives to double-check that everything is running smoothly, it gives them a confidential source to ask questions and get feedback, and it creates an impartial third party listener. There is always some additional knowledge to be gained from getting a second opinion. Most sales executives welcome additional resources to help fine-tune their sales organizations and head off any potential shortcomings. It's a process that those involved can learn from if they approach it with an open mind.

Reading this book is a step in the right direction when it comes to improving the sales management and sales leadership skills in any company. If you need consulting help to improve the sales efforts of your company please feel free to contact me via www.MentorPressLLC.com.

The Emerging Chief Revenue Officer (CRO):

One of the emerging trends in executive sales leadership today is the creation of the high-level sales quarterback—the "C" level sales executive. This new person is often being referred to as the Chief Revenue Officer (CRO). They are sometimes confused with the Chief Financial Officer (CFO), but couldn't be farther at the other end of the corporate spectrum. (The CROs are the ones tasked with bringing in revenue, not spending it.)

The CRO title has been created in companies to respond to the growing complexities of selling, an increased focus on accountability, and the creation of profitable revenue. The days of companies being built on a great concept but not delivering real revenue are over. CEOs who recognize this can create a powerful, revenue-focused organization by having finance, engineering, product development, marketing, and sales all working hand-in-hand to create revenue for the company and value for the shareholders. The point person to help make that happen is the CRO. Sales managers who understand this can create successful and lucrative career paths for themselves by stepping up to this challenge.

If you want to be a Chief Revenue Officer, having practical experience and understanding the ideas in this book will help you get there. Being a CRO is a rewarding and positive experience, and you will be in the center of the action. If you take the challenge, be prepared to clearly articulate to your CEO what you need to be successful, and demand the authority it will take to accomplish your goals, and then be prepared to stand by your convictions and make things happen. Creating profitable revenue is a company-wide team effort, not just a goal for the sales department.

Jeff Lehman